# ON ACCOUNT OF DARKNESS

# PRAISE FOR *ON ACCOUNT OF DARKNESS*

"More than just history, this book can teach us all something. *On Account of Darkness* is a powerful read about racism and overcoming prejudice, not just in sports, but in Canada. These untold stories need to be heard."

BOB IZUMI, sportsman and host of the *Real Fishing Show*

"These stories show that anything is possible, and good things can happen, no matter who you are. Growing up you see pro athletes on the news and you think it will never happen to you, but it can. Reading what these chapters are all about shows that through struggles, dreams can come true, and kids need to know that."

FERGIE JENKINS, member of MLB Hall of Fame

"A well-researched and often uncomfortable trip through Canadian sports history. Ian Kennedy's reporting about teams like the Chatham Coloured All-Stars will rekindle discussions about athletes from our country's past who deserve a more prominent place in history, and ought to also spark a debate about whether some of Canada's most prominent sporting legends deserve the pedestal they have been put upon."

RICK WESTHEAD, TSN Senior Correspondent

"I can't recommend *On Account of Darkness* enough. I also can't overstate how much I learned from Ian Kennedy's work. As a series of books have been trotted out echoing the same stories about the intersection of race and sports, it is so refreshing to read something that breaks new ground and discusses the issue from angles we have not seen. It is a deep dive into a vital topic that also contains such depth of feeling, depth of history, and depth of personal recollection to animate why knowing the past is so critical for the present."

DAVE ZIRIN, Sports Editor at *The Nation*, author of *A People's History of Sports in the United States*

"Voraciously researched, Ian Kennedy does an astonishing job of compiling and recounting incredible stories and achievements in sport that may have otherwise been forgotten. This book should live on every Canadian's bookshelf."

TARA SLONE, Co-Host, Rogers Hometown Hockey

"*On Account of Darkness* is a book we can all learn from. Overcoming obstacles such as racism as well as prejudice from different minorities. These are the truths that need to be heard across the globe."
BRIGETTE LACQUETTE, Olympic silver medallist, NHL scout and Indspire award-winner

"Ian Kennedy's *On Account of Darkness* is an important intervention that carries the difficult task of amplifying histories of racism and oppression that saturate contemporary sport . . . Kennedy reminds us how the truth of racism in sport is not only deeply steeped in our past, but also continues to shape a modern sport system founded on systemic racism, white supremacy, and racialized discrimination. *On Account of Darkness* offers a riveting deep dive into the intersections of race and sports through broad historical analysis and profound personal recollections to illuminate the ways in which a history of racism in sport is, quite frankly, a history of the present. When folks tell you to keep politics out of sport, hand them *On Account of Darkness* to show them how much of an impossibility that task is."
DEREK SILVA, JOHANNA MELLIS, and NATHAN KALMAN-LAMB, co-hosts of *The End of Sport* podcast.

"Ian Kennedy's book *On Account of Darkness: Shining Light on Race and Sport* is an important account of not only Black Canadians in sport but other racialized communities that are so often left out of mainstream texts. History needs to be taught truthfully and fully as it happened. Education and knowledge are a huge part of activism, and in order to break the continued cycles of racism that exist not only in sport but through all parts of society we need to continue to learn and share that history as it happened. Kennedy's book does just this and will be an important teaching tool and voice for lived experiences from racialized Canadians."
SAMANTHA MEREDITH, Executive Director, Chatham-Kent Black Historical Society

"Using the background of sports, a thorough telling of rampant racism over the decades in southern Ontario. A must-read to understand the injustices of yesterday and their effects still today."
RICHARD PEDDIE, former President and CEO of Maple Leafs Sports and Entertainment

# ON
# ACCOUNT
# OF
# DARKNESS

## SHINING LIGHT ON RACE AND SPORT

Ian Kennedy

TIDEWATER
PRESS

Published by Tidewater Press
New Westminster, BC, Canada
tidewaterpress.ca

978-1-990160-10-3 (paperback)
978-1-990160-11-0 (e-book)

LIBRARY AND ARCHIVES CANADA CATALOGUING IN PUBLICATION

Title: On account of darkness : shining light on race and sport / Ian Kennedy.
Names: Kennedy, Ian (Ian D.), author.
Description: Includes bibliographical references and index.
Identifiers: Canadiana (print) 20220187975 | Canadiana (ebook) 20220188955 | ISBN 9781990160103
(softcover) | ISBN 9781990160110 (HTML)
Subjects: LCSH: Racism in sports—North America. | LCSH: Athletes—Ontario—Chatham-Kent—
Biography. |
LCSH: Sports—Ontario—Chatham-Kent. | LCSH: Sports—Social aspects—North America. | LCSH:
Sports—
Social aspects—Ontario—Chatham-Kent. | LCGFT: Biographies.

Classification: LCC GV706.32 .K46 2022 | DDC 796.089/0097—dc23

Printed in Canada

To Stephanie and Ezra, for their immense patience and love, and to John and Katie, who were my original storytellers.

# TABLE OF CONTENTS

# AUTHOR'S NOTE

We acknowledge that Chatham-Kent, and all sport that takes place here, both past and present, as well as the stories in this book, occupies the traditional lands of the Anishinaabeg and Lunaapeew peoples. We acknowledge that their ancestral languages were antecedents to the language used in this book. We honour and thank the Chippewa, Odawa, Potawatomi, and Delaware Nations as stewards of this land, and as vital contributors to our community and society.

Unless otherwise indicated, quotes are drawn from first-hand interviews. Quotes from other publications have been reproduced exactly as printed in their original form, regardless of modern styles or usage, with the exception of those using derogatory slurs. Some of these have been altered to block out specific words.

I've placed myself in these stories, as someone who was admittedly oblivious and part of the problem for many years, on the recommendation of Black and Indigenous stakeholders. I've changed and, even though my town and our country are not perfect, I'm hopeful.

# INTRODUCTION

Sitting in church, I used to love hearing the parable of the wheat and the weeds. The story goes that a man sows "good" seed into the soil, but while he sleeps an enemy comes and sows weeds among the wheat. When they wake to see weeds have sprouted, the servants ask the farmer if they should pull them out, but he tells them pulling the weeds might also uproot the wheat. He decides to let both grow together until harvest. Only then can good and evil be separated.

Driving the dirt roads of Chatham-Kent, you can see the wheat and the weeds. Bounded by Lake St. Clair to the west and Lake Erie to the east, the community was built on agriculture. The region is the top producer of tomatoes, seed corn, carrots, cucumbers, Brussels sprouts, and pumpkins in Canada, and this diversity helps the economy flourish.

The biggest urban centre is Chatham, a town of about 45,000, three hours southwest of Toronto. The heart of the community, Chatham sits roughly in the centre of the municipality, sandwiched between Walpole Island First Nation and Delaware Nation, two Indigenous communities whose presence preceded white settlers and freed slaves by thousands of years. The region is also home to Dresden and Buxton, two important terminals on the Underground Railroad.

Katie and John, my mother's parents, landed in this community as poor immigrants unable to speak the language, having fled communist persecution in Slovakia following World War II. They worked any job they could, lived in a tiny shack that later became a one-car garage and were ridiculed for wearing the same clothes day after day. Eventually, they bought a farm halfway between Wallaceburg and

Dresden only a kilometer from where I grew up. My grandfather would wander out into his newly acquired field, fall to his knees and run the soil through his hands, praying for a good crop, enough to cover their mortgage and pay off their debt. Neighbours driving by would honk and laugh at him, knees in the dirt. He worked so hard to buy land that had been stolen by white settlers years before.

John moved here to become part of Canada. He had heard about the opportunity and the welcoming people. This country has told the same story for centuries, a multicultural discourse that emphasizes equity, inclusion, and pluralism. Chatham-Kent typifies that ideal—a well-established rural community sprinkled with prosperous small towns, a rich Black history and two independent First Nations. It was here that the Chatham Vigilance Committee prevented many Black residents from being returned to slavery, and it was here that John Brown came to lay plans for his raid on Harper's Ferry, often considered the first battle of the American Civil War. His Chatham Convention of 1858 was a blueprint for the revolution he hoped to spark and the government he hoped would succeed it.

Brown called Chatham a place filled with "true friends of freedom."[1] But the region was also home to Canada's first racial discrimination trial. It's an area built on conservatism that has resisted immigration and practised segregation longer than almost any other region of Canada.

The residents of Chatham-Kent are field people, growing crops on one field and chasing fly balls or sprinting across the finish line on another. They live and breathe sport: hockey, baseball, lacrosse, basketball, cricket, track and field, and, more recently, soccer, volleyball, swimming, and rugby. Sport, like Canada itself, has been placed on a pedestal allegedly oblivious to considerations of race and gender, where the playing field is level and merit is measured only by athletic ability. For some, it is true that sport has transcended racial constraints and provided opportunities that would have been otherwise unattainable. Physical prowess has provided avenues for change, platforms for protest, and visibility for the underrepresented.

But the area's whiteness has created a hostile environment for visitors. Like any home team, we've yelled, we've banged on the glass, we've used our home-field advantage against those who try to belong here with us, even those who were here before we arrived. Chatham-Kent, and the sports community that thrives here, typify the paradox of Canadian identity—celebrating our history as heroes of the Underground Railroad while ignoring the century of racism that followed. Touting the brave Chief Tecumseh who fought with local soldiers in the War of 1812, while ignoring the disenfranchise-ment and genocide of Indigenous peoples. We produce food for the world but fail to mention the years we forced Japanese Canadians to labour in those fields while their homes were sold to pay for their internment. We are the wheat, and we are the weeds, growing amongst each other.

Growing up, I visited my grandparents often, arriving in the after-noon, the sound of the door closing behind me announcing my presence.

"John! Ian's here!" My grandma would yell the same three words each time.

On the floor just inside their door was detritus from her garden. Clipped tulips and a basket of peas for me to take home, a pellet gun to scare the crows away from their cherry trees. Near the window a potato was growing in a shoe, a white runner with Velcro, the type you might see in a nursing home. No wonder she took it off. She would plant the potato in the spring because she was raised to waste nothing.

From my grandpa's bedroom, the voice of a preacher would boom from the television loud enough for neighbours, if they had any, to complain. When he finally found the remote control, his slow steps would move down the hall to the kitchen.

We'd sit at their table, and I'd brush away the crumbs they couldn't see, picking them from a stained lace tablecloth. Stacks of newspapers sat on top of a phonebook in the corner next to the old white fan they used to keep cool on summer days; air conditioning was not a luxury they would indulge in. Their walkers were parked beside each other.

I'd place a pizza on the table and my grandmother would weave her calloused, bruised, and bandaged hands together to pray over her food. Then we'd eat and they would begin speaking, taking turns leading a waltz through their history.

Never able to sit, used to serving her husband, my grandmother would lift her failing frame and pour coffee. When the pizza was gone, my grandpa would ask for a snack. Her John was always hungry, so she would pull leftover cookies from the fridge, placing them in front of him. His fingers felt for them, mistakenly grabbing this or that before landing on their target.

As they ate, they talked, rarely stopping for breath. The same stories told again. I knew each by heart. I'd heard them a thousand times but waited patiently for the finale of each, to hear them laugh, to see my grandfather smile as he recalled an ex-girlfriend named Monique. When he forgot, Katie would prompt him to start again. I'd sit and listen, memorizing every detail. Because soon they would be gone. Each time I said goodbye, my grandmother, who never reached five feet tall, stood on the steps to hug me.

Cancer would take my grandma. And with her passing went my grandpa's ability to remember. I'd occasionally see him return as I held his great-granddaughter over his wheelchair, his icy blue eyes briefly coming alive. He started singing, hymns so ingrained that not even dementia could take them. The night he died I tried my best to speak their stories into his ear. His vacant eyes flickered while his mind tried to keep pace. Now they were both gone, and their stories were mine to keep.

Storytelling is an art of the older generation, a legacy from a time when whiskey and dim rooms preserved our tales. Words moving from person to person, passed down through generations. I'd promised myself I'd write them down someday but, when I tried to do so now, I'd lost the nuance. I couldn't quite recall my grandmother's expression as she spoke her lines in their two-person play. The stories were fading; the gaps would stay unfilled.

My grandparents taught me to love stories. Not just the ones we'd seen played out hundreds of times in movies and books, but the stories of people who don't look like us, or sound like us. For more than a decade, I filled pages and airwaves for local media outlets with familiar sports news until I discovered a story I knew nothing about—the story of the Chatham Coloured All-Stars baseball team. I couldn't believe I'd never heard of Boomer Harding or Flat Chase or Ferguson Jenkins Sr., and I needed to know more. I found a new world of athletes and teams and soon, for me, the scores became irrelevant.

I was sitting in Chatham's Black Mecca Museum surrounded by documents and newspaper clippings, fact-finding for an article, when Dorothy Wright-Wallace, the longtime president of the Chatham-Kent Black Historical Society, walked in. She glanced over my shoulder and told me about the man pictured in the newspaper I had out. He was her brother, Eddie Wright, a famed Black hockey player and coach. As I listened, the intimate details of Eddie, who he was, came to life. The room was filled with the sights and sounds of Eddie's childhood, conjured by Dorothy's words. Dorothy had spent her entire life in Chatham's East End. She had stories to tell, stories she'd told many times before, but not to me.

Then seventy-eight years old, Dorothy had curly silver hair, faded freckles and was short enough for me to rest my arm on her shoulder. The first time we met, I saw a woman I knew; I recognized the mischievousness in her eyes. It was the look of a woman who did things her own way, who had struggled—and loved—deeply. As she spoke, I felt like I was sitting at my grandmother's kitchen table, and my hand instinctively swept invisible crumbs.

The next time I saw Dorothy, there was a sense of ease between us. Our conversation found a familiar rhythm, a metronome of breath I recognized and longed to have back. This time, our meeting was arranged. I was here to preserve her story, to learn about her life, the teams she'd grown up watching, and Chatham-Kent's Black history. I wanted to know what lay behind the final scores, behind the wins and losses of local athletes. I set a microphone in front of her, pressed record and began to listen.

It turns out there were other stories like the ones Dorothy told me that day. Perhaps they were parts of the same story that had been left out and erased. There were stories people had decided were best forgotten, things we don't talk about that stayed locked between axon and dendrite, unwilling to emerge. But, like societal vaccines, stories protect us. It's best to know the truth, to recognize the warning signs of illness, and to put up a fight.

I interviewed dozens of athletes, their families, coaches, and friends, compiling the oral histories of the many Black, Indigenous, and Japanese Canadian families in this region.

I often found the people I'd hoped to speak with were already gone, their stories lost, so I became a collector, a researcher, and a preservationist of many untold stories in sport. I listened and learned. I recorded. I wanted to know how we got here, even though I knew I couldn't really understand. I am white, so these are not my stories. But I am thankful for everyone who trusted me with them so that I can help keep them safe.

# Chapter 1

# UNDER THE PEAR TREE

Driving to hockey practice several times a week, we passed Uncle Tom's Cabin. I knew the name, but nothing else. My teachers never spoke of Black history. They didn't mention Uncle Tom's Cabin or the Underground Railroad even though our school was less than fifteen minutes from this historic site.

Years later, on an island in Botswana's Okavango delta, my wife and I met a member of the Houston Symphony Orchestra who, when we explained where we lived, said he wanted to visit us to see Uncle Tom's Cabin, a place filled with Black history that he'd read so much about. A few months after we all returned to North America, our friend flew to Detroit and took a train to Chatham. We drove to the site of the Battle of the Thames and read the placards on the monument marking the spot where Chief Tecumseh had died during the War of 1812. Then we drove to Uncle Tom's Cabin.

I'd seen it hundreds of times, but this was my first visit. By that point, I knew the history of slavery and the Black settlements in the area and I was embarrassed, ashamed that I'd never set foot on this spot. The tools of confinement and punishment on display unnerved me, and I was moved by the stories of freed and escaped slaves who built a new community, the Dawn Settlement, in the vicinity.

The first local Black residents in the region were four slaves owned by Sarah (Sally) Ainse, an Indigenous woman who arrived from Michigan in 1787 and purchased approximately 9,600 acres of land from the local Indigenous peoples. Free Black settlers and escaped slaves soon began to seek refuge along the Thames River, called Deshkan Ziibi (Antler River) by the Anishinaabeg, which runs from Lake St. Clair and through the city of Chatham. These Black settlers appeared in census records as early as 1791. By then, anti-slavery movements consisting of legal challenges and political lobbying were active in Britain and Canada. By 1793, the Act to Limit Slavery in Upper Canada had passed, banning the importation of new slaves and gradually phasing out slavery. In Canada, every Black person born after this act was deemed free by 1818.

In 1841, Reverend Josiah Henson, an escaped slave who was the inspiration for the titular character in Harriet Beecher Stowe's *Uncle Tom's Cabin*, established the Dawn Settlement near Dresden. His vision was to create a self-sufficient oasis of freedom with land for each family, agriculture, a church and school. The community thrived and soon boasted not only a school but a brickyard and sawmill that helped settlers clear land to grow wheat, corn, and tobacco while exporting black walnut lumber.

I wondered how many others, like me, lived so close and managed to remain so separated from the history in this area.

Forty kilometers south of Uncle Tom's Cabin in Raleigh Township lies North Buxton, originally known as the Elgin Settlement, another large, successful Black community. Near the local park stands an ancient pear tree. Every spring it is covered in white flowers that hint of fruit. And every fall since 1924 it has shaded generations of families, descendants of slaves with roots as deep as the tree's, who return to this spot from every corner of North America for the annual Buxton Homecoming. The town echoes with music as a parade proceeds through the village to the park. The smell of food is pervasive as hamburgers and hot dogs are pulled from nearby grills, tablecloths are spread across picnic tables, and colourful blankets are spread on the grass. Later, the pop of fireworks will accompany an array of colours bright against the night sky.

As with any homecoming celebration, there is sport. For Buxton's first homecoming, Father Robbins, whose descendants would play for the region's first all-Black women's baseball team and the famed Chatham Coloured All-Stars, used a horse to pull a grader across his dirt field. He temporarily relocated his livestock, but the bumps and divots they left behind created unpredictable conditions on the make-shift baseball field. A routine grounder, or a running player, could suddenly launch into the air, eliciting cheers or laughter from the crowd. The ball diamond, with the pear tree in view, is still filled with laughter as Buxton comes alive. Aunts, uncles, cousins, siblings, nieces, and nephews band together; family tree competing against family tree, each seeded by an ancestor who helped build a community founded on freedom and hope.

Shannon Prince, long-time curator of the Buxton Museum, remembers Buxton as an independent, close-knit community.

"Growing up here, we did things as a community. Not only baseball. We went down to the lake to go smelting. We would have picnics at the lake after church on Sunday, we would have square dancing and other events at the community hall—a talent show or a potluck, that sort of thing. When you did things you didn't do them as one family, you did them as a whole community. Everybody in the community was considered to be family, whether or not you were technically related, but we all were just about. It was a nice feeling to walk down the road and have somebody sitting on their porch ask you 'How was school today?' Even though we didn't have extracurricular things, we did the things that kids can't do today. Dodgeball, Red Rover, double dutch, jacks. And the boys had their marbles. So it was fun."

Buxton, named for Sir Thomas Fowell Buxton, who fought for an emancipation act in the British Parliament, began as the Elgin Settlement. It was founded by Reverend William King, an Irish immigrant who, appalled to have acquired fifteen slaves by marriage, began making plans to replicate the Dawn Settlement in the forests and swamps of Chatham-Kent's Raleigh Township, already a terminus on the Underground Railroad, in 1848.

King was popular in the area, having preached in Chatham, but found a formidable opponent in Raleigh councillor Edwin Larwill. A tinsmith born in England, Larwill was a widely respected community leader who considered himself a distinguished man. King's plan alarmed him. Larwill was convinced that if Raleigh and Chatham allowed Black settlements to flourish in the area, their towns would soon be "crowded with Negroes."[1] and circulated a petition against it. King's "City of God" would face fervent opposition from white settlers in the area.

King's popularity declined rapidly. Men he knew well refused to meet his gaze; heads turned away and people backed into storefronts at his approach. Riding through the downtown of nearby Chatham, King was stopped by an unidentified white man who warned King that his life was in danger. In response, King enlisted the help of Archie McKellar, another prominent Chatham citizen, and arranged a town meeting to highlight the benefits a Black settlement would bring to the community. A peaceful meeting took place at the Chatham's Presbyterian Church under the watchful eye of armed guards hired by McKellar and King, who thereafter would secretly follow their movements to ensure their safety.

Not to be outdone, Larwill planned a meeting of his own. He also circulated yet another petition that maintained, "the Negro is a distinct species of the human family . . . far inferior to the European . . . Amalgamation is as disgusting to the eye, as it is immoral in its tendencies and all good men will discountenance."[2] It was signed by 376 residents, 21% of Chatham's adult population.

Now the editor of the *Chatham Journal*, he began running editorials that opposed the settlement:

"Let lands be purchased in some isolated place, where no immediate intercourse can exist between the two races, and the contention and animosity which we are afraid will occur between both if they are sent here, will have no ground of existence."[3]

On August 18, 1849, more than 300 people from all corners of Kent County flowed into the barn behind the Royal Exchange Hotel. As soon as the meeting was called to order, King, who had not been invited to speak, pointed out that Black people had a legal right to own and purchase land in Raleigh. The first "boo" emerged from the crowd. It was followed by a shout from the corner, then others. Soon he could not be heard. As the crowd grew, the meeting moved outside to the front of the hotel.

Archie McKellar addressed the crowd from the balcony, demanding King be heard. The throng again erupted, refusing his plea. Then Edwin Larwill stepped forward, raised his hand, and quieted his supporters. Larwill asserted that King had no right to speak, further inciting his mob below. Shouts rose, fingers and fists pointed in the direction of the Reverend King, who now stood on the balcony near his friend McKellar. The space was electrified, the smell of sweat and loathing heavy in the air. King stepped steadily to the balcony railing, standing wordless as jeers rained over him until, one by one, the people below fell quiet. When only the hum of murmurs and the heavy breath of exertion were audible, King, with the ease of an experienced lecturer, spoke of the plans for Black settlement and the harmony that could exist at the Elgin Settlement.

With the crowd in flux, Walter McCrae, a future Chatham mayor, stepped forward to support Larwill. "Let the slaves of the United States be free, but let it be in their own country; let us not countenance their further introduction among us, in a word, let the people of the United States bear the burden of their own sins . . . the presence of the Negro among [whites] is an annoyance and amalgamation, its necessary and hideous attendant, is an evil which requires to be checked . . . [We do not want a] horde of ignorant slaves in the township of Raleigh."[4]

Following the meeting Larwill doubled down, sending

recommendations to the government to bar Black youths from public schools and to impose other restrictions on the rights and freedoms, including voting rights, of the Black population in Ontario. He continued to leverage his access to local media:

"Would such men submit to have 1,000 coloured paupers introduced into their community, to have the whole township government controlled and its officers selected by them, to have their sons and daughters educated under the same roof, with a black man for a teacher. Let Walpole Island be purchased from or an exchange made with the Indians, and let the African be as nearly by himself as possible."[5]

King was not to be stopped. In 1849, he moved to the Elgin Settlement with his fifteen former slaves, now free to live as his equal. When the United States passed the Fugitive Slave Act, which legalized the capture of escaped slaves and prohibited others from providing aid, the following year, Black migration via the Underground Railroad accelerated. The settlement built its first school, where Reverend King taught, and soon added a brickyard and sawmill that helped the settlement expand to 400 residents by 1852.

This success alarmed many among the local white population. Chatham residents seeing Black refugees settle in the area argued that property values would decrease because Blacks, "being lazy, would let their farms run down . . . Crime would increase, White Canadians would suffer from the Black odour. Blacks would try to marry white girls, with the result that a 'mongrel' population would be produced and the white race would be downgraded."[6]

Edwin Larwill parlayed this anti-Black sentiment into leadership roles in the community, serving first as school commissioner in Chatham and, after 1854, as a member of the Legislative Assembly of the Province of Canada representing the people of Kent. Two years later, he introduced a resolution demanding that "all negro or coloured, male or female quadroon, mulatto, samboes, half breeds or mules, mongrels or conglomerates" be banned from public institutions, and ideally returned to the United States. Despite widespread anti-Black sentiments at the time, this went too far for the House of Assembly, which required Larwill to retract the request.[7]

In 1857, with an election on the horizon, Black community leaders began organizing to defeat Larwill and replace him in the Legislative Assembly with Archie McKellar, who had stood alongside Reverend William King in defence of the Elgin Settlement eight years earlier. Among them was Martin Delany, who moved to the city of Chatham from the United States in 1856, had worked alongside famed Black abolitionist Frederick Douglass to publish the anti-slavery newspaper *The North Star*, and was one of the first three Black men admitted to Harvard Medical School, only to be removed weeks later after protests by white students. On the day of the election, Delany's grassroots campaign in Chatham paid off when 300 Black voters arrived at the courthouse to support McKellar, helping him secure a decisive victory. When the American Civil War broke out, Delany returned to the US and fought for the Union army, where he became the first Black officer to receive the rank of major.

By the onset of the American Civil War in 1861, the city of Chatham's Black population had reached 1,252—28.4% of the community's total residents and almost a third more than Toronto's Black population of 987. But proximity did not bring tolerance. Reverend James Proudfoot, a prominent local minister, condemned Chatham specifically: "There is not a place in Canada where the whites are more prejudiced against the blacks than Chatham."[8]

Now out of politics, Larwill continued to advocate for segregation, now primarily through sport. He and Walter McCrae worked to uphold "the restrictions placed on certain sports by a class-oriented society" in Chatham, with considerable success. According to historian Robert Douglas Day, despite representing more than a quarter of Chatham's population in the 1850s, "the Negro remained largely alienated from Chatham's sporting circles."

In his 1977 thesis, *Impulse to Addiction: A Narrative History of Sport in Chatham, Ontario, 1790-1895*, Day chronicles early occurrences of Black athletes participating in organized sport in Chatham-Kent. According to his research, which stemmed from an examination of local newspapers, the first recorded interracial sporting event in Chatham-Kent history was, fittingly, a grudge match. On April 17, 1862, an Irishman and a Black fighter took to the ring to settle a voting dispute. Sixty spectators watched the 44-round match, which lasted over an hour with no clear winner. The next record of a Black athlete competing against a white opponent in Chatham-Kent didn't appear until several years later when, in May of 1868, a white runner from Ottawa defeated Buxton's Isaac Williams in a footrace at the Chatham Barrack Grounds. Williams lost his $20 wager. A year later in 1869, a Black Chathamite listed only as Parker defeated a runner from Dawn Mills, capturing a $10 prize.

While Larwill and his supporters no doubt found these events distasteful, it was Base Ball, as it was called during this period, that truly alarmed them. This new game derived from the British game of rounders and North American town ball. Town ball, in turn, had originated as a low-risk activity for slaves to play on special holidays.[9] It used materials commonly found on the plantation and appears regularly in slave narratives. Balls were made from cotton, with the main variation being that, to earn an out, defenders would attempt to hit runners with the ball.

As the president of the Chatham Cricket Club, Larwill found this game particularly "palatable to Canada's colonial merchants and aristocrats" because it upheld the traditional power and class structures transported to Canada from Europe.[10] Cricket had long been part of the "colonizers' search for authority" responsible "for communicating English moral worth with 'races' less civilised than our own" and as a "means to a civilised world, promoting teamwork, obedience to the rules, and respect for 'fair play'."[11] A star player himself, Larwill and his sport had long been a beacon for upper-class Chatham, with numerous players advancing to represent Ontario and Canada. Larwill promoted cricket, and appropriate traditional white attire, as a tool to uphold the hegemony of Canada's race relations, a bulwark against this new game that threatened to provide Black athletes with an accessible entry to sport—and society.

While Larwill focused on defending the community against baseball through cricket, his old ally Walter McCrae promoted the merits of the velocipede, a variation on the bicycle that became a worldwide craze in the 1860s. In 1869, McCrae, described as a "pillar of the community," umpired a day of velocipede races that "signified the intense, captivating powers of the sport" in Chatham.[12] Prohibitively expensive, velocipedes effectively maintained the class and race barriers that Base Ball was threatening.

The Black community was equally aware of the racial underpinning of sport. As Frederick Douglass observed, slave owners permitted slaves to spend time on holidays "in sports, ballplaying, wrestling, boxing, running foot races, dancing, and drinking whiskey" but only for the purpose of "keeping the minds of the slaves occupied with prospective pleasure within the limits of slavery."[13] Now, Base Ball was challenging the social norms and traditions cherished by white community leaders and providing opportunities for Black athletes to compete as equals.

"Baseball . . . was as much Canadian as it was American in the nineteenth century. The sport, its athletes and ideas all passed freely across the border . . . the diamond became another avenue for Blacks to reach personal fulfilment and public acclaim."[14]

On June 27, 1871, an all-Black baseball team of local residents took to the field on the Barrack Grounds, traditionally reserved for the town's cricketers. Chatham's Royal Oak Club played the Detroit Unexpected Base Ball Club. Despite a ninth-inning rally that scored fourteen runs, the home team lost 34-30. The following month, the team played another game, this time falling to a well-established team from nearby Ridgetown. Not only were these the first baseball games in Chatham, they are the first recorded games featuring an all-Black team in Chatham-Kent. And although the race of the Detroit team is unknown, the game against Ridgetown definitely featured a white team facing Black opponents. Two years prior, the Goodwills of London were thought to be the first all-Black baseball team in action in Canada when they played an organized game against another all-Black team, the Rialtos of Detroit.

Even as local newspapers "shunned the intrusion of America's pastime into a British-oriented sporting tradition," and maintained that, "Base ball is a degenerate game, compared with good old cricket,"[15] Base Ball continued to gain popularity as a working man's sport. In 1876, *The Chatham Tri-Weekly Planet* reported that the "base ball plague" had infected other communities including London and Guelph, and hoped it would not spread to Chatham, despite the fact that local clubs had been forming for the past five years.

Following the Royal Oak Clubs, another all-Black team emerged in the 1880s, the Jubilee Base Ball Club. In 1884, Black teams from Detroit and Pittsburgh came to town for games and that summer the Chatham Base Ball Club, an all-white team, began organizing. Local papers, as explained in Day's 1977 thesis, continued the narrative of class, stating the club was headed by Chatham's lower class working men compared to the upper class participants of the Cricket Club. In the United States, the Cuban Giants became the first Black professional baseball team when they formed in 1885, and in 1887, the short-lived National Colored Base Ball League organized. As William Humber stated in his 2004 book *A Sporting Chance: Achievements of African-Canadian Athletes*, "Formal separation of Blacks and whites was not as yet accepted practice" in this era. Black teams were forming leagues, and barnstormed against Black, white, and Indigenous teams. Formal separation occurred in 1887, when rules were implemented to keep Black athletes off of "white teams."

The game remained segregated through the turn of the century, but teams from Negro Leagues in the United States began challenging white Canadian teams. In 1898, this included a game between the all-white Chatham Reds, an independent semi-professional team, and the Page Fence Giants, then considered the top Black team in the United States, having won a miraculous 82 straight games the previous year. In front of 1,000 Chatham fans, the Giants defeated Chatham 9-1, even though Chatham's pitcher was Rube Waddell, who would go on to have a storied Major League Baseball career earning himself a spot in the Baseball Hall of Fame. The following year, another all-Black team, the Chicago Columbia Giants, barnstormed through Chatham. One of the members of the Page Fence Giants and Chicago Columbia Giants to play in Chatham was William H. Binga, one of the foremost outfielders and hitters in the era. Binga's family had escaped slavery in Kentucky, with some members, including his father, settling in Detroit, and the remainder settling in Chatham and nearby Amherstburg.

Despite the emergence of Black team sports, and the occasional mention of individual Black athletes, sports records in Chatham-Kent remained largely white through the 1800s. According to Robert Douglas Day, "Sport, for the most part, was a product of the British contingent in Chatham. The English and Scottish elements in the town implanted their traditional sport forms. Such sporting pastimes became substantiated as the most popular activities in the town . . . The Blacks simply could not, or probably more correctly, were not allowed to find a niche in the diversified sport model."[16]

Indigenous teams were similarly excluded. There is a record of the Walpole Island Indian Clipper Club playing against a Chatham baseball team in 1876, and a Toronto team in 1877. In 1878, a new iteration, the Walpole Island Oil Stockings defeated a team of white players known as the Chatham Stars 10-7. Reporting on the game, the *Chatham Tri-Weekly Planet* wrote, "The catching of Cole and first base playing of Frawley scalped several of the Indians in crossing home plate."[17]

Edwin Larwill died in 1876. A road in Chatham, Park Avenue, was originally known as Larwill Avenue and in old Guelph there are still two one-block roads named Edwin Street and Charles Street, named for Larwill and Charles Smith, stars of the Chatham Cricket Club, following their outstanding performance in a cricket match in Guelph that impressed fans and distinguished guests including the Lieutenant Governor. But Larwill's true legacy lived on through one of his successors as president of the Chatham Cricket Club, H.A. Tanser.

An educator who earned his doctorate at the University of Toronto in 1939, Harry Ambrose Tanser steadily climbed the ranks of the Chatham School Board serving first as Inspector and then as Superintendent. He was in charge of all schools in Chatham for nearly thirty years and was a regular speaker at educational events across Southwestern Ontario. Nicknamed "Mr. Education" by the media, Tanser's contributions were formally acknowledged when, upon his retirement in 1962, the Chatham Board of Education named a newly opened school after him. As *The Windsor Star* put it, Tanser was a "man of vision" who "helped shape the lives of thousands of boys and girls."[18] Although the school was later torn down to make way for a subdivision, a road, Tanser Court, still marks the location.

Tanser shared Larwill's conviction that baseball was a lower-class activity that, left unchecked, would corrode the social order. In the February 18, 1935 edition of *The Windsor Star*, he published an editorial for the Ontario College of Education advocating that cricket, a sport with "fine ideals of sportsmanship, esprit de corps, and teamwork," be adopted in all Canadian schools. Leading by example, he started cricket teams for boys at all Chatham schools and banned any student from playing on both school softball and cricket teams.

Tanser sought to buttress endangered "whiteness" through sport even as he argued that racial identity and heredity were the sole determinants of intellectual capability. In the years leading up to World War II, Tanser used his position as Chatham's Inspector of Public Schools to recruit teachers to help test Black and white students in Kent County. In his 1939 publication, *The Settlement of Negroes in Kent County, Ontario, and a Study of the Mental Capacity of Their Descendants,* he claimed to have discovered the "marked superiority of Kent County whites over the Negroes."[19] He considered white students to be superior in all ways, "followed in order by Japanese, the Indians, the Chinese, and the Negroes."[20]

Tanser's work, which was later turned into a book, was sponsored by noted eugenicist Peter Sandiford from the University of Toronto, a man whose own publications included *The Mental Capacity of Southern Ontario Indians.* Another noted local school trustee and author, Victor Lauriston, commended Tanser's research for taking the "unprejudiced approach of the teacher" to ensure that "conclusions are drawn from evidence carefully gathered."[21]

Two years later, Tanser published a paper titled the *Intelligence of Negroes of Mixed Blood in Canada,* arguing that intelligence varies with "white blood." Ranking Black students as full-bloods, mixed bloods, three-quarters bloods, half-bloods, and quarter-bloods, he argued for breeding Black populations with white as a way to improve the general lack of achievement on the part of "full-blooded Negroes."[22]

The same year, 1941, Tanser addressed a crowd in Windsor, Ontario, calling upon Canadians to be vigilant in their defence of the white population against immigration because "we are not numerous enough in this country to be masters of our own destiny." He stated that Canada would do well to avoid repeating the problems that arose with the "infiltration" of escaping slaves.[23]

In her book, *Seek the Truth,* local Black historian Gwen Robinson recalls Tanser's tenure, and the impact it had on

Chatham's Black community. "The system has done a good job of convincing some blacks that they are inferior . . . Tanser's printed word is a part of that system perpetuating the myth of racial superiority."[24] Robinson began writing her book, a compendium of Black history in Chatham-Kent, when her son Drew received an assignment in elementary school to write a report on Black history. He soon found there was little to no information in the local library, an omission that may well have reflected Tanser's ongoing influence.

Dorothy Wright-Wallace clearly remembers Tanser visiting her Grade 3 classroom when she was eight years old. She sat on the floor by the window listening to him read *The Story of Little Black Sambo*, a caricature of a Black youth who lives with his parents Black Jumbo and Black Mumbo. The book's illustrations made her feel ill.

As she speaks of him, she is transported back to that room. Every nuance and sound is vivid, every piece in its place. She remembers piercing blue eyes that were focused largely on her, a little Black girl among mostly white classmates. Even after so many years, her confusion and sadness are clear as she places her hands on the table and leans in, a few freckles showing above the blue mask she is wearing amid a global pandemic. Her voice breaks only for a second. "It hurts when I think of him. It's just like he's there, and I can't get him out."

I have a photo of H.A. Tanser. In it, he's kneeling with a cricket bat propping him up on one side and batting pads strapped to his legs. I can't see his eyes. He's wearing spectacles and squinting, likely looking into the sun. He's dressed all in white, as are the nine other men surrounding him, part of Chatham's cricket team. A few of them are wearing suspenders, but not Tanser, who looks more youthful than most of his teammates. His posture is impeccable, proper. He's almost smiling, and I can't help but think he looks complacent, secure in his superiority. One of the highest paid men in town, president of a sports club he loves, with the power to do as he pleases.

## Chapter 2

# IT WAS NEVER OUR GAME

A wave of smoke and stale beer would crawl across you, sticking to your hair and skin as you entered Sam's Hotel in Wallaceburg. Marking you. Above the bar in rented rooms were drug addicts, the residents who validated the "hotel" moniker. On the main floor, the thud of music would fill your ears, slightly tinny with simultaneously too much bass. Nameless and hapless bodies rubbed against each other on the dance floor, watched by older men with crude mouths. On the right was a long bar lined with cheap liquor and bargain beer; to the left there were a few pool tables. A dive bar that was only palatable in an inebriated low light, Sam's was not the kind of place you told your mother about, although she had probably been there at some point as well. It was where we went when we wanted the darkness to hide us.

Sam's Hotel opened in 1947 as the Lord Selkirk Ballroom, named in honour of a man who devised a plan to expropriate nearby Indigenous lands for a Scottish settlement. Before my first visit I was told to lower my gaze and walk straight through to the back of the club where tables lined the dance floor near the stage. This is where the white people sat. I was taught not to make eye contact with the people who inhabited the front half of the space; this is where the Indigenous people were.

Sam's had a reputation. This was where fights happened, where people got stabbed. I never did see a stabbing, but I saw fights, and I saw someone run down by a car in the parking lot, right next to the No Frills grocery store shopping cart return. And I read headline after headline about assault, attempted murder, and more. As the clock crept past midnight, pores filled with smoke and cells swelled with alcohol. The intolerance held in the fatty parts of the body was released as muscle memory moved opponents from the dance floor to the parking lot. Sometimes it was one person fighting another, sometimes it was group versus group, always white versus Indigenous. I'm not sure I ever knew of a motive. It was years before I realized I didn't know how we'd got here, how Canada got here.

The Lenape were the original inhabitants of lands stretching along the Delaware River, across the modern states of Pennsylvania, New Jersey, New York, and Delaware. It was the Lenape, renamed Delaware by arriving colonists, who sold Manhattan to the Dutch and deeded land to William Penn. The Lenape of Pennsylvania were later colonized by Moravian German missionaries who, as pacifists, were viewed with suspicion by all combatants during the Revolutionary War. In 1782, ninety Lenape people, thirty-four of them children, were massacred in Gnadenhutten, Ohio by American militiamen. The survivors moved north, eventually joining the Chippewa, Odawa, and Pottawatami along the banks of the Thames River. Delaware Nation at Moraviantown, Eelünaapéewi Lahkéewiit, was founded on May 2, 1792.

Shortly after the Lenape were attacked in Pennsylvania, in 1796, the British created the Chenail Ecarté Reserve by purchasing twelve square miles of land along the St. Clair River from local Chippewa chiefs in anticipation of a significant influx of Indigenous refugees from the United States. In 1804, when it was clear that the expected migration would not occur, Lord Selkirk devised his plan to convert a portion of the Chenail Ecarté Reserve to a Scottish settlement. In the eyes of the British, Indigenous people had no need of land that had supported their economic and cultural practices for generations.[1]

In the coming years, deforestation, urbanization, and the dispossession of land by settlers all combined to undermine the

Indigenous way of life. Researchers McDougall and Valentine provide a comprehensive history of this process: "The politics of the settler world transformed the reserves from home bases from which one could move out to hunt to insecure islands in a settler sea."[2]

During the War of 1812, many Indigenous peoples supported the British, hoping to achieve greater autonomy. However, the British delegation to the Treaty of Ghent (1814) that ended the war was unable to secure American support for an Indian territory. Throughout the early years of the 19th century, the Indigenous population endured numerous murders, sexual assaults, and other acts of violence perpetrated by white settlers who began pressuring the government for more restrictions on Indigenous people, a sentiment that coincided with the arrival of the first Protestant missionaries in the 1820s.

Historians Eamon and Marshall maintain that, "for Indigenous peoples living in British North America, the War of 1812 also marked the end of an era of self-reliance and self-determination. Soon they would become outnumbered by settlers in their own lands. Any social or political influence enjoyed before the war dissipated. Within a generation, the contributions of so many different peoples, working together with their British and Canadian allies against a common foe, would be all but forgotten."[3]

Indigenous people resisted the impending threat of further colonization and the pressures from missionaries. Bauzhi-geezhig-waeshikum, hereditary chief of Walpole Island during the 1820s and 1830s, pointed out the hypocrisy of the Methodist church:

"The white man makes fire-water, he drinks, and he sells it to the Indians, he lies and cheats the poor Indian. I have seen him go to his prayer house in [Fort] Malden, and as soon as he comes out I have seen him go straight to the tavern, get drunk, quarrel, and fight. Now the white man's religion is no better than mine. I will hold fast to the religion of my forefathers."[4]

Despite their protests, new restrictions continued to be imposed.

Indian Agents were introduced in the 1830s and were given sweeping powers to regulate most aspects of Indigenous life. By the 1840s, Indigenous people no longer had access to the Chenail Ecarté Reserve or surrounding lands, leaving only a group of islands collectively referred to as Walpole Island. This land was—and remains—unceded territory.

In the 1840s, the Anglican Church sent missionaries to build a church on Walpole Island. One of them, Reverend Andrew Jamieson, served as a missionary on Walpole Island for forty years, baptizing as many as 400 of Walpole Island's 750 residents. The Anglicans were followed by the Jesuits. Missionary Dominique du Ranquet and his assistant claimed to have "learned that a great number of still heathen savages were living on this island and they resolved to Save them."[5] Convinced that Indigenous culture and beliefs were primitive and inferior, the Jesuits cut down a large grove of ancient oaks on the Island's traditional burial grounds and replaced them with a steeple. At a meeting in 1849, orator Ochaouanon pointedly responded:

"You, Black Robe, the man who wears a hat, what have you done? You have dishonoured the most beautiful part of this island, which is ours. You have cut down some ancient trees, trees which we respected. What do you intend to do with them? Build a large prayer lodge? But what would you say if we went to the other side of the great water to force our customs on you? When have Whites ever taken part in our dances, our celebrations, our customs and boasted about it? Black Robe. . . you have come to ridicule our customs right here on our own land . . . You mock the remains of our ancestors."[6]

Chief Petwegizhik, Walpole Island's last hereditary chief, led the opposition to the Jesuit missionaries and, in 1850, burned the Jesuit church to the ground. Dominique du Ranquet left the island and never returned.

White society's disdain for Indigenous culture extended to sport, seen as another space to hegemonize. Early French colonizers were quick to adopt the game of baggataway, which had been played among the Anishinaabe and Haudenosaunee Nations in the area as long as memory existed. They renamed it lacrosse, after the French term for field hockey, *le jeu de la crosse.*

In the 19th century, the game became firmly aligned with British influences in the country, largely due to the efforts of William Beers, who published standardized rules for the game in 1860. A Montreal-born player and enthusiast, Beers saw a tool that could be used to establish a unique Anglo-Canadian identity. He explained his reasoning in his book, *Lacrosse: The National Game of Canada,* published in 1869.

From the moment lacrosse "had its first existence in his wild brain," Beers believed "that the Indians of Canada know nothing whatever about the origin of their native field game." For Beers, on and off field colonization went hand in hand. "When civilization tamed the manners and habits of the Indian, it reflected its modifying influence upon his amusements, and thus was Lacrosse gradually divested of its radical rudeness and brought to be a more sober sport."

"The Indian never can play as scientifically as the best white players and it is a lamentable fact, that lacrosse, and the wind for running, which comes as natural to the red-skin as his dialect, has to be gained on the part of the pale-faced, by a gradual course of practice and training." Once suitably trained, however, "there is no reason an Indian feat may not be done by a white player."

The National Lacrosse Association was formed in 1867, the same year Canada became an independent country, becoming the first governing body of sport in the new Dominion. In *Lacrosse: The National Game of Canada*, Beers stated that Canadians "claimed their field game as the national game of our dominion" in the same way they had claimed the "rivers and lakes and land" once owned by Indigenous people. He lobbied strenuously—but unsuccessfully—to have lacrosse officially recognized as Canada's national sport. "As cricket, wherever played by Britons, is a link of loyalty to their home, so may lacrosse be to Canadians."

Lacrosse was no longer an Indigenous game in the eyes of settlers. Just as language and ceremonies were stripped away through residential schools, so too was the spiritual nature and value of lacrosse. Indigenous people viewed baggataway—the Creator's game—as a spiritual activity intrinsic to their culture. It was played for healing, to resolve disputes, for social purposes, and for political reasons. In the hands of white Euro-Canadians, lacrosse was reduced to entertainment and became subject to the hyper-competitive, results-driven hierarchy that underpins western sport. What was originally a borderless game was hemmed in, defined and given structure where none previously existed.

Europeans favoured Christianity, and through residential schools attempted to Christianize Indigenous peoples, so it is no wonder that the Creator's game, often viewed as a spiritual ritual, was something to be erased and colonized. In her 2020 paper *The Appropriation of Lacrosse: Competitive Lacrosse and The Creator's Game*, Chloe Anderson argues that, "Europeans prioritized Christianity and secularization, so even if they saw lacrosse as spiritual rather than merely a game, they likely did not see the appropriation as the travesty and injustice it is because of their skewed views of what fit the category of important and religious."

In his 2018 thesis, scholar Andrew Narraway writes that "the history of lacrosse is a history of trickery, where Euro-Canadians appropriated it for their own identity purposes yet continue to struggle to define themselves."[7] Within a decade, lacrosse was being played in the United States, Australia, and the United Kingdom, an export from Canada. A tour organized by William Beers brought the game to the United Kingdom in 1876. That same year, another Canadian, Lambton L. Mount brought forty lacrosse sticks to Australia and created the Melbourne Lacrosse Club. By 1879, the

American Lacrosse Association had been founded with nine clubs. Today, almost fifty countries compete internationally in lacrosse.

The Chatham Lacrosse Club was formed in 1868. By the 1880s, local teams including the Blenheim Kents, Chatham Dodger Club, and Ridgetown Howards, all exclusively composed of white players, were competing in "sudden death" single goal contests. Teams and athletes from settler communities on both sides of the border now pitted themselves against those from Walpole Island and Delaware Nation. Walpole Island's lacrosse teams did not compete in league competition but they played many challenge matches, often from teams arriving via steamer. In 1887, the Detroit Lacrosse Club went to Walpole Island and, according to the July 21 edition of the *Detroit Free Press*, "crossed sticks with a team of Indians." The headline read "The Detroits Take Two Scalps at Walpole Island" and the accompanying story proudly proclaimed that "the redskins were outplayed at every point." In 1893, Windsor's YMCA Lacrosse Club travelled to play Walpole's team in a match that would become an annual Dominion Day tradition.

In the 20th century, lacrosse was once again modified to meet the needs of white society. Communities across the country were building indoor rinks as the popularity of hockey continued to skyrocket and were anxious to use these facilities during the summer months. In the 1920s, Montreal's Paddy Brennan began experimenting with a new, indoor version of the game that was faster paced and required fewer players, mimicking Canada's other growing passion, hockey. This new game of box lacrosse quickly supplanted the traditional, field-based version in popularity and, in 1931, was adopted by the Canadian Amateur Lacrosse Association as the official form of the sport in the country. By moving lacrosse indoors, onto iceless hockey surfaces, the appropriation of the game was complete. According to the 1996 Report of the Royal Commission on Aboriginal Peoples, "recreation was re-creation," and Beers, among others, had appropriated the game, recreated it into a westernized tool of colonization and assimilation, and then touted it to the world as distinctly "Canadian."

While lacrosse wasn't proclaimed Canada's national sport during his lifetime, William Beers' constant promotion lodged the notion in the public consciousness where it continued to compete with hockey. In 1994, The National Sports of Canada Act resolved this rivalry, officially recognizing lacrosse as Canada's official summer game and hockey as its official winter game.

Indigenous culture is slowly reclaiming spaces long associated with oppression. Just as a forest fire devastates ancient trees to create an opportunity for dormant seeds, the demolition of Sam's Hotel in 2020 provided an opportunity for renewal. Everyone had a story of something that happened there—a first kiss or a black eye—and when the rubble was removed a part of our shared history went with it. On a spot once soaked in blood and beer, a new foundation was poured and the Ska:na Family Learning Centre arose. Ska:na means "Creator's peace" and the centre is dedicated to providing childcare infused with cultural practices and traditions for Indigenous youth. From the truth of the division that was once here comes the reconciliation of learning, and youth beginning again. Where there had been countless fights, there is now peace.

## Chapter 3

# A BIBLE IN MY HANDS

I grew up learning jokes about Indigenous people. Teachers, coaches, and friends used a myriad of slurs to explain that Indigenous people could not support their families, were drunks, could not be trusted, and were liable to steal or burn cars. Indigenous youth who were bussed from Walpole Island First Nation to "our" school were "lazy." Entering high school, older students told us what hallway to avoid because it was where the "Native" students hung out. Walpole Island, its forested areas interspersed with houses, many of which could be best described as derelict, was a place we went to play hockey or to reach the ferry to the United States.

Entering junior hockey as a fourteen-year-old, I was terrified of my new Indigenous teammates. I soon learned what a status card was, and that they could buy hockey sticks without paying taxes. Thanks to the influence of my church, my school, my town, and my teams, I had built a caricature of an Indigenous person. It was sport, in the form of my teammates, that helped the unknown become known.

Louie and Luke Blackbird, among others, were members of our Wallaceburg Lakers team. They were tough players with Ontario Hockey League experience who called Walpole Island home. In one of my first games, I got into trouble on the ice, caught in the corner as I was repeatedly cross-checked by a much older and larger opponent. Louie, my defence partner, swooped in, grabbed the player, dropped his gloves and, within seconds, had landed several punches. He lay on top of my tormentor while I held on to the next closest player, tussling with a new foe closer to my size. Without a word, Louie got up and skated toward the penalty box. He was assessed five minutes for fighting while I was handed two minutes for roughing. As we sat side by side in the penalty box, he looked over, a smile forming at the edges of his mouth like a comic ready to deliver his punch line, and said, "If I ever have to do that again, you're next." He tapped me on the shin pads, with a chuckle. I took a drink of water and exhaled. From that moment on, I played knowing I had Louie on the ice with me, and that he was a friend, not an enemy.

In my early twenties, I volunteered and then briefly worked at Walpole Island First Nation Elementary School. The school grounds were an oasis: a baseball diamond and climbing equipment bordered by tall grass and shaded by oak trees. Standing in that field, watching First Nations youth roll a ball across the plate in a game of soccer-baseball, I realized that I knew nothing about the land I was standing on, and less about the people I was with. It had been easier not to listen, or at least not to hear.

At the end of that school year in 2008, some of the Walpole Island staff organized a field trip to watch the Detroit Tigers play. I sat alone near the back of the bus talking to two boys named Ernie and Wolfgang, surrounded by the laughter and excitement of children. When our bus stopped at the border, the customs officer took my passport—and mine alone—to be scanned. I was the only non-Indigenous person on the bus; everyone else was simply moving through their ancestral territory. I was the white settler whose ancestors had created this imaginary division between people, along with an educational system that had perpetrated incalculable harm. I'd been raised in the church, had played and coached sport, and was now beginning a career in education sitting on a bus full of children whose grandparents had survived residential school. I looked down at my passport and knew which side of this border I had come from, but was unsure of where I, and these Indigenous kids, were headed next.

From the beginning of their relationship with Indigenous populations, churches considered education as integral to their mission.

In 1828, the Anglican Church of Canada opened a day school, the Mechanics' Institute, for boys from Six Nations of the Grand River Reserve. Three years later, it would become the Mohawk Institute, Canada's first residential school. At first, the Mohawk Institute operated for boys only, but Indigenous girls were brought to the facility after 1834.

In the years following confederation, the newly formed government endorsed the churches' efforts to "civilize" Indigenous people. In the words of Prime Minister Sir John A. Macdonald, the 1876 Indian Act sought to control Indigenous communities so as to "wean them by slow degrees, from their nomadic habits, which have almost become an instinct, and by slow degrees absorb them or settle them on the land."[1] In 1883, the residential school model became official government policy. Making the announcement, Public Works Minister Hector Langevin told the House of Commons that, "In order to educate the children properly we must separate them from their families. Some people may say that this is hard but if we want to civilize them we must do that."[2]

An early target of this "civilizing" effort was Elijah "Ed" Pinnance who was brought to Shingwauk Residential School near Sault Ste. Marie, 635 kilometers from his home on Walpole Island in 1894. Shingwauk Industrial Home was originally opened in 1873 in Garden River First Nation but burnt to the ground only six days after opening. The new facility, which would become Shingwauk Indian Residential School, opened two years later in 1875 on what is currently the site of Algoma University. Pinnance was among the first of 534 Walpole Island students who would be taken to residential schools, 370 of whom would attend Shingwauk. Close to two dozen Walpole Island and Moraviantown youth would die there. Those are the documented deaths.

Shingwauk was operated by the Anglican Church with a goal to "raise the Indians from their present low degraded position, & place them on an equal footing with their white neighbours, to make in

31

fact Canadians of them."[3] This was to be accomplished through forced confinement in cold and unsanitary living conditions, abuse, sexual assault, starvation, neglect, and isolation. "Making Canadians" required lopping off braids, banning traditional languages, and meting out physical punishment for any behaviour that could be deemed Indigenous, something previously unheard of. According to one Walpole Island survivor, "physical punishment of children was not practiced in our culture before the arrival of Europeans. Children were cherished because they were closest to the Creator, and they represented our future."[4]

Sport was integral to school life both as recreation and as a useful disciplinary tool. In the summer months, children who behaved would be allowed to play baseball or basketball or participate in track and field days. "Deserving" children could momentarily run free or swim in local lakes. When the lakes froze, boys could strap on skates and play hockey, each glide of the blade a stride toward assimilation.

In a 1890 edition of *Our Forest Children: Published In The Interest Of Indian Education And Civilization*, a monthly periodical published in Shingwauk's printmaking shop and edited by the Reverend in charge, school administrators use of sport as a recruitment tool was described, promising that youth would "play games like white boys do" and confirming that "base ball was all the rage; a large piece of ground in front of the Home had been levelled and made a capital ground for playing on, and there every spare moment seemed to be spent both by master and boys."

The Shingwauk Buckskin Base Ball Club had been formed the year prior in 1889 and included at least four Walpole Island residents: Joseph Sampson, an eighteen-year-old who worked in the bootmaking shop Pinnance would later run; William Riley and John Solomon, both seventeen; and nine-year-old Louis Issac. Upon their release, the boys who played for this team would bring the game back to Walpole Island.

Principal George Ley King was proud of the boys' performance.

"They excel at football and base ball, their favourite games, and are rarely beaten by outside teams." In a letter to stakeholders of the school included in the 1890 report, Sampson confirmed that, "we Indians boys made 26 runs and the White boys made 22 runs." In the year ahead the Buckskin Club was slated to play "against . . . the white people." Sampson said, "I hope we will beat them."

During his years at Shingwauk, Pinnance participated in all sports, including football, but his first love was baseball. In an 1897 letter to his family, Pinnance's passion is clear: "The snow is not all gone yet but it is going very fast. We are all anxious to get at our games," he wrote. "The boys have organized a Foot Ball Club and are collecting money to buy a ball . . . They are going to organize a Base Ball Club too."[5]

Leaving Shingwauk in 1900, Pinnance was recruited to play baseball for the Carlisle Indian Industrial School located in the traditional Lenape territory of Pennsylvania. Like its Canadian counterparts, Carlisle aimed to extirpate Indigenous culture, language, and beliefs. Operated by the US government, the school was administered by a former military officer named Richard Henry Pratt who believed: "It is this nature in our red brother that is better dead than alive, and when we agree with the oft-repeated sentiment that the only good Indian is a dead one, we mean this characteristic of the Indian. Carlisle's mission is to kill this Indian, as we build up the better man."[6]

For Pratt, the best way to demonstrate Carlisle's success was through sport—strong men playing American games. So, in 1879, he travelled to Dakota Territory to "recruit" the first students for Carlisle from the Oglala Sioux and Brule Sioux. Within three years, the school had formed a football club and baseball team and began cultivating a reputation in the sporting world by competing against Ivy League schools such as Cornell, Harvard, Princeton, and Yale. The success of these teams on the field and in advancing Indigenous athletes to professional teams soon did the recruiting for Carlisle.

As David Wallace Adams wrote in *More than a Game: The Carlisle Indians Take to the Gridiron, 1893-1917*, the school's competition against, and victory over these schools was a demonstration of Pratt's hopes for acculturation and the "potential for football to win white friends for the cause of full Indian acceptance into the American system."[7] Sport was an opportunity for Pratt to "gain wider support for his ideas on Indian progress," his idea to "kill the Indian, and save the man."

The school's football, baseball, and track teams were coached by the legendary Glenn "Pop" Warner. Most closely associated with football, Warner and the Carlisle team are credited with pioneering the forward pass, the three-point stance and the overhead spiral. In one famous game in 1911, Carlisle upset Harvard 18-15 in front of 25,000 fans, with future Olympic gold medallist and Football Hall of Fame member Jim Thorpe scoring every point for the school.

Warner clearly understood the role sport played at Carlisle. In one infamous speech, recorded in Sally Jenkins' book *The Real Americans*, Warner addressed his football team before they played Army: "Your fathers and your grandfathers are the ones who fought their fathers . . . These men playing against you today are soldiers. They are the Long Knives. You are Indians. Tonight, we will know if you are warriors."[8] Carlisle, again led by Thorpe, easily won the game 27-6, defeating a team that included nine future Army generals, among them Dwight D. Eisenhower.

At least twenty Carlisle alumni, including Ed Pinnance, would go on to play professional sports. According to an account from Nin.Da.Waab.Jig, a research project based on Walpole Island, "after developing his playing skills at various schools, [Pinnance] returned to the Walpole area where he caught the attention of a pro baseball scout." Only months after leaving Carlisle, Pinnance played his first professional baseball games for the Lawyers in Mount Clements, Michigan. He later played for Nashua and New Lebanon in the New England League.

It was while he was playing in New Lebanon that Pinnance received the call to play for the Philadelphia Athletics in the Major Leagues. Until then, only two Indigenous athletes had competed in Major League Baseball: Louis Sockalexis (1897) and Bill Phyle (1898). Sockalexis is often identified as the first Indigenous player in Major League Baseball history, spending three seasons competing for the Cleveland Spiders and his presence in Cleveland, is often cited as the reason the franchise later chose the name "Indians" in 1915.[9] Bill Phyle pitched a shutout in his major league debut in 1898, and spent time with the Chicago Orphans, New York Giants, and St. Louis Cardinals, ending his Major League career in 1906.

At twenty-two, Pinnance made his debut pitching for the Philadelphia Athletics against the Washington Senators. In the only two appearances he made in the Majors, Pinnance struck out two batters, and finished with a 2.57 ERA. He allowed only five hits in the seven innings he played and earned a save in his lone decision.

The September 15, 1903 edition of *The Philadelphia Inquirer* reported that fans took note of their new pitcher and began mocking his name, calling him Peanuts instead of Pinnance. "As soon as Pinnance stepped to the rubber he was christened 'Peanuts' by the bleacherites and this name will probably stick to him for all time."

In *The American Indian Integration of Baseball*, Jeffrey Powers-Beck describes the press conference after the game. When a Washington reporter asked him about the jeering, Pinnance replied with humour and wit. "Why should that name annoy me? I'll be roasted more or less, and from what I've been able to observe, the roasting process vastly improves the peanut." The press took jabs at Pinnance and fellow Indigenous player Charles Albert Bender, condemning them as "foreigners" even though they were playing on their ancestral lands.

Charles Bender had played with Pinnance at Carlisle and was reunited with him when both joined the Philadelphia Athletics in 1903. Bender would go on to a Hall of Fame career, winning three

World Series titles with the Athletics. Despite its brevity, Pinnance's appearance is considered significant because he was the first "full-blooded" Indigenous athlete to play Major League Baseball, a reference to the longstanding measure, especially in the United States, of blood quantum.

Blood quantum claims to determine race according to ancestry or "bloodlines." It's a measure used by white settlers to determine Indigeneity by identifying what percentage of blood comes directly from Indigenous ancestry. Prior to colonization, no such measure was used by tribes or nations for assessing cultural inclusion. For Black Americans, racial classification had been enshrined in law since the 1800s, particularly during the Reconstruction era following the Civil War. To defend whiteness, anyone with even "one drop" of Black ancestry was considered to be Black. Even though the concept of blood quantum for Indigenous peoples was not formally recognized in US law until 1924 through the Racial Integrity Act, and later in the 1934 Indian Reorganization Act, the societal definitions had long been in place.

The same concept that was used to segregate Black citizens became a measure of assimilation for the Indigenous population. In a 2021 *California Law Review* article, Maya Harman argues, "Using blood quantum allowed the government to turn independent nations into racialized groups, which thus enabled the government to subordinate them. . .The government hoped that using blood quantum would eventually eliminate Native peoples—that intermarriage would 'dilute' the amount of 'Indian blood' in the population, causing descendants of Native peoples to become indistinguishable from the rest of the population."[10]

While the concept of blood quantum would seem outdated, it continues to be used as a standard in the sporting world. The Baseball Hall of Fame refers to blood quantum in the official biography of Charles Bender and, in a November 2021 feature for NBC, Max Molski's *Get to Know the History of Native Americans in Baseball* claims "there have been 52 major league players who were verifiable full-blooded American Indians."[11] In Canada, teenager Josiah Wilson, a member of the Heiltsuk First Nation, was barred from the 2016 All-Native Basketball Tournament because he had been adopted from Haiti, and therefore did not have Indigenous blood.

In the eyes of white officials, Pinnance was "full-blooded" and his success in spite of his undiluted "Indian blood" made him a novelty. Without blood quantum, Sockalexis might be the only Indigenous athlete remembered as a "first," while Bender would be discussed only for the racism that followed, and his exceptional on-field play. Pinnance's brief Major League appearance might have been completely forgotten.

After his appearance with the Philadelphia Athletics, Pinnance went on to play professionally for Portland in the Pacific Coast League, Amsterdam and Troy in the New York State League, Bay City in the Southern Michigan League, and Davenport in the Illinois-Indiana-Iowa League. He retired in 1910 due to health issues related to diabetes.

After returning home, Pinnance farmed on Walpole Island and Squirrel Island, worked in marine contracting and as a blacksmith, and used his calligraphy skills to create posters and business cards for local establishments. He became a community leader, serving on the Band Council for six terms, from 1916 until 1931, and was tasked with coordinating the use of a tractor, plough, and threshing machine donated by Henry Ford, who regularly visited Walpole Island on his yacht.

When his health allowed, Pinnance would pitch to local kids, including his son, and wow them with his famous curveball that did "magic dances" as it approached the plate. From time to time, he would suit up for a game as well. At the annual Walpole Island Fair in 1921, Pinnance, now older and heavier, became the first player to ever hit a home run out of the fairgrounds. "The spectators they said that's even a longer drive than Babe Ruth with a home run,"

Robert Kiyoshk, a Walpole Island elder recalled. "Everybody was just yelling and jumping and clapping their hands . . . As stout as he was—Elijah Pinnance—he walked around the diamond. He didn't have to run."[12]

Pinnance's success inspired others on Walpole Island and at nearby Delaware Nation. Indigenous youth began taking balls and bats into open fields and creating makeshift bases.

Teams from Walpole Island had been competing in formal leagues since the turn of the century; by 1905, they were a dominant force in Kent and Lambton Counties and played American teams from Algonac and Port Huron, Michigan. The 1905-1906 Walpole Island Base Ball team "won many victories" and were "probably the champions of any Indian team in the Dominion of Canada."[13] This was the first local Indigenous team to leave behind a team photo and a record of their roster.

Ed Pinnance passed away in 1944, but his passion for baseball lives on in Walpole Island students like Ernie and Wolfgang. As we watched Justin Verlander throw a spectacular game from the mound, we stole French fries and chicken strips from each other, dipped nachos, shucked peanuts, and laughed as a group of white women in front of us became more intoxicated with each inning.

When the game ended, we weaved through bodies and boarded our bus home. Again, I was the only passenger who needed a passport to cross this arbitrary border. When we returned to Walpole Island, a staff member and parent handed me a gift, a thank you for my months of volunteering, and for chaperoning this year-end trip. For a moment, I felt like the borders had disappeared, that I was immersed in Indigenous culture, and my presence was not out of place.

When I opened the gift, I saw a beautiful Bible bound in white fabric. Inside, laid across a blank page, was the signature of every student on the bus that day. Some printed, some in cursive, all written with the abandon of a youth passing the book on to the waiting hands next to them. It was then I realized how wrong I'd been. I didn't belong here, even though I would always be here. I was standing on unceded territory, a descendent of white settlers who had committed atrocities against Indigenous people that remain largely unacknowledged. I went to elementary and secondary school ten minutes from Walpole Island, alongside Indigenous students, and I'd never heard of a residential school until my final year of university. And yet there I stood, with a Bible in my hands.

## Chapter 4

# THE GREAT WHITE HOPES

Growing up in Wallaceburg, it was a Wednesday tradition for teens to watch the local junior hockey team play. Teenagers would line the area behind the visitors' bench to see the fights on the ice, and then start their own in the stands. Sometimes it was teenage bravado, but more often race was involved in the fracas. The following day, in coffee shops and in our classrooms, the score was an afterthought to the drama in the stands.

At school, on our lunch break, differences were again settled with fists. The ring was an alleyway or the parking lot behind an old building. A kid from Walpole Island with a group of friends behind them, and a white kid from town supported by his friends. They'd fight, the circle around them cheering and catcalling. If either combatant collided with the spectators forming the ring, it was likely they would join the fray. When the last punch was thrown, when the combatants were exhausted, or a level-headed spectator intervened, we'd return to our classrooms. Somewhere in the room a student with scuffed knuckles, and another with a swollen eye, would sit dazed. The fight was not over; rather, the combatants had simply retreated to their corners, waiting for the bell to sound at the end of class, and for another round to begin.

Boxing, or pugilism as it was originally known, has a storied history in Canada and elsewhere. In Chatham-Kent, the earliest recorded bout occurred in 1845, with the first Black fighter on record competing in 1862. Both matches were bare-knuckle affairs, a popular format that was never officially sanctioned in either Canada or the US. The only "governing body" was a tabloid-style magazine called the *National Police Gazette*. The magazine, which focused on all things lurid, covered sport, murder, and other sensational events and included photographs of prostitutes, strippers, and burlesque performers considered scandalous at the time. A hugely influential forerunner of later lifestyle magazines, it also promoted spectacle-style competitions, particularly bare-knuckle boxing. Founded in 1845, the *National Police Gazette* "sanctioned" bare-knuckle fights until 1894, when it became clear that gloved boxing would prevail.

In 1872, International Boxing Hall of Fame members Billy Edwards and Arthur Chambers, both from England, fought a bare-knuckle bout for the Lightweight Championship of America, an event described in the September 5 edition of the *Chicago Tribune*. The fight began in Detroit but was broken up by authorities. Unwilling to end the event without a victor, the fighters and their supporters, a group of roughly 200 people, crossed the border into Windsor, boarded a steam-powered propeller boat and headed north up the St. Clair River. The following morning, the steamer arrived off Walpole Island, where small boats ferried those aboard to shore.

Confident that Walpole Island's unceded status would prevent interference, organizers immediately "went ashore, to pick the spot and pitch the ring." While there is no evidence that local residents were involved in the planning, they did watch the fight and catered to the guests. One enterprising local sold cantaloupe to the fans for five cents each while they waited for the bout to begin.

At 10:00 a.m., Edwards, dressed in white silk with blue trim, met Chambers, wearing cream and red. Edwards, the defending champion, drew first blood and pummelled Chambers, round after round. In the twenty-sixth round, an exhausted Chambers fell to the mat, claiming Edwards had bitten his shoulder. At that, the referee called the match in favour of Chambers, awarding him $2,000 and the Lightweight Championship of America. Edwards, who immediately "commenced to cry with madness and took a solemn oath that he never even thought of biting," never fought again. Chambers would hold the Lightweight title until his retirement in 1879.

Chambers was not the only championship boxer to compete in and around Chatham-Kent. In 1884, Canadian Lightweight Boxing Champion Harry Gilmore travelled from Toronto to Chatham for a three-bout boxing exhibition against a Black Chatham heavyweight recorded only as Peters. According to the February 26, 1884 *Chatham Tri-Weekly Planet*, Gilmore "thumped" Peters. At this time, interracial matches were extremely rare. This fight, and perhaps the high visibility of Black and white men competing on the same stage, sparked a ban on the sport in the city that lasted four years. Anyone caught participating in a public exhibition of boxing was subject to arrest.

In the early years of the 20th century, another Ontario boxer began gaining recognition. Tommy Burns was born three hours north of Chatham-Kent in the small Ontario town of Hanover. He remains the only Canadian-born heavyweight boxing champion in history. Burns won his title in February of 1906 defeating the reigning champion, Marvin Hart, on points in Los Angeles. Unlike his contemporaries, Burns did not restrict himself to white opponents, proclaiming: "I will defend my title against all comers, none barred. By this I mean white, black, Mexican, Indian, or any other nationality. I propose to be the champion of the world not the white, or the Canadian or the American. If I am not the best man in the heavyweight division, I don't want the title."[1]

Over the next two years, Burns defended his title thirteen times, including twice in one night. In 1908, he faced Jack Johnson, the son of former slaves from Galveston, Texas, in front of more than 20,000 fans in Sydney, Australia. During the fight, Johnson reportedly turned his back to Burns to address the crowd. He also invited Burns to take his best shot, standing with his arms open "as if to hug the man," and allowing him to punch.[2] When Johnson finally decided to fight, police had to stop the match to save Burns, and stop the predominantly white fans in attendance from rioting. Johnson defeated Burns in fourteen rounds.

Johnson's victory sparked race riots in more than twenty-five states and fifty cities. Angry white mobs killed at least twenty people and injured hundreds more. Conversely, Black populations across North America held impromptu parades, prayer meetings, and celebrations.

At the height of the Jim Crow era, a Black man stood alone atop the world of boxing, a position the white sporting world could not allow. Writing in *The New York Herald* on December 27, 1908, author Jack London wrote, "Personally, I was with Burns all the way. He is a white man, and so am I. Naturally I wanted to see the white man win. He played and fought a white man in a white man's country, before a white man's crowd." He then called for a "great white hope" to rescue the white man from a Black champion.

London's article became a rallying cry and the search for a Great White Hope began. Attention turned first to former World Heavyweight champion Jim Jeffries who had been sharply critical of Burns' decision to face Johnson. "Burns has sold his pride, the pride of the Caucasian race. The Canadian never will be forgiven by the public for allowing the title of the best physical man in the world to be wrested from his keeping by a member of the African race."[3]

Jeffries had retired undefeated in 1905, beating every white challenger, but not Johnson, who he refused to fight at the time. "I refused time and again to meet Johnson while I was holding the title, even though I knew I could beat him. I would never allow a Negro a chance to fight for the world's championship, and I advise all other champions to follow the same course."[4]

When the public began claiming Johnson was the superior fighter, Jeffries did the only thing he could—he answered the challenge. Jeffries came out of retirement in 1910 stating, "I am going into this fight for the sole purpose of proving that a white man is better than a Negro."[5]

Johnson's response was simple. "Every fighter on the eve of his fight declares that he hopes the best man wins. I am quite sincere when I say that I do."[6]

What was dubbed the "fight of the century" has been described by many as the most lopsided championship bout in history. After fifteen rounds, the outcome was clear and Jim Jeffries' corner threw in the towel. *The New York Times* announced that "The fight of the century is over, and a black man is the undisputed champion of the world."[7]

Now, North America needed a new contender to defend whiteness. With no clear candidates identified, an elimination tournament of "white hopes" was held in New York in 1911. Johnson sat in the stands at the National Sporting Club of America, watching his prospective challengers, one of whom was Canadian boxer Andrew Arthur Pelletier, who went by the name of Arthur Pelkey.

Pelkey was born in Pain Court, a small, predominantly French-speaking village only ten kilometers outside of Chatham. Pelkey defeated five fighters during the tournament before being eliminated by Al Benedict in a controversial decision.

Many observers, newspapers, and Pelkey himself believed he should have won that decision, and that the tournament was rigged in favour of another contestant, Al Palzer, who was managed by the organizer. "The decision rightfully belonged to Pelkey who gave his opponent a good beating, flooring him in an extra round that had been ordered," *The North Adams Transcript* wrote on July 27, 1911. The crowd at the tournament booed the outcome, which was called "the poorest decision of the evening."

Sitting ringside, Jack Johnson laughed.

"There was something about the scene that made the negro title holder, who was occupying a seat close by, just double up with laughter, and his outburst attracted Pelkey's attention." According to *The North Adams Transcript*, it was at this moment that Pelkey found "the inspiration for becoming a champion," and "longed for the day when he might crawl through the ropes and rob Jack Johnson of his heavyweight crown."[8]

Pelkey's first move was to challenge Al Palzer, who had indeed been declared the White Heavyweight Champion of the World at the elimination tournament. Although no record exists that this bout took place, Pelkey continued fighting, hoping to earn his chance against the top "white hopes" of the time. Meanwhile Al Palzer defended his title until 1913, when Luther McCarty scored a TKO victory in the 18th round of a bout in Vernon, California.

Pelkey immediately put forth a challenge. "I am ready to go out to California any time and fight Luther McCarty and if I can't lick him, I don't want a cent, I will be perfectly willing to walk all the way back home," Pelkey said, adding that he had a group of friends willing to make a $5,000 side bet that he would be "McCarty's master," and that all he wanted was "a chance to get inside the ropes with this so-called 'white champion of the world.'"[9]

While Pelkey was on a visit home to Chatham-Kent, he received a telegram from Tommy Burns offering to promote, train, and manage him so that he might become the White Heavyweight Champion of the World. First, however, Burns wanted to fight Pelkey himself.

Pelkey agreed and, in April of 1913, the two men squared off at Manchester Arena near Calgary, nicknamed Tommy Burns Arena for the man who built and ran it. The event marked Burns' long-awaited return to the ring and ended in a six-round draw, with both boxers scoring knockdowns.

Pelkey injured his hand in the match, which prompted his father to offer him a farm worth $1,000 adjoining to his own near Chatham "if he will retire and settle down to a less strenuous vocation."[10] But the fanfare Pelkey received from fighting Burns, along with their new relationship, finally put his goal in sight. In May of 1913, Burns received confirmation via telegram that Luther McCarty had accepted Pelkey's challenge.

McCarty was confident and planned to defeat Burns after his victory. But only one minute and forty-five seconds into the bout, Pelkey knocked the champion out with a punch that most described as harmless. McCarty hit the mat and did not move. Supporters moved him outside believing fresh air would revive the fighter, but he was pronounced dead. A distraught Pelkey was soon charged with manslaughter.

Chatham-Kent's Arthur Pelkey was now the World White Heavyweight Champion and the next "great white hope" but he was a changed man. The coroner's report eventually exonerated him but his defence had nearly bankrupted him and the shock of killing an opponent broke his spirit. He lost his title to Gunboat Smith in his next fight and went on to lose the next nine before leaving boxing and returning to Windsor where he became a police officer until his death in 1921 at the age of 38.

The same year Pelkey won his World White Heavyweight title, the Amateur Athletic Union of Canada asserted that Canada's boxing title would be a white-only honour, further dividing the sport by race. The boxing world had learned its lesson, announcing unequivocally that "No coloured boxer will be allowed to compete in the Canadian championships . . . Competition of whites and coloured men is not working out to the increased growth of the sport."[11]

The era of the Great White Hopes came to an end on April 15, 1915, when Jess Willard, who had once given Pelkey a "terrific thrashing" in a ten-round fight at Madison Square Gardens,[12] defeated Jack Johnson to claim the World Heavyweight title. No Black fighters would get the chance to contend for the heavyweight title for more than twenty years, until Joe Louis faced Germany's Max Schmeling.

Louis' parents were born of freed slaves and Schmeling, a former heavyweight champion of the world himself, came together in a pair of fights riddled not only with athletic importance, but with political and social consequence. In the first fight, which occurred in 1936, Schmeling shocked the world and Louis, handing Louis the first knockout of his otherwise undefeated career. After the fight,

Louis gifted his gloves to his friend and employee Earle Cuzzens, whose wife Beulah hailed from North Buxton. The gloves now reside in Washington's Smithsonian Institute, where they were donated by Beulah and Earle's nephew, Ken Milburn.

By the time Louis and Schmeling fought again in 1938, things were different. As American-German animosity intensified, Louis had transformed from a Black boxer to an American hope.

"White Americans, even while some of them were lynching Black people in the South, were depending on me to KO a German," said Louis in a June 19, 1988 article in *The New York Times*. "The whole damned country was depending on me." In *I Know Why the Caged Bird Sings*, Maya Angelou recalls, "If Joe lost, we were back in slavery and beyond help. . . We didn't breathe. We didn't hope. We waited."

Darkness hung over Yankee Stadium as Louis traded blows with Schmeling. The stadium lights illuminated only the ring, shining on Louis' Black body as he knocked out a white German. While Schmeling himself refused to join the Nazi party and was cleared of Nazi connections by a British court, he met with Adolf Hitler and gave the Nazi salute following bouts. He was a chosen representative of the Nazis and Joe Louis became a hero, embraced enthusiastically by the Black community and more reluctantly by racist segments of the white community. At least temporarily, nationalism had trumped racism.

Tommy Burns saw Joe Louis win his title; so did Jim Jeffries. And Jack Johnson was there. John Roxborough, Louis' manager, was very aware that Louis could not be another Johnson. His managers needed him to be a Black athlete who would not need to be vanquished. They needed him to be acceptable to white people. When Johnson appeared at one of Louis' training sessions leading up to that championship bout, he was told to leave, with Roxborough telling him he had "held up the progress of the Negro people for years with his attitude, how he was a low-down, no-good n-----." He reminded Louis that white people had not forgotten the boxer they hated so much. Louis had to be a Black man who knew his place, unlike Johnson, who was too exuberant, too confident, too unapologetic. "You know, boy, the heavyweight division for a Negro is hardly likely . . . If you really ain't gonna be another Jack Johnson, you got some hope. White man hasn't forgotten that fool n----- with his white women, acting like he owned the world . . . And for God's sake," added Roxborough, "after you defeat a white opponent, don't smile."[13]

Matthew Brown, in his thesis examining the complex relationship between the two heavyweight champions, wrote, "Louis' managers set out to create a dominant boxer accompanied by a perfectly acceptable and humble public image. They were well aware of the public backlash that had occurred after Jack Johnson had become the first black heavyweight champion of the world by embarrassing nearly every white opponent he faced . . . As long as people were unable to see or hear about his indiscretions, then Louis would continue to be publicly portrayed as the acceptable black man. The media obviously felt it beneficial to continue to uphold Louis as a model black citizen who could be idolized by black America and potentially lead to the next generation of blacks embodying this non-threatening lifestyle and personality."[14]

In the wake of Louis' success came a long series of Black Heavyweight Champions that largely resolved the issue of race within boxing. But the question of Indigenous sovereignty has reappeared within the context of a new sport, mixed martial arts (MMA). Prior to 2011, MMA bouts were banned across Canada but the question of unceded territory provided "jurisdictional ambiguity, allowing grey-market businesses . . . extreme fighting—to thrive, a legal blind spot hidden in plain view."[15]

In 2008, promoter James Procyk defended the hosting of MMA events on unceded territory in front of the Ontario Athletic Commission. "For the Ontario Athletic Commission to say it has jurisdiction over a reserve territory, which is a sovereign nation, oversteps its authority, and it becomes even more distasteful in light of land claims issues that have been going on."[16] His argument prevailed and, in 2010, the Xtreme Cagefighting Championship was held on Walpole Island. The matches featured Chatham-Kent's Chris "The Menace" Clements, who would advance to fight in the Ultimate Fighting Championships (UFC).

The majority of the fans and fighters present were white. As Jeremy Beal recalled in his January 3, 2011, article for *This* magazine, the event underlined how little had changed since Edwards met Chambers in 1872: "[T]he reserve still carries a stigma among outsiders; I was surprised at the friends and family members who warned me of the dangers of setting foot on the reserve. Some expressed concern for my safety, others refused an invitation to come along. An astonishing number recited hearsay about the calamities that had happened to friends of friends who 'went over there.' Of course, it was all disturbingly bigoted nonsense: whatever problems exist on this reserve, the urge to rough up white MMA fans with money to spend is not one of them."

Leaving Joe Louis Arena as a child, I felt a similar fear, one perpetuated by implicit bias I could not locate. I'd step out into the night beside my father, the high of a Red Wings win still coursing through my veins, uneasy as we walked through Detroit to find our car. Growing up in a predominantly white area, there were things inside me I couldn't explain, that were not built on experience, feelings that embarrass me now. Back in the perceived safety of our vehicle, we drove down Jefferson Avenue past the monument to Joe Louis, "The Fist," a twenty-four-foot statue created to commemorate Louis' win over Schmeling and his place as a representative and hero for *all* North Americans, not just the Black population. Soon, we'd cross through the Detroit–Windsor tunnel. Back in Canada, my father would guide us to the highway, and I'd drift into a peaceful sleep.

# Chapter 5

# THE HOME TEAM WEARS WHITE

"Amen. Go in peace."

Those magic words marked a transition. The doors to the Baptist churches would open and Stirling Park, the heart of Chatham's East End, would begin to bustle. It was time for baseball. People would enter the park from every direction, packing the bleachers. Lawn chairs and overturned milk cartons would fall into formation along the baselines. Across Scane Street, which ran the length of the park, people would climb onto the roofs of homes. If a train was stopped on the tracks, as it often was, people would clamber onto the railcars for a better view of the field. One by one, the neighbourhood stars would emerge, gloves in hand, ready to take to the field in front of hundreds, and often thousands, of fans. And so it was on Sundays, church and baseball.

Stirling Park was only a few blocks from Chatham's downtown, but for the Black, Japanese, and immigrant families of the East End, the intervening train tracks and roads were borders guarded by police officers, realtors, politicians, and white residents. To move from one territory to the other, you needed to have a reason for coming, and a plan to leave. During early Black settlement in Chatham in the 1860s, Chatham's Mayor Cross explained that, "the coloured people generally live apart. There has been, hitherto, a very strong prejudice against them, and the result is that they are, generally speaking, confined to a particular locality in town."[1]

According to researcher Dr. Carmen Poole, Chatham's East End "was impoverished spatially, economically, and historically by powerful whites who believed that the East End space and the working-class whites, immigrants, and African Canadians who resided in it could not thrive, by virtue of their race and/or class, and were therefore worthy of neglect and contempt."[2]

Despite its economic disadvantages, the East End was home to a thriving community that revolved around the park. "It was always busy, and always there for the game of baseball," recalls Dorothy Wright-Wallace, who spent her entire life in the neighbourhood. "That park, that was the centre of our activity, something to go and do. It was loved by everybody, we just seemed to gravitate there, everybody knew everybody, it was our meeting ground. Not only were the churches important to us, but so was Stirling Park."

In the winter months, the diamond at Stirling Park would be flooded and neighbourhood kids would speed across the ice, skating all day. When their fingers and toes got too cold, they'd step off the ice and stand beside an old pot belly stove placed in the centre of the park each winter.

"Stirling Park in this area was the home base for everything. It was community. It was just the centre of who we were, it was a place that was," said Wright-Wallace. "I was born in '43, and that's all I've ever known my whole life, and as time went on with baseball, that was our second home."

Black baseball teams had been formally organized in Chatham since 1871. The original Royal Oak Club was followed by the Chatham Coloured Giants in the 1920s, an integrated team composed of Black and white athletes before this practice was accepted, that won the Coloured Amateur Michigan and Ontario Championship in 1925. As an alternative to leagues, as there were not usually enough all-Black teams to form a circuit, all-Black teams from the 1880s onward travelled from city to city, challenging teams to exhibition games in order to find competition, while earning money for the players. By the 1920s, this practice was known as barnstorming, named after roving aviators who used the same business model. Basketball's Harlem Globetrotters, who many years later would include Chatham's own Fergie Jenkins on their roster, also started barnstorming during this period.

Travelling from town to town, barnstorming promoted one of the earliest forms of integrated sport. Black teams primarily faced white opponents, earning respect in at least some circles. Dizzy Dean, the National League MVP who led his St. Louis Cardinals to a World Series title in 1934, was outspoken in his praise of Black baseball players. He maintained that if "big leaguers believed that they were better than the best Negro players they had another thought coming."[3]

During the Depression, barnstorming allowed professional players to make extra money. Future Hall of Fame pitcher Satchel Paige, then playing for the Pittsburgh Crawfords, was a noted barnstormer, jumping from team to team, often as the main attraction drawing crowds and opponents.

In 1932, the Chatham Coloured All-Stars, successors to the Chatham Coloured Giants, began their inaugural season of play by barnstorming through towns and across borders, both real and imagined. Crowds of up to 4,000 people would surround the diamond to see them play, many taking the day off work to be part of the event. For some it was sport; for others it was a minstrel show, Black performers providing entertainment that reinforced white superiority.

"They were coming to see us get beat and they also wanted to clown about it," said Wilfred "Boomer" Harding, Chatham-born star of both baseball and hockey, in a 1977 interview archived within the University of Windsor's Breaking the Colour Barrier research project. "When we went to Strathroy they used to write on the sidewalks that we was coming to town. But I guess, and everything else they were out to beat us."[4] In an interview in *Chatham-Kent This Week* (June 10, 2017), Boomer's daughter-in-law Pat Harding said, "There was prejudice . . . back then when they played in different towns they wouldn't let [the players] sleep in town."

Blake Harding, Boomer's son told me the hostility, as the team travelled from town to town, extended to the stands. "Before I was born, my mother Joy Harding, she would go with her sister and sister-in-law to all these games, and they would have to sit on the stands and listen to all this garbage. The boys would be playing ball, they'd be doing what they had to do on the field between the lines. And they'd be sitting up on the bench and they'd be getting into it, they had to fight just as much as the boys, and they would fight. She took it harder than my dad, and I remember her just sitting there and saying, 'Boomer, you be careful out there'."

Boomer's sister, Beulah Cuzzens, recalled one particular game. "The Stars were treated just like Jackie Robinson. I went into Blenheim one day to watch the Stars play ball. I taught down in Shrewsbury, so I got there a little early and the kids along the road said, 'Well, I see the darkies are arrivin'. That was me. And a little later, our team came along, and we were called all the names that they called people in those days."[5]

Leaving town following a game, the All-Stars would often literally fight their way out, standing back-to-back and shoving through hostile mobs, throwing punches where necessary. Gradually, however, crowds that came to jeer left with respect, recognizing that many of the players on this team were professional caliber. Earl "Flat" Chase was a major league talent in the eyes of everyone who saw him. Following one stellar performance, the *Chatham Daily News* dubbed Chase the "Kolored King of the Klout," recognizing his achievement even as it invoked the Ku Klux Klan. In an interview with *The London Free Press* published on September 7, 1978, Boomer Harding said, "There's no question in anybody's mind who ever saw him [Chase] that he would have been a major leaguer had it not been for the colour barrier." Ferguson Jenkins Sr. was another talented player for the All-Stars who would only see Major League Baseball through the eyes of his son, Fergie Jenkins Jr.

After spending the 1932 season exclusively barnstorming, the

1933 Chatham Coloured All-Stars were admitted into Chatham's City League with the help of white business owner and local Ontario Baseball Amateur Association representative Archie Stirling. The following season, 1934, the Coloured All-Stars defeated the C.C. Braggs Insurance team three games to none to win the Chatham City League. Stirling continued his support of the team after they captured the city league title, setting his sights on the provincially sanctioned playoffs. In addition to owning a variety store in Chatham's East End, and founding the city's first playground and pool, Archie Stirling would spend a lifetime building baseball and hockey teams that became ongoing sources of civic pride. As the sponsor of the team, Stirling offered free ice cream to any youth bringing back a home-run ball from an All-Stars game.

In most leagues of the time, including Major League Baseball and the Ontario Baseball Amateur Association (OBAA), the colour line was well defended but unwritten. Stirling made sure his team got a chance to compete for a provincial title by removing "Coloured" from the team's name as it appeared on the entry form. "They worried that they may not be accepted because of their colour, but we got around that," said Stirling, who would later be nicknamed Mr. Baseball in Chatham. "We just signed the certificates and mentioned nothing of the Coloured All-Stars. They were entered as the Chatham All-Stars."[6]

Allowed into the competition, Chatham was not to be defeated, first ousting the Sarnia Red Sox, then the Welland Terriers. As the team continued winning, the tone of the local media started to change. By the time the All-Stars faced Milton in the semi-finals, the newspapers considered the team as a representative of Chatham and a source of civic pride. The crowds grew larger, with a number of genuine white baseball fans dotting the fences and stands.

The team beat Milton and advanced to the Ontario championship representing the Western Counties. No Chatham team had ever won an Ontario baseball title, and no all-Black team had won a Canadian provincial championship. Once the Ontario title was in sight, the Chatham All-Stars became even more determined. In the first game of the OBAA final, the All-Stars defeated Penetang in extra innings in front of throngs of hometown supporters. After they lost the next game in a hotly disputed one-run contest, the stage was set for a third and deciding game, scheduled to take place on neutral ground in Guelph.

In his interview with the University of Windsor's research team, Boomer Harding described that final game. "They wouldn't have us in Penetang, they were very prejudiced, that was the only trouble. In Guelph on that day, we moved into the same hotel they were, and they moved out as soon as they found out we moved in."

On a sunny afternoon in mid-October, the teams took to the field, neither willing to concede. Tied 2–2 in the top of the eleventh inning, the Chatham All-Stars came to bat and scored a run, edging ahead 3-2. The players and crowd could feel victory approaching. Flat Chase had already struck out twelve batters; now he had a chance to close out the series.

Penetang came to bat and Chase threw a dagger. Strike one. A few pitches later, Chase had struck out the first Penetang batter. The All-Stars' dugout hummed with nervous excitement; a celebration was only minutes away. Victory seemed imminent until the home plate umpire and the umpire standing behind second base simultaneously raised their arms, stopping the game. They called the game "on account of darkness," inexplicably reverted the score to a 2–2 tie, and hurriedly left the field.

"It's hard to believe but I can still see the two guys throwing up their arms in the air, they must have had a pre-arranged signal because they just took out running. There was no talking to them, they just jumped in their cars and were gone. There was no way we were going to win that game," Harding recalled.

As Harding's son Blake explained to me, "The Penetanguishene series. Why'd they call the game on account of darkness? Well, it was dark because there were nine Black players out there, that's why it was too dark."

With a fourth and deciding game now slated for the next day, Archie Stirling had a new umpire and officiating crew brought in from Hamilton. This time, the Chatham All-Stars overwhelmed their opponent, winning 13–7 and capturing the provincial title. On the mound, Flat Chase bested Penetang's Phil Marchildon, who would go on to play seven seasons of Major League Baseball in the 1940s. Flat Chase—widely recognized as a Major League-quality talent—went back to driving a garbage truck and playing as an amateur. Later, he'd become the first Black player in team history to win a Canadian title with the renowned London Majors.

Every town loves a winner, even if they don't love the players on the team, and 2,000 people greeted the champions when they returned to Chatham. "When they won the series and they came into town they were riding on the sides of the cars and everything and the whole town was jammed at King and Fifth Street to meet them. And they just hollered and cheered them because nothing like that had ever happened in Chatham before and they had all kinds of white fans, coloured fans . . . They were all-Ontario winners and everybody jumped on the bandwagon," said John Olbey, the younger brother of All-Stars member Cliff Olbey during a 2016 interview for Breaking the Colour Barrier.[7]

Mayor Isaac Davis opined that, "Chatham will win other ball championships, but we'll always remember it was the coloured boys who led the way."[8]

In nearby Buxton, where several members of the All-Stars were born, the win was celebrated with equal zeal. The Black community was not only visible, it mattered. "We won!" said Pauline Williams, whose uncles, Hyle and Stanton Robbins, were members of the 1934 team. "It was a happy time—a big, big, big thing. Buxton won."

In Legacy to Buxton, Arlie Robbins writes, "The winning of this Championship brought a great boost to the morale of the coloured people of southwestern Ontario whose spirits were at a low ebb because of the discouraging effects of the Depression and local prejudices."[9]

Men who worked as chauffeurs, waiters, porters, and bellhops were treated like kings. Team members received jackets and were honoured at the William Pitt Hotel, a place where many had worked but none had been allowed as guests. While such recognition was short-lived, Black players and teams were no longer barred from league competition. All-Stars captain Don Washington, for instance, was recruited to play in nearby Strathroy, quickly becoming a fan favourite.

Boomer Harding recalled team manager Happy Parker urging the many businessmen and leaders present at the William Pitt celebration to help the All-Stars as they had helped the city: "We've brought baseball back to the city of Chatham for the first time—the first championship . . . OBA championship. And he says, 'Now give the boys some jobs.' Now some of the merchants give the boys jobs. Cause all we had was hotel work, which was tips. And shining shoes and working in garages. Painting cars or something."[10] Nonetheless, some of the notable names from the 1934 All-Stars would move to other, more accepting cities for work in the years that followed.

Despite their title, racism continued to dog the team throughout the following season. During another barnstorming tour, the All-Stars were turned away by the Toledo Mud Hens, a minor league affiliate of the Detroit Tigers, because Major League Baseball refused to allow games with Black players. On another occasion, a team featuring multiple members of the Detroit Tigers was also set to refuse a game until Willie Shaugnosh (Shognosh), an Indigenous player who joined the Coloured All-Stars that year, provided an out. As described by Boomer Harding, "the Detroit manager said we'd better all be Indians in a hurry or his guys wouldn't take the field. So, for a day we were Indian."[11]

Black baseball players had always enjoyed a close relationship with their Indigenous counterparts and often met men of Delaware Nation at Moraviantown such as Omer Peters to eat, socialize, and, of course, play baseball. The smoke in the pool hall would be thick and the baseball stories would fly in every direction when Peters got together with Flat Chase. The way his father spoke of his friend, Omer's son Gordon was sure that Chase was Indigenous. Shaugnosh, described in an August 6, 1935 *Chatham Daily News* article as "the best pitcher in the Western Counties League" would earn a tryout with the Detroit Tigers before serving on the Walpole Island Band Council.

The All-Stars would stay together through the decade. They won the 1935 city title, and in 1939 they again advanced to the Ontario finals, but a dispute over the location of the deciding game against Meaford arose, and no championship was awarded. With World War II already underway overseas, All-Stars players began enlisting and were soon playing both baseball and basketball at the Basic No. 12 Training Centre in Chatham. This included Boomer Harding and two All-Stars who joined the roster in the late 1930s, Gerald Browning and Bill Henson, grandson of the founder of the Dawn Settlement, Josiah Henson.

The Basic No. 12 baseball team also included Hank Biasatti, who would eventually play in the National Basketball Association for the Toronto Huskies and in Major League Baseball with the Philadelphia Athletics. Biasatti was the first Canadian ever to play in both the NBA and MLB.

Of the group, Henson spent the most time overseas. He served in England, France, and Belgium before being captured in Germany and imprisoned in Stalag 11-B for four months. Repatriated to Canada in 1945, he joined the Taylor A.C. baseball team, the successor to the Coloured All-Stars formed in 1946 and soon renamed the Kent Panthers. Boomer Harding also went overseas, serving in Holland and Belgium until D-Day, and remaining in Europe to play hockey on a touring Armed Forces team. After returning to

Chatham, he played alongside Henson and Browning on Taylor A.C. and the Panthers while continuing his hockey career.

Sport and war are two of the world's greatest equalizers. For members of the Chatham Coloured All-Stars, both only levelled the playing field temporarily. Following their fabled 1934 season, and after a world war ostensibly fought in the name of freedom, things returned to normal. The battle for equality was far from over.

# Chapter 6

# LEARNING TO PLAY BALL

Growing up, there was a rack of hockey pucks above my bed, each cupped by wooden dowels glued into a board. Organized chronologically, each represented a National Hockey League, Ontario Hockey League, or other game I'd gone to see. I'd get a puck from any new team I watched. At night, as I slept, the pucks would rattle as the train passed close to our house. From time to time, one would jump from its place, striking me awake. I'd turn on the light to see which memory had hit me.

Pliney Stonefish kept a similar collection of memories in the top drawer of his dresser. His were baseballs. After a win, when he felt he'd pitched particularly well, he would tuck the ball into his glove, bring it home and place it neatly into his drawer. Most were surprisingly clean because, when Stonefish was pitching, the ball had a way of evading the thwack of the bat.

From time to time, his son Darryl would open the drawer and stand in awe of the stash of baseballs, some obviously older than others, memories collected over years, across multiple provinces and from numerous championship runs. He'd run his fingers over the stitching, like a pitcher preparing his offering, and occasionally sneak a ball out from the drawer for a pick-up game. As time went by, the baseballs in the drawer became more worn, and a few holes formed in the collection when Darryl and his friends lost a ball. Pliney never said a word: not about the origin of the baseballs themselves, the dirt added to his drawer or the missing memory.

Pliney, an Indigenous man from Delaware Nation, had grown up around baseball, inheriting his passion from his father Walker who, like Ed Pinnace, attended Shingwauk Residential School in the 1890s. The Eelünaapéewi Lahkéewiit people have long been associated with successful baseball and fastball players, and the diamonds in Delaware Nation at Moraviantown have been a central feature in the community for over a century. The All-Ontario Native Fastball Championships, founded in 1971, have called these fields home, and championship teams have rounded the bases to the cheers of adoring fans.

The first photographic evidence of an all-Indigenous baseball team from Delaware Nation dates from 1922 and features a number of veterans returned from World War I. Even though the Indian Act of 1876 clearly stated that, "the term 'person' means an individual other than an Indian, unless the context clearly requires another construction," the young men of Moraviantown enlisted in significant numbers. Allies of the British since the War of 1812, Indigenous men, perhaps enticed by the similar constructs of fraternity, discipline, and rules that characterized sport, enlisted: 53% of eligible Indigenous men enlisted compared to a national rate of 31.6%. According to the Annual Report of the Department of Indian Affairs for 1919: "Forty-two Moravians of the Thames went to the front from a total adult male population of seventy-nine. One of their number who won fame as a sniper, Private George Stonefish, of Moraviantown, was tendered a civil reception by the city of Chatham on his return to Canada in recognition of his exceptional services. Another of their number, Corporal Albert Tobias, also was awarded the Military Medal. He is the son of ex-Chief Walter Tobias, who was killed at Ypres. Two other sons of ex-Chief Tobias also served with the expeditionary forces. One of the Moravian Indian soldiers, Private Roy Snake, enlisted at the age of sixteen with a forestry unit. He was afterwards transferred to the infantry and participated in the battle of Cambrai . . . the Chippewas and Pottawatomies of Walpole Island sent seventy-one to the front from a total adult male population of two hundred and ten."

Both Delaware Nation and Walpole Island also supported the war effort financially. The Annual Report is clear that: "From the outset of the war the Indians, both as bands and as individuals, have been very generous in proportion to the means at their disposal in contributing to the Patriotic, Red Cross, Belgian Relief, and other war funds." The "Moravian Band of the Thames" contributed $200 and Walpole Island contributed $125.

World War I provided an opportunity for men and women, in spite of race, to work together against common foes and toward common goals. After the war, baseball diamonds became places where Indigenous and white athletes interacted in ways that had not been seen before. Top Indigenous players including Albert Tobias, Sam Lascelles, Roy Snake, and Omer Peters found their skills were in high demand. In 1927, Albert Tobias and Omer Peters became some of the first athletes to go "off-reserve," winning the Kent County Intermediate Baseball championship as members of the Ridgetown Base Ball Club. A decade later, Pliney Stonefish would be playing for teams in Windsor and Detroit, and Peters would win an All-Ontario title playing for the Bothwell Cougars.

Omer had learned to play baseball by using a stick to hit stones his father Archie would pitch to him. Omer's son Gordon explained to me that "on Sundays, he was not supposed to be working, not supposed to be playing sports. But he broke that religious domination in the family and he went and he played baseball. He said to his dad, 'I can make more money playing baseball for teams around here than I can working in the fields.' That's how he started playing baseball."

Unlike their parents and siblings, Tobias, Stonefish, and Peters were not forced to attend residential school. Instead, they attended the Moraviantown Indian Day School, which operated from 1867 until 1990 and was run at various times by the Moravian, Methodist, and United Churches. Day schools had been the original mechanism used to assimilate Indigenous youth and shared a common philosophy and approach with their residential school counterparts. They were often places of abuse, in all forms. As Pliney's son, Darryl, explained, "We had church-run schools here all the time. Sometimes our schools were like residential schools right here."

When World War II began, many First Nations men again elected to go to war. "They chose to go because they saw two things happening. First in defence of our lands from potential German occupation," said Gordon Peters, "and second, there was a notion that our peoples were allied with Great Britain and Canada."

Omer Peters enlisted and is thought to be the first Indigenous man accepted into a flying position with the Royal Canadian Air Force. Until then, Indigenous people were barred from service in the Royal Canadian Air Force and Royal Canadian Navy. Official air force policy was, "All candidates must be British subjects and of pure European descent. They must also be the sons of parents both of whom are (or, if deceased, were at the time of death) British subjects or naturalised British subjects."[1]

After war was declared, the policy was modified to "enlisted applicants must be of pure European descent with the exception of the North American Indians." On May 16, 1941, *The Windsor Star* acknowledged Peters' achievement: "Like his forefathers who hunted those seeking to oppress them, Omer Peters, 32-year-old full-blooded Indian, hopes to track down German fighter planes and 'scalp' them with his machine gun from the gunner's seat of a Royal Canadian Air Force plane."

Serving with the Canadian Forces and playing baseball on integrated teams allowed Albert Tobias, Omer Peters, and Pliney Stonefish to learn how to "play ball" in other ways as well. All three would become chiefs of Delaware Nation; Omer Peters in particular would leverage the clout and connections he acquired as a baseball player to break barriers for other Indigenous people.

"My dad was very much a working man," said Gordon Peters. "He came from that environment and passed that on to us. If there's something to be done, let's just do it; if the barn needs to be painted, let's just do it. When I was twelve years old, he took me to work, and it was not uncommon for him to take men to work with him. Because people knew him, he would get hired at the cannery in Ridgetown, for instance, and he'd take someone in there and get them a job. I didn't realize until after that what he was doing was breaking the colour barrier. He was getting Indigenous people jobs."

Peters advocated tirelessly to bring solidarity to Indigenous people and "always expressed his undying faith in the First Nations people across the country."[2] At the Provincial level, Peters was a founding member of the Union of Ontario Indians, serving as president and then executive director of the organization. He also helped to establish the National Indian Brotherhood, which later evolved into the Assembly of First Nations, a key advocacy group composed of leaders from First Nations across the continent.

One of Peters' largest contributions came during the fight against the 1969 White Paper, a federal document that proposed the full and mandatory integration of Indigenous youth into existing education systems in the provinces and territories, along with the elimination of First Nations reserves. Indigenous leaders, including Omer Peters, recognized the White Paper as a clear violation of existing treaties and developed the Red Paper in response. The Red Paper asserted that Indigenous education was a right guaranteed through treaties with the Federal government and Crown, and that First Nations communities were not prepared to accept integration under the guise of "equality." The White Paper was withdrawn in 1970 after galvanizing a generation of Indigenous leaders who would be increasingly outspoken and effective in the coming years.

Tobias, Peters, and Stonefish all left a legacy of excellence and a blueprint for using sport as a gateway to political influence. Gordon Peters would become one of the best athletes to ever emerge from Delaware Nation at Moraviantown and one of the most ardent supporters of Indigenous rights in Canada. Gordon was a college hockey star for the Ohio State Buckeyes and went on to play professionally. Following pro hockey, he became president of the Association of Iroquois and Allied Indians (AIAI) and was elected Ontario Regional Vice-Chief of the Assembly of First Nations in 1985, a position he held for twelve years.

In 2015, when the Truth and Reconciliation Commission of Canada released ninety-four calls to action in order to "redress the legacy of residential schools and advance the process of Canadian reconciliation," Peters used his role as Grand Chief of AIAI to speak clearly. "You can't have Canada built on a foundation of lies," Peters said. "That's what Canada is right now. They teach these lies to the children."[3] The year before, he had said, "We have to be able to enjoy the same quality of life as the people who have come to inhabit our lands . . . They called it a dark chapter in history. The Canadian public needs to know there's a whole mitt full of dark chapters."[4]

Pliney's sons, Darryl and John Lee, both loved sport and also used it as a pathway to community leadership. John Lee Stonefish, who was elected Chief of Delaware Nation in 2005, excelled at hockey, soccer, and baseball, but became obsessed with track and field. In 1960, at age fifteen, John Lee won the junior title at the Western Ontario Secondary Schools Athletic Association track and field championships and was awarded the Tom Longboat Award for Southern Ontario as one of the top Indigenous athletes in Canada.

Established in 1951 by Indian Affairs and the Amateur Athletic Union of Canada, the Tom Longboat Award is named after a famed distance runner from Six Nations of the Grand River who won the Boston Marathon in 1907 and was named the World Professional Marathon Champion in 1909. Although intended as an honour, scholars such as Janice Forsyth, author of *Reclaiming Tom Longboat: Indigenous Self-Determination in Canadian Sport* (2020), argue the award allows the Canadian government to control Indigenous identity through sport.

Longboat's own story is similarly ambivalent. While his

achievements were lauded, he was personally denigrated. In a January 4, 1909 article for the *Toronto Star*, Lou Marsh described Longboat as "the imperturbable Indian . . . smiling like a coon in a watermelon patch." Marsh often used racist stereotypes and depictions in his writing, and credited Longboat's white coaches, including himself, for the Indigenous runner's successes. He wrote that Longboat "must be handled, not treated" and that Longboat "will wind up in a circus."[5]

Lou Marsh and Tom Longboat both fought for Canada in World War I. Marsh, an officer promoted to major, soon returned home after being diagnosed with a heart disorder, while Longboat remained and was twice injured on duty as a dispatch carrier. Despite Longboat's valour, Marsh, who interviewed him upon his return, accorded him no respect. In a May 21, 1919 *Toronto Daily Star* article titled "Interviewing Big Indian a Tough Job. Tom Longboat more taciturn than ever—two years in France," Marsh wrote, "In my time I've interviewed everything from a circus lion to an Eskimo chief, but when it comes down to being the original dummy, Tom Longboat is it. Interviewing a Chinese Joss or a mooley cow is pie compared to the task of digging anything out of Heap Big Chief T. Longboat."

Marsh was not alone in his denigration of Indigenous soldiers. Even after thousands of Indigenous people had served in two world wars, the Canadian Army's recruitment manual for 1944 made special mention of the "Enlistment of Indians and Half Breeds": "Care should be taken when accepting applications from or approaching Indians as prospective recruits. Here education standards are strictly adhered to. Experience has shown that they cannot stand long periods of confinement, discipline, and the strenuous physical and nervous demand incidental to modern army routine. On the other hand, some very fine Indians have been enlisted, but these are usually persons who have had their schooling and training in an Indian Residential School."[6]

Black Hawk and Chief Tecumseh fought on the side of the British before Canada was a country. Tom Longboat was a dispatch carrier, serving in France during World War I. Omer Peters, Albert Tobias, and Pliney Stonefish were among hundreds from Delaware Nation and Walpole Island who enlisted. An estimated 7,000 Indigenous people fought for Canada in World War I and World War II. Yet these veterans struggle to receive the respect they have earned, then and now.

I grew up watching Don Cherry on *Hockey Night in Canada* each week. He embodied Canada's national identity—a tough no-nonsense white male who loved hockey and was an ardent supporter of the military. Each year, as Remembrance Day approached, his colourful lapel would be adorned with a poppy and he would deliver stirring tributes to Canada's soldiers and veterans, even as he criticized anyone or anything that did not conform to his vision of a white, male-dominated society. When co-anchor Ron MacLean suggested, "A lot of First Nations kids go to bed at night and wake up in the morning thinking they won't get a fair shake," Cherry replied, "Fair shake in life! Go out and get your own fair shake in life and work for it. Don't give me that stuff." It wasn't until 2019, on Remembrance Day no less, that public outrage over Cherry's comments accusing immigrants of not wearing poppies finally resulted in his termination.

I watched Don Cherry each weekend, and I believed him. Now I believe something different, that perhaps Canada needed Cherry as an example of what we don't want to be—a bigot who once represented a large percentage of Canadians, but whom we've moved beyond, a sign that people can change. I don't know what happened to Pliney Stonefish's baseball collection but my pucks are in a box now, buried away. The train doesn't run on that track anymore.

# Chapter 7

# THE HOME STRETCH

Down the gravel roads of Chatham-Kent, you can judge the changing of the seasons by the corn. Each July, throngs of teenagers head into the fields to detassel corn. It's a rite of passage—hats and gloves, thermoses full of water, corn rash and heat stroke. All for a summer of wages.

In other fields, orchards, and greenhouses, migrant workers from Mexico, Jamaica, Honduras, and other nations arrive by the planeload to pick tomatoes, prune trees, and labour in sweltering fields, sometimes in unsafe and illegal conditions. Like the Japanese Canadians who were interned here during World War II, migrant workers are often unwanted, despite performing essential jobs others won't. In the fading sun, you can often see these workers using spare moments to play cricket or soccer outside of their bunkhouses.

By August 1, the seed corn has been detasseled, and stands of sweet corn dot roads and laneways to farms. The rest of the corn, grown for silage or ethanol, has crept toward the sun, now over six feet tall. Soon, harvest will come, and the green of these fields will turn brown, marking the passage of time.

In Buxton, a bell rings each August 1 to signify the day in 1834 when slavery was abolished throughout the British Empire. Emancipation Day has been recognized in Buxton, Dresden, and Chatham ever since. Initially, celebrations consisted of parades, music, and dancing that were temporarily acceptable in the eyes of white society, provided they were conducted with the "greatest decorum and regularity was preserved."[1] The celebrations must have become indecorous because, in 1874, a protest involving 2,000 white citizens led to the cancellation of the annual Emancipation Day parades in Chatham, which would not resume for eight years.[2]

Over time, baseball was added to the festivities. During a 1936 Emancipation Day celebration in Windsor, famed boxer Joe Louis, the Chatham Coloured All-Stars, and a group of North Buxton men all took to the field at Jackson Park. The North Buxton Stars squared off against Louis' Brown Bombers in a softball game, which was followed by the Chatham Coloured All-Stars playing another baseball team, the V8s.

The other sport that became integral to Emancipation Day celebrations was harness racing, long associated with the Black community. "From the beginning of harness racing . . . Negroes have been identified with the sport as grooms, trainers and drivers, and now and then as owners and breeders."[3] Josiah Henson himself raised and trained a Hambletonian stallion, a lineage that dominates the standardbred horses used in harness racing. In harness racing, trotting or pacing standardbred horses pull a driver on a sulky in contrast to thoroughbred racing that features a jockey on the saddle of a galloping horse.

During slavery, plantation owners trained both horses and men to perform for their entertainment. Some slave owners "groomed particular Negroes for local bouts, much as they bred and trained horses to challenge the trotters of neighboring racing enthusiasts."[4] Initially restricted to feeding, breaking, exercising, and grooming horses, smaller slaves were eventually selected to perform as jockeys for genteel white men.

Thoroughbred racing became the first sport to blur the racial divide in America. The first known Black jockey was an enslaved man called "Monkey" Simon who was often hired out to a white breeder named Colonel George Elliot, famous for his rivalry with future president Andrew Jackson. From 1811 to 1815, Simon, aboard a horse named Haynie's Maria, beat the best horses and jockeys Jackson could find nine straight times.[5]

A decade after the abolition of slavery in America, Oliver Lewis, a Black jockey, won the first Kentucky Derby in 1875, a race where fourteen of the fifteen jockeys were Black. Lewis' winning horse, Aristides, was trained by a former slave named Ansel Williamson. Perhaps the most noted Black jockey, however, was Isaac Burns Murphy, who won the Kentucky Derby in 1884, 1887, and 1890. In total, Black riders won the Kentucky Derby fifteen times between 1875 and 1902 until the new Jim Crow laws took hold. Soon, Black drivers and jockeys became a rarity, rather than the norm in horse racing. On July 29, 1900, *The New York Times* reported that, "As a matter of fact, the Negro jockey is down and out not because he could no longer ride, but because of a quietly formed combination shut him out. Gossip around the racing headquarters said that the white riders had organized to draw the color line. In this they were said to be upheld and advised by certain horse owners and turfmen who have great influence in racing affairs."[6] When Henry King rode in the Kentucky Derby in 1921, he was the last Black jockey to do so for 79 years.

Harness racing was more closely aligned with work than its thoroughbred counterpart. "The horses used for slave labor on the plantations were the strongest and fastest horses available in the country. Slave owners kept the horses in closed locations because if slaves were able to steal the horses they could quickly escape from the plantations. Due to these reasons, horseracing was limited. Horsemanship was also the mark of a gentleman. The social competition between races created a boundary between whites and blacks."[7]

Slaves became involved in harness racing through auxiliary, caretaking roles before being allowed to drive. While thoroughbred racing had many Black jockeys, including enslaved men, in premiere races throughout the 1800s, harness racing remained segregated. Stemming from chariot races and cart racing in Europe, the sport of harness racing did not include a Black driver in the sport's top race, the Hambletonian, until 2000 when Detroit-born DeWayne Minor drove in the event.

In Chatham-Kent, harness racing as practised at Dresden Raceway was preceded by impromptu "scrub" races held between area farmers on roads and frozen rivers on Sunday after church. The Chatham Turf Club was formed in 1845, and ground was cleared and levelled for horse racing on the east side of Chatham.

As one of the organizers was Edwin Larwill, the club was clearly intended for white riders only. Another founding member, Oliver Dauphin, offered to race his horse, Jim Crow, against any nag in the county. That same year, 1850, Dauphin posted a public challenge to any "white male" willing to compete in a foot race. The racial stipulation was made as Dauphin "detested mingling" with Black athletes.[8] Neither challenge was accepted.

The number of street races in Chatham forced the town to enact laws against racing horses down the main thoroughfares. Races became more organized and dedicated facilities were built. By the 1850s the Chatham Peninsular Club was reporting crowds of more than 5,000 racing fans.[9] While tracks became a venue for white riders and drivers, the local Black population was forced to continue using informal, and now illegal, spaces. In 1865, unlawful street racing produced the first record of a Black man participating in local horse racing. He was charged with racing a horse on King Street in Chatham, while his white opponent, who had access to legalized local tracks, went free.

The Mineral Springs Driving Park opened near Chatham in 1864 in addition to the Peninsular Club and harness racing began to evolve from a leisure activity to a profession, including in Black settlements. The 1901 Chatham census stated that two Black men were employed in horse racing, one as a trainer and one as a jockey. In Dresden, the sport was increasingly popular at the annual fair, and plans for a formal track began. The official Dresden Raceway site was surveyed and made into a regulation loop in 1913.

In 2021, 187 years after the first celebrations, Emancipation Day was being formally recognized in Canada for the first time, and I was driving to Dresden Raceway, where an event had been organized to honour Black harness racing drivers, trainers, and horse owners. I chose a leisurely drive along the back roads and watched the fields roll by. I could see a rusted barn ahead, a pasture fenced around it. Closer to the road sat a small farmhouse with painted blue batten board siding. Hanging above the man working at the barn was a flag: triangles of red, intersected by a blue X, and thirteen white stars. This man had woken on Emancipation Day and climbed up his ladder to hang a Confederate flag on the door of his barn. An above-ground pool sat behind their house, and a plastic car, the kind toddlers propel with their feet, was tucked along the side of the house. Children lived here; another season of hate had been planted.

Dresden Raceway is located on the corner of Josiah Henson's Dawn Settlement. This very location had been home to freed and escaped slaves in the 1840s while emancipation in America was still decades away. A century later, these grounds were used to intern Japanese Canadians. As a youth, my hockey coach had brought us to the track to run laps and then climb the stairs of the grandstand carrying our teammates on our backs. A horse owner and trainer himself, he wanted us to have standardbred legs that could outskate our competition. Today, it would be the site of Black Heritage Day.

At the raceway, fans were already lining the fences with lawn chairs. A Black man in a dark gray suit stood at the rail surrounded by families laying claim to the track-level picnic tables. In the bleachers of the grandstand, a family sat wearing matching Uncle Tom's Cabin t-shirts. A son was helping his elderly mother up the stairs with her walker. They moved with intent, like people who had sat in the same seats at Dresden Raceway for generations. The smell of hot dogs permeated the space. All around me was the hum of stories and shared memory coalescing.

One of the Black trainers being honoured was Terry McCorkle, whose father Lonnie was a noted Black driver at the track. He recalled the rich Black history of the track. "When I was a kid around Dresden, there were some coloured guys training and driving—Grineage, List, an old guy named Herb Davis—they'd all have one or two horses a piece, but there was all kinds of Black people involved."

Another multi-generational harness racing family were the Lists; today's guest of honour was Fred List. Born in Chatham in 1942, List grew up spending his summers in barns working as a groomer and handler, and urging his father Harry on at racetracks across Ontario and the United States. His first experience training a horse came when his father allowed him to take the family horse for the three-kilometer ride to his rural school. After a few weeks, the horse would stop at a neighbour's house, and no amount of coaxing could get it to continue. List would tie the horse to the fence and walk the rest of the way to school. After he told his father this, Harry rode with him, and when the horse stopped, Harry worked with the horse until he continued on. From that day forward, Fred List rode the entire way to school, and his love for training horses was cemented.

As the son of one of the most accomplished harness racing drivers in the province, young Fred List was accepted at the track. But in Dresden, he was still a second-class citizen. On one occasion, he cooled down a horse that had been brought to Dresden by two Indigenous men. As a gesture of appreciation, they offered to take him downtown for food. Only twelve years old at the time, List was unprepared for what happened next.

"We went down to a restaurant in Dresden. We went in and sat down, and they ordered. They asked me, 'What do you want, Fred?' I said, 'I'll just have a hamburger and French fries.' The waitress said, 'We can't serve him in here,' looking at me. They said, 'What do you mean?' The waitress repeated herself, 'We can't serve him in here.' They said, 'Fred, you go on out and wait in the truck, we'll bring you a hamburger.' I don't know if they ever opened that restaurant up again. They tore that place apart and threw tables and chairs out into the street, and they brought me out a hamburger and fries. The police chief came along and just shook his head."

Dresden wasn't the only place. List can remember walking into a barber shop while on a racing trip with his father. The barber told him that if he cut his hair the men in town would burn down his shop.

Even on the track itself there was inequality. "My dad was a great racer, better than me," recalls List. "They'd give him the horses no one else would touch, and he'd win. He never got good horses, but it didn't matter, he'd win races all over the place."

Terry McCorkle, who is too young to remember the height of discrimination in Dresden, knew that Black participants like his father and the Lists continued to face inequality within the sport. "They never really had breaks, because you never had good owners. You've got to have good owners with money to buy the good horses."

"As far as driving and training, I don't think we really do get a fair shake with things," said famed Black harness racing driver and trainer DeWayne Minor in 2020. "I've produced some nice horses and had some decent owners, but they don't stay as long as they would with a white trainer. If you don't produce right away, they'll pull out."[10]

Perhaps the most famous Black driver in harness racing history is Lewis Williams who, starting in 1963, put together a career that included more than 2,000 wins. The American Harness Racing Hall of Fame called Williams, the only Black member, "the most successful African-American in the primarily Caucasian world of harness racing," saying, "Williams always felt his skin color hampered him from attracting new owners as easily as his white counterparts." In Williams' own words, he did not receive the "same trust and respect afforded white trainer-drivers with equivalent or even lesser talents."[11]

Across the border in Canada, Fred List would go on to win countless races in Ontario, setting new records at Dresden Raceway as he went. Despite its local roots, however, the future of Black involvement in harness racing is uncertain. In a June 19, 2020 interview with HarnessRacing.com, George Teague Jr., another successful Black driver, said, "I don't see the next generation of Blacks (in harness racing). Maybe it's not a sport for African-Americans since it's such a white game. This game has a long way to go, or shortly it's going to be an all-white game."[12]

On that August day in 2021, I stand talking to Fred List as the horses trot onto the track for a race that honours him and his father, the colours of each jockey's jersey bright in the sun. Fred smiles as he watches the horses pull their drivers down the home stretch, and across the finish. When it is over, his name echoes through the grandstand as he steps onto the track and drapes a green blanket embroidered with his family name over the panting winner. It was Black Heritage Day, and he was no longer separate, or secondary; he was the guest of honour.

## Chapter 8

# NOT CANADIAN ENOUGH

I was leaning over the glass, dangling a photo to be autographed by a hockey hero. We were in St. Thomas, Ontario for the 1997 NHL Top Prospects Game. Bobby Orr was coaching and stood behind his bench signing autographs during intermission. Joe Thornton was the marquee name on the ice, a soon-to-be first overall selection, but it was Orr I recognized.

I was at the game with my best friend who, ten inches shorter, could not push his way through the crowd. He wanted Orr to sign his autograph book, so I wedged myself into the mass of human bodies and reached my arm over the glass. Orr took the book, looked up at me, and then jammed it back into my hands. "Get lost, I already signed something for you," he shouted. Youthful faces and a few adult ones looked around for the cause of the commotion and saw me, eyes welling with tears. Dejected, I handed the unsigned book back to my friend and sat quietly beside him watching Orr and Don Cherry, the coach of the other team in the event, wave at fans, pat future Hall of Famers on the back and model what it meant to be Canadian.

I looked over and saw the blank page of my friend's book, one his dad had purchased especially to have Orr sign. Now, I envy the blankness of that page. For years I treasured the signatures Orr, Cherry, and Joe Thornton gave me that day. I held them as valuable and often acted out the story of Bobby Orr telling me off to laughter at parties. Now I know the signature on that page is worthless. Ink on paper from a straight white settler who would eventually purchase a full-page advertisement endorsing Donald Trump and mount a vigorous defence of his friend Don Cherry, a man who made sure everyone on the other side of the glass was an outsider.

I still have the photo Orr autographed for me. It's hard to know what to do with it. Part of me wants to burn it, to leave no trace of my existence alongside his. I want to forget my involvement in the systems he helped to build, and the ideology he perpetuated. But I was part of that oppression. I was part of the Canadiana, the national identity tied to a game, that looked to exclude any person who didn't look like me or sound like me.

World War II brought global attention to the issue of white supremacy. On foreign soil, the blood of Black, white, and Indigenous Canadians soaked into grass and sand. There was equality in death where there wasn't in life. And when, more than two years into the war, Japan attacked Hawaii's Pearl Harbor, Canadians began identifying enemies by the colour of their skin.

In the days following Pearl Harbor, Japanese language schools in British Columbia were closed and thousands of fishing boats owned by Japanese Canadians were seized. As the calendar flipped to 1942, the Canadian government, following the lead of the United States, invoked the War Measures Act and forcefully dispersed over 22,000 Japanese Canadians living in British Columbia. To pay for their internment, which lasted for the duration of the war, the government dispossessed Japanese Canadians, selling their businesses, land, fishing boats, vehicles, and homes.

Curfews were imposed and by March of 1942 the first group of Japanese Canadians were brought to Vancouver's Hastings Park, the site of the annual Pacific National Exhibition. Inside the livestock building, rows upon rows of tightly packed bunk beds were constructed. Women and children slept here, amid the stench of animals and urine. The toilets were troughs without partitions or seats, and 1,500 women shared ten showers. Privacy and dignity had been confiscated along with their belongings.

The men and teenage boys were housed in the Forum, home to the pre-NHL iteration of the Vancouver Canucks. Bunk beds filled the arena where up to 5,000 spectators usually watched hockey. In the open space between buildings, men would throw baseballs. Children would run and kick makeshift soccer balls. Beyond the barbed wire that now enclosed the grounds, the prisoners could spot white golfers playing at Hastings Park Golf Course and white spectators still enjoying horse races on the adjacent track. Their confiscated trucks and cars were being stored on the track's infield, waiting to be sold.

Across the country in Chatham-Kent, men were being sent overseas at an increasing rate. The ground had been tilled and planted, but a shortage of field labour was emerging; government officials decided to meet the need with interned Japanese Canadians. Ontario was far from vulnerable Canadian coasts and its large sugar beet crop was deemed essential to the war effort. Some communities in Niagara and Eastern Ontario welcomed the assistance of Japanese Canadians and applied for more Nikkei workers, but not Chatham-Kent. Local government and citizens wanted nothing to do with internment camps, nor the Canadians who would be held at these facilities.

Towns in the area bristled with racist sentiments. Chatham's council pointed to what they believed to be the inherently deceitful nature of the Japanese. There was no room for "pests and traitors" in Kent County.[1] One Chatham alderman moved "that the infiltration to Kent County by citizens of Japanese origin be eliminated and that steps be taken to have all Japanese removed from the district."[2] Citizens, the mayor, and councillors did not want Japanese Canadians infiltrating their communities, not as internees and definitely not as residents.

The Minister of Agriculture at the time, P.M. Dewan, was unmoved. "Being a national problem, it seems only reasonable that Ontario should not shirk its share of responsibility, and certainly the difficult task of locating Japanese evacuees from the west coast should not be aggravated either by provincial obstacles or local prejudices."[3]

Chatham-Kent's desire for whiteness would eventually be outweighed by their need for field labour; five of the nine farm camps constructed in southwestern Ontario were located in the area. The *Chatham Daily News* ran a headline that read "Citizens Object to Japanese Labor Site in the City," quoting residents concerned that property values would be affected, and that the presence of the Nikkei, or any person of Japanese ancestry regardless of birthplace or citizenship, would "frighten children."[4]

Japanese Canadians were brought by train to Tilbury, then immediately boarded Dominion Sugar Company trucks destined for a camp near Valetta. Here, the local opposition was so intense Graham Pipher, the region's representative for the British Columbia Security Commission, a government agency responsible for the forced dispersal and internment of Japanese Canadians from British Columbia, recommended that workers be immediately transferred elsewhere for their safety.[5]

One of the new arrivals was Satoshi Izumi, nicknamed Joe because his teachers had found his given name too difficult to pronounce. A fisherman from Chemainus, Joe had been brought to Hastings Park with the rest of his family. But single men, including Joe and his brothers Kaname (Harry) and Mitsuo (Roy or "Mits"), were destined for labour while his parents, sisters, and youngest brother Herbie would be sent to Lemon Creek internment camp in British Columbia's Slocan Valley. Standing on the platform at the train station, Joe Izumi handed money to his sisters through the window of the train car and then ran alongside, holding their hands as far as the platform would allow. Then they were gone.

Joe first arrived in Jackfish, Ontario on the shores of Lake Superior. From there, it was south to a camp outside of Toronto, then St. Catherines and finally, Eatonville in Chatham-Kent. He and fifty-four others were each assigned bunk beds at the Eatonville Roadhouse, originally the Park Hotel, near Rondeau Provincial Park. Unlike large-scale internment camps designated for families, roadhouses and farm camps housed single men required as labour. Located on Highway 3, the main route to Toronto, prior to the war travellers would stop at the Park Hotel for one dollar chicken dinners and bootlegged liquor.

Joe was sent where labour was needed. He worked clearing timber and brush for new roads inside Rondeau Provincial Park, then in Dover, near Chatham. He used a hoe to cut a row of sugar beet seedlings into blocks while another Nikkei labourer on his hands and knees beside him thinned the cluster of seedlings so that only a single plant remained, an intensive process known as "blocking beats." The hours were long and the food and shelter insufficient, but there was a diamond to be used for baseball and softball.

Similar to residential schools, sport at internment camps provided both entertainment and respite. For the Nikkei, sometimes also referred to as Nisei, a term identifying Japanese Canadians, it remained a source of identity, a remnant of pre-war life. In the years following the rise of the Vancouver Asahi team of Japanese Canadians in 1915, baseball had become a fascination in Japanese Canadian communities in British Columbia. The Asahi team, which would eventually be inducted to the Canadian Baseball Hall of Fame, featured prominently in everyday life.

Beginning in 1935, Joe played third base for the Chemainus Nippons, an all-Japanese Canadian baseball club, one of two in a five-team league. In 1939, his oldest brother Harry was catcher, and his brother Mits, the star of the trio, rotated between second base, shortstop, and pitching. Mits' ability had also drawn the attention of white teams in the area, and he did double duty, playing with the Duncan Cubs as well. In 1940, as tensions started to rise against Japanese Canadians, the Izumis and the Nippons moved to the Mid-Island Japanese League. Harry was no longer playing, but younger brother Herbie joined Joe and Mits at second base.

After Pearl Harbor, Japanese Canadians could only play

baseball in internment camps and teams formed at Dresden, Valetta, Chatham, and smaller roadhouses as well as in neighbouring communities such as Glencoe and Petrolia.

In Dresden, the reverend of the local United Church bought four bats and four baseballs for the interned men. Games commenced immediately and included competition within each camp, between camps, and later between internees and local teams. As early as 1942, games were recorded in the *Chatham Daily News* between the Dresden "Japanese Labourers" and a team of internees from the Harwich Township camps.

Dresden, however, did not want these Nikkei playing baseball, or even working in local fields. On April 27, 1942, members of the Dresden Legion wrote a letter to Ontario Premier Mitchell Hepburn hoping to stop the admittance of Japanese Canadians into the area, saying, "They can never become real Canadians. That once here they would stay. Our standards of living would be lowered due to their competition in the labour market and elsewhere. It is our aim to keep Canada British and oppose the admission of any person or persons that cannot become British subjects in mind and deed."[6] Similar letters were penned by groups across Chatham-Kent, including Bothwell and Blenheim.

That summer in Chatham, local baseball teams started challenging the Nikkei farm teams after the 1942 harvest season. Following losses at Northridge and Chatham, the area Nikkei teams began winning games, beating teams from Petrolia, Florence, and an all-Black team from North Buxton. According to researcher Stephanie Bangarth, "Competitions were organized against teams from other towns, and the teams always played to a receptive audience. While the athletic prowess of the Nisei ballplayers impressed the local residents and their opponents alike, so too did their generosity."[7]

During a 1942 game between the Glencoe Farm Service Nisei Team and the Ridgetown All-Stars, the Nisei team raised $27.50

from gate proceeds, which they donated to the Queen's Canadian Fund. In another game, the Petrolia Nisei team donated proceeds of $7.00 to the Legion to support troops overseas.[8]

Off the field, sentiments in local communities did not change, even as the need for labour and the contribution of Japanese Canadians in local communities grew.

As the need for farm labour remained acute, Canada's Department of National Defence and Department of Labour agreed to deploy German prisoners of war. From 1944 to 1946, Chatham was home to a prisoner of war camp, Camp 10. In total, 325 German prisoners of war worked on farms in Chatham-Kent, at Wallaceburg's Dominion Sugar refinery and for the Libby McNeill Company. According to researcher Jordyn Bailey, Chatham area farmers were so happy with the work the prisoners of war were doing that they requested more during the fall of 1944.[9]

Article 38 of the Geneva Convention mandates that "Prisoners shall have opportunities for taking physical exercise, including sports and games, and for being out of doors. Sufficient open spaces shall be provided for this purpose in all camps." When Neys Camp 100, initially used to house Japanese Canadian internees, was converted to a prison primarily for high-ranking German officers, the recreation facilities were upgraded. POWs had access to "an athletic field ninety by fifty meters; a gymnasium and recreation hut; a tennis court and a skating rink. In the gymnasium they have parallel and horizontal bars; vaulting horses and mats."[10]

According to historian Michael O'Hagan, "Prisoners in most internment camps set up their own teams and leagues and began playing football (soccer), baseball, volleyball, basketball, tennis, and . . . hockey. In an early report of the War Prisoners' Aid, director Jerome Davis remarked, 'One Canadian manufacturer out of the generosity of his heart, contributed two hundred pairs of skates. The result was that we were aided in building skating rinks in almost every prison camp in Canada.'"[11] Some POWs were given unsupervised access to the bush in order to hunt. Guards at the camps would go so far as to "loan us their rifles and off we'd go, because we were trusted like that."[12]

One of those who took part in sport was Paul Mengelberg, a crew member on a U-boat who was held at Ontario's Angler Camp 101. Paul participated in figure skating, high bars, and pommel horse. He described sport in the camp: "The recreational field was used for football [soccer] in summer and for ice skating in winter. Prisoners played hockey against the guards, who always won." When Mengelberg returned to Germany, he was not met with the warmth he felt in Canada, "because I was a Nazi," and so he returned to work and live permanently in Toronto.[13]

Mengelberg was not alone. Canada treated German POWs so well that, following the war, many did not want to return to Germany. Of those who did, many hoped to soon return. In a *Legion Magazine* article titled "The Happiest Prisoner," which looked at the lavish treatment of German POWs during World War II, Graham Chandler writes that "35,046 German soldiers, sailors, airmen and potential insurgents were incarcerated under a program one later called 'the best thing that happened to me.' It's how many of them felt about their time here; and it's partly why more than 6,000 wanted to stay after the war ended."[14]

By 1945, POWs in Chatham had access to weekly concerts, biweekly movies, and a sports field used for football, running, boxing, and discus. Prisoners were brought to the Cedar Springs Range, a military rifle range, where they could swim in Lake Erie; they were free to visit Chatham whenever they wanted.

Nikkei labourers, by contrast, were only allowed into town ten at a time and under RCMP surveillance. As Ken Adachi notes in his book *The Enemy that Never Was: A History of the Japanese Canadians* (1976), this was to protect the Japanese Canadians from overt acts of violence, because the "hostility was more marked in Chatham than anywhere else." He quotes Chatham's mayor at the time telling a Police Commission meeting that "that 99 and 9/10 of thinking people of Chatham do not want the Japanese here, and that they should all be interned, and that public opinion has not changed since the Japanese first arrived here." Chatham city council banned Japanese Canadians from being in the community after sunset.[15]

While Japanese Canadians were treated as other, German POWs were made to feel that Canada was their home, including at Chatham, where "several POWs openly stated they had no desire to return to Germany after the war."[16]

Recalled Horst Braun, a U-Boat wireless operator, "I was terribly homesick for Canada! I couldn't wait to get back here."[17] Siegfried Bruse, a former U-Boat officer and POW who returned to Canada and started a successful real estate firm in North Bay, Ontario stated, "I like Canadians. They made my life as pleasant as possible from the day I came here as a prisoner. Later, when I returned as a landed immigrant, I knew this was my country. There was also the feeling that you could create something here, that you could achieve what you wished in this land."[18]

For German POWs, including Nazis, Canada provided opportunities that were withheld from Japanese Canadians, citizens identified as enemies because of their race.

According to researcher J. Bailey, "German POWs were ultimately accepted in post-war Canada because their racial status ranked them above prospective Jewish and Asian immigrants . . . If many communities came to view the German enemy as productive members of society over the course of the Second World War, there was no similar transformation in attitudes to other internees. Anti-Japanese sentiment was palpable in many of the same places that welcomed the Germans, and this notion of a 'natural difference' was structured along racial lines. In no region is this clearer than Kent County, the most vocal region in Canada in its opposition to the use of Japanese Canadian internees as labourers."[19]

They were not Canadian enough.

## Chapter 9

# TURNING THE TABLES

On a December morning in 2021, I crossed the bridge to Walpole Island, parked across from the arena, and climbed into Alyssa Sands' jeep. She was wearing a green ribbon skirt, with gold bands and pink flowers. Her father, Bill, sat behind me, our unofficial tour guide for the day. We drove to the Highbanks, where the Snye and St. Clair rivers meet, Michigan visible across the water. Nearby, two small islands belonging to the First Nation used to regularly be blanketed with horses, wading through the water to cool off, chasing bathers from beaches. Stallions would fight for command of a herd or mating rights to a mare.

The three of us drove past baseball diamonds and headed into the bush, passing the place where Alyssa has spotted the biggest deer she has ever seen. We walked out into the old oak savannas near the location where Bill's childhood home used to stand. As children, Bill and his friends would walk through this bush, following the paths the horses cut, their hooves pounding down the undergrowth to form *miikanan*, or little roads. When they heard the familiar thunder of a herd, they would climb into the trees, feeling the heat from the horses' bodies and their breath rising into the branches.

Bill and his older brother, Butch, helped their father build corrals for the wild horses that still roamed the island, working to break them. Both Butch and Bill would race their ponies at the annual Oneida or Walpole Island fall fairs. Butch would often win.

The horses, however, were not loved by all. The missionaries thought the sight of them breeding in front of children was indecent, a sin to be cleansed, and so the first horses were killed.

As traditional hunting and gathering grounds became restricted off reserve, agriculture became a primary source of food on, and the economic driver for, Walpole Island; these once beautiful and free horses became a nuisance to farmers. They kicked in fences, pulled clothes from drying lines and ate crops. They needed to go. Anyone who wanted a horse could catch and keep them. Then they sold them off for $10.00 a head.

By the time Bill Sands was born in 1946, the wild Ojibwe spirit horses were already declining. Eventually they were rounded up and killed. Screaming truckloads of the horses were driven to nearby Chatham and destroyed at the glue factory.

Today it was cold, but the sun was shining. White tufts of clouds hung low above us. In the summer, this space would be lush with undergrowth. Now leaves covered the ground as light tumbled through the trees. To our right was a pond, hidden by invasive phragmites.

"It's beautiful," I said. "So many people from the mainland never see this part of the Island, they only drive from the bridge to the ferry."

"A lot of people are still scared to come out here," said Alyssa.

"They might run into some Indians," Bill added, laughing at his own joke.

In the quiet of the forest, I admitted to them that I would have been one of those people. I used to be one of those people but on that day I felt no fear, only peace.

From here, we headed along kilometers of dirt roads. Alyssa showed me the field where she shot her first deer. Bill told me about riding the Ojibwe ponies through these areas. When we pulled off next, we were in fields and open space. Every inch held a hunting story for Bill; he began to tell his stories and the stories of his ancestors.

In 1957, eleven-year-old Bill Sands got on the school bus that picked him up at his home on Walpole Island First Nation and dropped him off outside his school in Wallaceburg. When the bell rang, Bill went inside and took his spot. As the quiet of the lesson began, he heard footsteps and looked up to see the familiar face of Fred Hall, Walpole Island's Indian Agent. Fred wanted to buy Bill lunch in London.

"Lunch in London, why? I don't want to go," Bill replied, hesitant.

The Indian Agent grabbed him by the collar and replied, "You're going."

Fred Hall did take Bill to lunch in London. Afterward, instead of bringing him home, he drove east to the Mohawk Institute near Brantford. Pulling up the long drive, the building cast a shadow much darker than that of the oak trees on Walpole Island. White pillars stretched into the sky, framing the front door.

When the school bus returned to Walpole Island that night, Bill wasn't on it. "I was eleven years old, and I didn't get off the bus. The Indian Agent was gone, there was no telephone at the time and my parents didn't have a car. My sister said my mother almost died from that shock. It was the worst thing ever in her life."

In 1920, attendance at residential school became mandatory for all Indigenous youth in Canada. As Deputy Superintendent General of Indian Affairs Duncan Campbell Scott explained, "I want to get rid of the Indian problem. I do not think as a matter of fact, that this country ought to continuously protect a class of people who are able to stand alone. That is my whole point . . . Our object is to continue until there is not a single Indian in Canada that has not been absorbed into the body politic, and there is no Indian question, and no Indian department, that is the whole object of this Bill."[1] By the time Bill Sands was taken to Mohawk in 1957, not every Indigenous child was being forced to attend. Bill was one of the unlucky ones.

When the school bell rang on that first day, Bill was introduced to life at the Mush Hole, the nickname given to Mohawk Institute by students due to the mushy, often worm-infested gruel they were fed. That first day, Bill was beaten twice by other students before he could even get to the residence. After dinner, he was beaten again. "I got beat up like that every day for the first two weeks, before school, after school, after dinner, it was just a common thing. Not just me, a lot of the other boys as well. There were always fights. And the staff promoted it—they pushed the big guy into the little guy or pushed the little guy into the big guy and then the fight was on. That was pretty tough."

At the end of that second week, Bill was one of dozens of older boys crammed into a room to participate in that most Canadian of traditions, watching *Hockey Night in Canada*. Researcher Andrew Narraway argues that "hockey provided the schools with a uniquely Canadian disciplinary technique that taught specific expressions of Canadian masculinity such as toughness, perseverance, and loyalty. Furthermore, the artistry of hockey mixed with its inherent tendencies towards physical aggression made it the perfect sport for assimilation as it channeled Indigenous 'weakness' and 'aggression' into disciplined bodily movement."[2]

Bill recalls, "We had a room there where we'd watch the hockey games, and a guy knocked me off my chair and jumped on me and was beating me up. I just covered up my head and I had my hands behind my head. This guy was punching me. Anyway, I felt him lift off my body, I turned around and looked up and a big guy was holding him by the belt, he was holding him up in the air." Bill had made his first friend, an older boy named Woody Snake from Munsee Delaware Nation. From that moment on, Bill's beatings stopped.

Mohawk became the new norm for Bill. He worked in the fields, ate the sticky mush and occasional root vegetable—their only fresh food—and did his best to avoid the powdered milk and eggs that tasted of sulphur, a smell that came from the water they drank. Like many, he waited for the respite of sport to break the monotony of days and to forget about the hardships they were facing. "I played sports, everything that came up I got involved in. We played hard-ball, baseball. I played basketball, I played hockey, I played floor hockey, whatever the sport, I got involved in it. I remember, I was probably about thirteen years old. I'd been there about a year already and nobody wanted to get in goal when we'd play hockey. They'd allow Six Nations teams to come in and play us at the school, you know we couldn't go out, but they could come play with us, and I was the goalie. No one would get in goal, I don't think we had much proper equipment, but I stuck it out. All the while I was there, I stayed the goalie all the time, and I guess I got a little bit better. And I played basketball, and that was fun; met a lot of kids from Six Nations and had fun."

When Bill was released from Mohawk, he brought his trauma with him. "I was there for four years, it was the toughest four years of my life, and it still affects me today, and it affected my children, and my ex-wife, my parents. Especially my parents." He longed to be outside, a free man no longer confined by walls. He returned to Walpole Island, a hunting and fishing mecca that has been protected and stewarded for centuries by the Indigenous people of this land. The Island forms part of the Atlantic and Mississippi flyways and the 8,300 hectares of coastal marshlands and wetlands that border Lake St. Clair provide prime habitat for fish and mammals such as muskrat and mink.

Bill returned to Walpole Island in 1961 and got a job at the local gas station. That December, and every one that followed, he set hundreds of muskrat traps, hoping to sell their pelts and meat. He'd tend these traps until he saw the red-winged blackbird arrive in the early spring, a sign that meant only a few snowy days remained and hunting season would soon return.

Early one morning, when the border between sleep and wakefulness was dulled by the lack of light, Bill heard his brother rise. He heard the sounds of a shirt and pants being pulled on, Butch's feet descending the stairs and the door closing as he went out into the morning. Bill closed his eyes again, but Butch was soon shaking him awake.

"Billy, you gotta guide."

"What time is it?" Bill's voice was heavy with sleep.

"Five o'clock."

"I'm sleeping. Get out of here."

"You gotta guide. You'll get $10 if you take some duck hunters out," Butch urged, who was already scheduled to work that day.

Bill propped himself up on his elbows. "Can I do it?"

"Sure you can," his brother replied. "I'll tell you how."

Neither could know it was the first morning of a six-decade career for Bill.

Hunters returning from the marsh would talk as they pulled into the gas station and Bill filled their tanks. Soon Bill's name was being passed among the white visitors to the island. They'd heard he could call ducks, find pheasants and quail, and that he knew fishing spots where perch and bluegill were always biting.

"Hey, Bill, how do you like working here?" a man called from his vehicle.

Bill walked over, pulling the gas pump from its hold.

"I heard you can blow a good duck call," the man continued. "How much do you make here?"

Bill recognized him. He was a white man from Wallaceburg who ran a hunting and fishing club on the island.

"Thirty-five dollars a week."

"If you can blow this duck call, I'll double it. I'll pay you $70 a week if you can blow this call."

"You give me the job, and then I'll show you I can blow the call," Bill replied, full of teenage confidence.

That same year, Bill, now sixteen, took another job guiding for William Clay Ford Sr., the grandson of Henry Ford and owner of the NFL's Detroit Lions, who also owned a lodge on Walpole Island. In the years that followed, Sands' reputation continued to precede him, until a major American company, the National Steel Corporation, offered to build a lodge next door to Sands' home to entertain employees, investors, and executives. Sands would also run Drake's Only, a popular guiding service operating out of the National Steel Lodge, which became known as Big Shooters.

The lodge became a mecca for celebrities, and Bill Sands assumed the lustre of stardom. Steven Spielberg, Prime Minister Paul Martin, and Cher all stayed on the Chematogen Channel at Big Shooters. On one occasion, Sands picked up his phone to hear Brent Ladds, president of the Ontario Hockey Association, offering him any favour if he'd guide a hockey player. A few days later, Bobby Orr arrived. Not many years after he sat crowded around a television watching hockey greats Gordie Howe and Alex Delvecchio play, he found himself in a duck blind issuing instructions to both of them. When the thunder of the guns ruptured the early morning silence, the remaining mallards took to the sky. Like any good coach, Bill praised Alex and Gordie before wading into the water to retrieve the ducks.

During the afternoons following a hunt, Bill's children played catch with Kirk Gibson and other Detroit Tigers players. On quieter days, Sands would walk through the prairies of Walpole Island with his dogs, Casper and Dancer, successors to a pair of hunting dogs gifted to his grandfather by double Olympic gold medallist, Major League Baseball alumnus, and football Hall of Famer Jim Thorpe.

"My dad went to work with Henry Ford in Detroit, and he worked with Jim Thorpe there. They became friends and Jim Thorpe would come to the Island on weekends with my dad, and he became really good friends with my grandpa, Walter Sands. Jim raised giant Airedales and he gave my grandfather two. They were hunting dogs, pheasant dogs, upland game. They were ferocious, not to people, but they could really fight. When my dad was hunting on St. Anne's Island, hunting pheasants, those two dogs were great. They could flush the birds and retrieve them for my dad."

By 1977, only four Ojibwe spirit horses—Lilian, Biizhiki, Diamond, and Dark Face—remained. They were destined to die as well after Canadian health officials deemed them a health risk. To save them, a group of men drove across a frozen lake at Lac Lacroix, in Northern Ontario, where the horses were being kept, and took them under cover of darkness to a farm in Minnesota in what would be called the "heist across the ice."[3]

They were bred to a mustang and survived until Terry Jenkins, who owns TJ Stables near Chatham, and her husband, John, who is Métis, found the descendants of the surviving horses living as a small herd near Fort Frances, Ontario. Terry Jenkins had spent her entire life searching for the small, shaggy ponies that her father had told stories about, and when she found them, she immediately felt their healing power. Stepping into the pasture for the first time with them, Jenkins was overcome.

"Their heads came up out of the lush grass and immediately they started towards us, circling around me, surrounding me with a power I had never experienced in all my six decades," she said. "Their tiny hooves beating a rhythm of power. An unmistakable flush came through my body from these little horses of an overwhelming love that I only experienced when I held my newborn infant in my arms."

From those four horses, fourteen descendants remained for the Jenkins to purchase in 2019 but, within twenty minutes of their arrival, the matriarch of the herd gave birth to a new foal, that Jenkins named Eshquemaatogan, Ojibwe for "new beginnings." Someday, they hope to return this herd to Walpole Island.

Until then, Bill visits them in the pasture at TJ Stables, his grandson in his arms. Alyssa stood next to me as we watched Bill and the horses. "For as long as I can remember my dad talked about the horses," Alyssa tells me. "It was an emotional experience for me to see him reconnect to something that brought him so much happiness as a little boy. I think about his childhood, being stolen and taken from a good life—and then I think about my own son, even myself. My dad's history impacts three generations today. Watching and walking with him on his healing journey is helping all three of those generations heal."

Both Bill and the horses were forcibly removed from Walpole Island. But they both survived. And now they're coming back.

# Chapter 10

# RAGGING THE PUCK

The room smelled of wet clothes, sweat, and the disinfectant that had been used to mop the floor. Blue jeans and sweaters hung on hooks above the wooden benches that lined each wall, shoes tucked underneath. My fingers were wound in skate laces as I weaved and pulled, threading the aglet through each hold, until I gave one final tug, crossed the laces, and tied a bow. I pulled my shin pads down to the laces, taped them at the top and bottom before looking up to see fifteen of my friends, my teammates, at various stages of dress.

From the time I started at five, until the time I walked away from competitive hockey at twenty-three, I played with several hundred different players in six towns in Southwestern Ontario. Almost all of them were white. When we played against a team from Nashville that had multiple Black youths on the roster, our coach made racist comments on the bench, trying to make us laugh. Some did. In the dressing room, we were told that we should be beating this team by a wider margin as Black people can't even play hockey. I was fifteen before I competed against a Black hockey player on a Canadian team. He was from Kitchener.

The first time I played against an Asian player was at a tournament in Toronto. Our coach gave us an in-depth scouting report: Asian players were "sneaky" and "tricky." Because they were small, they couldn't take hits so we should play physical.

The whiteness of hockey remains evident, a legacy inherited from team owners and league officials who worked to keep it that way. Without barriers, there were at least two players tied to Chatham-Kent who could have played in the NHL. Boomer Harding could have preceded Willie O'Ree, and George Chin could have played before Larry Kwong.

George Chin was born in Lucknow, Ontario—two hundred kilometers north of Chatham-Kent—to Rose and Charles Chin, Chinese immigrants who arrived in the early 1920s just before the Chinese Immigration Act of 1923 effectively closed the door to newcomers from China. They opened Chin's Restaurant, serving Chinese food to the community, and started a family that grew to include fourteen children, eleven of them boys. The basement of the restaurant was prone to flooding and, in the winter months, would freeze to form an indoor ice surface where the Chin children and community kids would come to work on their hockey skills and play games.

George, Albert, and Bill Chin were the hockey stars of the bunch. In 1944, Detroit Red Wings' scout Freddie Cox observed that, "the three Chin boys from Lucknow are going to surprise everyone this winter. They'll be ready for the big time before long."[1]

He was right. The talented trio earned an invitation to attend Toronto Maple Leafs training camp prior to the 1944–1945 season. "The ones attracting the most attention in the games have been the three Chinese brothers, Albert, George, and Bill Chin from Lucknow. Although on the small side and several steps away from top-flight hockey, the Chinese line made a big hit with the crowd with its clever passing, good stickhandling, and aggressiveness," reported the *Toronto Daily Star*.[2]

After a strong showing, the trio were released, a move that was mocked by Toronto media when George Chin, only fifteen at the time, went home and started lighting up his juvenile league. "George Chin, a 15-year-old who laughed his way through Leafs training camp last fall, scored all 12 of his juvenile team's goals at Kincardine Saturday night. Hadn't we better send for him, Hap?"

the *Toronto Star* wrote, calling on Leafs manager Hap Day to bring Chin back.[3]

Only two days later, George Chin scored an additional six goals in another game, prompting *The Star* to again call, this time on Maple Leafs scouts, to bring the brothers back. "Maybe Squib Walker should hustle out to Lucknow and scout the kids all over again as a Leafian front line threat!"[4]

Had George, or either of his brothers, been signed to an NHL contract and appeared in a game in 1944–45, he would have been the first non-white player in NHL history. Instead the Chin brothers became an attraction at visiting arenas, including in Chatham-Kent where their Lucknow Juveniles played an Ontario Minor Hockey Association playoff series against the Tilbury Juveniles. The March 14, 1949 edition of *The Windsor Star* promoted the game as "Featuring the Three Chin Brothers All Chinese Hockey Players."

Outside the dressing room there would be lines of children waiting for George's autograph, but from the stands, the parents of these children would spew racist slurs. "When we played in places like Goderich, Kincardine, and Hanover, we heard the occasional racial taunt. It was stuff like, 'Kill that ch----!' We just shrugged it off and tried to score another goal to beat them," *The Toronto Star* quoted George Chin in an October 2, 2016 article about his youth playing days.[5]

The following year, 1946–47, George Chin joined the Windsor Spitfires in their inaugural season, scoring thirty-one points in only twenty-four games. Two seasons later, he joined the Chatham Sr. Maroons, where he helped the team win the International Hockey League's Turner Cup over the Sarnia Sailors, playing in front of packed houses at the new Chatham Memorial Arena.

The NHL colour barrier was broken the following year by another player of Asian descent, Larry Kwong. Like Chin, Kwong was born into a large family. The fourteenth of fifteen children,

Kwong advanced to senior hockey in British Columbia, playing for the Trail Smoke Eaters, a team that typically compensated players by getting them well-paying jobs at the local smelter. Kwong however, was relegated to lower paying work as a bellboy. "I made the team, but they wouldn't give me a job because I was Chinese," he said.[6]

In a January 5, 1944 article in the *Edmonton Journal*, Kwong said, "The fans like to see a Chinese player as a curiosity. That's my good luck. But it has its disadvantages. There has always been a player or two trying to cut off my head just because I was Chinese. And the bigger the league the bigger the axe they use."

Despite the racism of the time, Kwong became the leading scorer of the New York Rangers' farm team and was called up for a game against the Montreal Canadiens. Kwong was benched the entire game, before playing a single shift in the final minute of the game, his first and only shift in the NHL.

Following his season in Chatham, Chin was recruited by the University of Michigan and went on to win back-to-back national championships in 1952 and 1953, leading the team in playoff scoring both years and earning NCAA All-Tournament First Team honours. That same season of 1953, back home in Lucknow, brothers Jack and Charlie Chin helped the Lucknow Midget team win an Ontario Minor Hockey Association D championship, defending their 1952 Bantam OMHA title. In 1954–55, Morley Chin would follow in George's footsteps and play for the University of Michigan Wolverines.

After graduating, George Chin played one year of professional hockey for the Nottingham Panthers in England before retiring from the game having scored an incredible total of 268 points in 176 games. In 1977, he was inducted into the Michigan Dekers Hall of Fame and, in 2018, was listed as the 36th best player in Michigan Wolverines history. The Dekers Club, a non-profit organization, has been recognizing University of Michigan hockey players with an annual Hall of Fame class since 1964. The Hall of Fame features dozens of NHL alumni and international stars, including Chatham native Mel Wakabayashi.

Despite never having played in the NHL, the Chin brothers left their mark. One of the many children who honed their skills in their Lucknow basement rink was NHL All-Star and Team Canada hero Paul Henderson. The Chin family gave Henderson his first set of equipment, and one or another of the Chin brothers coached him throughout his minor hockey career. Referring to the goal that defeated the Russians at the 1972 Summit Series, Henderson said, "If it wasn't for a Chinese Canadian family, I would never have scored the most important goal in Canadian hockey history."[7]

Boomer Harding has been called Chatham-Kent's own Jackie Robinson many times. Growing up, he wasn't only a star baseball player. Harding also excelled in soccer and hockey, helping his high school team win regional championships. While playing with the Chatham Coloured All-Stars, Harding also played hockey with the Chatham Adanacs, and won a Kent Hockey League title in 1937 with the Chatham Queens A.C. After joining the war effort and completing his posting at Basic Training Number 12 in Chatham, Harding was sent to London, Ontario where he started playing hockey for the London Army All-Stars. Next, he was posted to Kingston where he played baseball and soccer for the Kingston Ponies, and hockey for the Kingston Vimy.

Near the end of the war, Harding was shipped overseas to Holland and Belgium and was recruited to play hockey for a Canadian Armed Forces team that featured NHL players from the Detroit Red Wings, New York Rangers, and Montreal Canadiens. The team embarked on a tour of Europe, playing professional teams at each stop.

Returning from Europe, and with time to spare before baseball started, Boomer joined the other local veterans on the Legion soccer team. They won the city and county championship before travelling to Toronto for the Ontario Cup, which, with Harding on the field, they won as well.

According to Harding's son Blake, "They had an old highway cruiser that took them down to Toronto and the wives went. After their win they went to the host Legion for a celebration and to get presented with the trophy. They walked in and—nope, you're not getting served."

"That one hurt, that one hurt him," continued Blake, who himself served as a Chief Warrant Officer and Regimental Sergeant during a twenty-two-year career with the Canadian Armed Forces. "And so, the whole team turned around and said, 'Come on, we'll just grab something on the road somehow, and this is not where we're going to be.' When he came back here, he thought, I served four years in the military, I'm a veteran. And to be refused the right to go into a Legion. I know that one hurt him. When he talked about it, he didn't want to talk about it much."

Boomer Harding enjoyed the respect of his peers. It was Adam Brown, one of his teammates from the army team who had won a Stanley Cup with the Detroit Red Wings in 1942-43, who recommended Harding to the Red Wings organization. Initially signed by the Detroit Auto Club, he was traded to the Windsor Staffords when the team found out Harding was Black. In 1946, Harding became the first Black player in the International Amateur Hockey League, playing for the Detroit Red Wings' farm team, the Windsor Staffords.

That season, Boomer Harding became the first Black athlete to play at Olympia Stadium, the home of the Red Wings for 52 years, from 1927 to 1979. Only two years before, Harding, along with his sisters and brothers, had been turned away from public skating at the same arena because, according to the attendant, "public" meant "white." The next Black player to compete at Olympia Stadium would be Johnny Utendale in 1957.

Playing on the Windsor Staffords, Detroit's top farm team, the

NHL was within reach. Harding could become the first Black player in National Hockey League history, all he had to do was score. Early in the season, Harding stepped on the ice and scored a pair of goals in the first period. However, a third goal would not come because Harding would not be allowed to play another shift. He was benched without a word. Prior to the season, Windsor's owner had promised a new fedora to anyone who scored a hat trick. It quickly became evident that this honour would not be bestowed upon a Black man.

A few games later, Harding again scored two early goals to propel his team into the lead, but instead of continuing to ride their top player, Windsor's coaching staff again put Harding on the bench, keeping him there until the final buzzer. Harding soon came to realize that, although the team wanted to benefit from his skill, the fedora—and the NHL—would be withheld.

Because he wanted to play the game he loved, Harding abandoned scoring attempts early in games. He would pass off the puck in every situation, racking up assists. When the third period arrived, Harding would return to his own game, taking his chances to score. At least this way, there would only be minutes left on the clock on the nights Harding managed to score a pair of goals and was called off the ice. Harding finished his lone season in the International Hockey League as one of the top scorers on his team, despite only trying to score in the third period.

According to Harding's son Blake, the ice was a lonely place for a Black hockey player in the 1940s. "It was that feeling of maybe Jackie Robinson, that I'm out here all by myself, there's nothing I can do to hide it. I'd take my helmet off—well, they didn't wear helmets—so a Black man on white ice sticks out. And back then it really stuck out. Dad, I think, was a real pioneer in hockey, and didn't have the community behind him. And I think it was a really . . . he was on his own in that."

This was the difference for Harding. With the Chatham

Coloured All-Stars, he had been one of fourteen players, all in the same boat. In hockey, he was alone, the only Black man in an otherwise white sport. Initially, his teammates would not pass him the puck; that came later, after he'd earned their respect. While his teammates received cheers and adulation from the fans, slurs and jeers would rain down on Harding. He was an intruder. Harding would continue to play, just not at the professional level, and became a long-time, no-nonsense referee. At least in this role, he controlled the rules.

Boomer Harding would become the first Black mail carrier in Chatham; his brother Andy, who also played baseball for the Chatham Coloured All-Stars, the first Black police officer. They were a family of achievers but, despite Boomer's talent, those achievements would not extend to the highest levels of sport. Blake recalls many people, including himself, asking "Are you bitter about not making the National Hockey League? Are you bitter about not making Major League Baseball?" Without speaking, Boomer would rub the skin on his arm. He didn't need to speak to be heard.

Willie O'Ree broke the NHL's colour barrier in 1958 when he played forty-three games for the Boston Bruins. It would take another sixteen years for the second Black player to make an appearance. That would be Mike Marson, who appeared in seventy-six games for the NHL's Washington Capitals, scoring twenty-eight points in 1974.

Marson grew up in Wexford, a neighbourhood in Scarborough, Ontario, a city that today has a non-white population comprising over 70% of residents, including more than 65,000 Black people. "I remember the first time we all watched Willie O'Ree and I said to my uncle and dad, 'I want to do that.' I want to be a hockey player," Marson recalled.[8]

After playing minor hockey in Wexford and Scarborough, Marson chose to join the Southern Ontario Junior Hockey League that would allow him to start playing Junior hockey a season earlier than he could locally. Soon, he was skating with the Chatham Maroons alongside fellow future NHLers Ken Houston and Randy MacGregor. That season, he caught the attention of the Ontario Hockey League's Sudbury Wolves who selected him fourth overall in the draft. Marson would move to Sudbury the next year, spending two seasons with the Wolves, scoring 94 points in 69 games in 1973–74.

Marson was inspired to strive for the NHL, not only by Willie O'Ree, but also by Canada's Prime Minister at the time, Pierre Trudeau, whose message helped him to see possibilities in his own future. "We had the original 'Trudeau-mania' going on, and its message was that you could do anything you want regardless of your race, creed, or colour as long as you applied yourself to it. The whole thing in Trudeau's perspective was, 'Why shouldn't you be allowed? You're Black? Well, why shouldn't you be able to play in the National Hockey League and play at Maple Leaf Gardens? Why not?'"

Reality was not so rosy and Marson faced many of the barriers that had dogged O'Ree. "It was like one man against the entire social order of life in North America. And how does he stand up against it? It was endless," Marson said in a February 14, 2020 interview with Sportsnet.[9]

When the Washington Capitals drafted him in the second round, nineteenth overall in 1974, Marson became the first Black person drafted by an NHL team, and later that same year, he was in the National Hockey League.

As the nineteen-year-old stepped onto the ice that season, there was a downpour of slurs from fans, his opponents, and coaches. As described by Cecil Harris in his book *Breaking the Ice: The Black Experience in Professional Hockey* (2007), "When Marson first hit the NHL ice, taunts of 'n-----,' 'monkey,' 'coon,' and 'spear-chucker' were just part of the cacophonous soundtrack that accompanied his games."

"I was the first contemporary Black hockey player," Harris quotes Marson as saying. "So everywhere I went it was very novel, and I felt like a target. The same people who were yelling 'N-----s, go home!' to the Black kids being bussed to school . . . were going to our games at night. Those people were racist to begin with and they would feel frustrated because they couldn't keep the government from sending Black kids to school with their kids, so what did they do at the games? They let off steam yelling 'n-----' and every other name in the book at me.

"There were times when I was refused lodging in hotels and the team would have to stick up for me. Or entering an arena . . . and being questioned by security staff because there were no Black hockey players . . . For me, this was a daily thing. You'd go to pre-board an airplane and you're questioned—'Well sir, I'm sorry this is just for the hockey players.' I dealt with this kind of business all the time."

In total, Mike Marson played 196 games in the NHL, all but three for the Capitals, and over 400 professional hockey games in his career before leaving the game he loved when he was only twenty-five years old. While he inspired countless other players the way O'Ree had inspired him, the white ice of hockey was too much. What felt so natural for him was too unnatural for society.

"For me, it seemed normal to be a hockey player. I grew up in Canada. I played hockey. A Black hockey player? So what? But I found out people looked at me like a Martian. Not Mike Marson. Mike *Martian*. Because I was a Black hockey player."[10]

For white hockey players, a love of the game, talent, and a little luck can be enough. For Black and Asian hockey players, it takes more—it also takes courage, perseverance, and inspiration from those who went before.

# Chapter 11

# JUMP JIM CROW

My teacher sent me out of the classroom with an empty bucket in my hands. I descended the first flight of stairs to the school's entrance where, just inside the doors, sat the school's piano, played for us to sing songs about Easter, Christmas, and Remembrance Day. A photo of The Queen hung next to a trophy case of plaques and awards. Turning the corner and descending the next flight of stairs, I entered a zone that smelled of stale coffee, urinals, and bleach. On my left was the staff lounge, where my mother would volunteer to boil hot dogs for school events. To the right was the boys' bathroom. Beyond these public spaces, and through an arched stone doorway, was a hallway forbidden to students. A boiler that hummed as it kept our school alive, exposed pipes and walls painted with leftover colours no one would see—these were the spaces that could both scare and thrill a seven-year-old. I had been told to follow this path to find our school custodian, who would fill my bucket with soapy water to wash our desks and erase faded lessons from the blackboard.

I saw no one until a voice called to me from a tiny desk pushed into an alcove. There, sitting in front of me, was the first Black man I'd ever met. He had a mustache, large ears, and gentle eyes. He was wearing a blue shirt, with a pen and pencil tucked into a pocket protector. He smiled.

His name was Mr. Cook. Over hundreds of return trips, my visits slowed. It took longer for us to fill my bucket; we talked more each time and sometimes, when Mr. Cook needed a second pair of hands, we'd escape to another unknown corner of the school where he'd teach me as we worked. Soon Mr. Cook knew all about my passion for hockey, which he told me he had played. In the basement of the school, he grabbed a broom, standing in for a hockey stick, and showed me how to do a spin-o-rama like the legendary Denis Savard. Each time after my bucket was filled, I'd do a spin-o-rama as I walked away, trying not to spill, and we'd both laugh.

Outside of this dark and secluded space in an aging building, we rarely spoke but, whenever he saw me, Mr. Cook would do a spin-o-rama from down the hall with a mop or broom in his hands. He signed my cast when I broke my arm playing soccer in Grade 4 and I'd see him watching as I dribbled through the key and tucked a lay-up into the net for our school basketball team. On the field outside, I'd gain favour with my friends from my unspoken relationship with our custodian, who would rescue our lacrosse balls, baseballs, soccer balls, and balls of every other shape, tossing them down from the roof of our school. I confided in him, but our relationship was not reciprocal; I knew nothing about his life. Like most children, I took from him without question.

Thirty years later, I reached out to a woman named Valerie Cook to interview her dad, then eighty-seven years old, who had once been a prominent Black athlete in Dresden. When she got back to me, she asked if I had been a student at D.A. Gordon Public School in Wallaceburg. Her dad had been a custodian there and remembered my name. After all these years, I'd been reconnected with the man who showed me the spin-o-rama and took a sincere interest in my life. His name was Jarvis Cook.

Dresden was a key terminus on the Underground Railroad, and home to Uncle Tom's Cabin and Josiah Henson's Dawn Settlement, a haven for Black refugees escaping slavery. For decades, it was also home to some of the most overt acts of racism in Canada. The Chatham-Kent area, which also includes Wallaceburg and Chatham, was a hub for Ku Klux Klan activity, and during the summer of 1925, hundreds of crosses were burned across southwestern Ontario.

Paradoxically, Dresden was also one of the first communities to integrate baseball. In 1939, when the Chatham Coloured All-Stars were still playing as an all-Black baseball team, the Dresden Juniors defeated Walkerton to win the town's first ever provincial championship. Their roster included a pair of Black athletes—Wayne and Walter Lambkin.

Hockey, however, was a different matter. "Many years ago my brother really had an interest in playing hockey, and I remember my dad and a couple of uncles kind of dissuaded him from even wanting to, because they said he truly wouldn't be welcomed on a hockey team," recalls Ruth (Lambkin) Dudley.

Schools were integrated in the 1940s and some churches followed suit, but "white only" signs still appeared in windows and over doors of shops and restaurants. In 1943, a local Black man, Hugh Burnett, decided to combat racial inequality in the region by forming the National Unity Association (NUA) of Dresden, Chatham, and Buxton. The NUA made progress: the following year, their campaign led to the passing of Ontario's Racial Discrimination Act, which banned any signage or publication expressing discrimination based on race or religion.

It was a step in the right direction, but not far enough. The signs were down, but Jim Crow still lived in Dresden. Named after a minstrel show character, Jim Crow laws were a collection of written and unwritten rules that originated in the southern United States in the 1880s to bar Black people from jobs, voting, and educational institutions, as well as from stores and restaurants. Jim Crow kept Black youth from pools, beaches, and arenas, and told them what fountains to drink from, what bathroom to use, and what bench to sit on.

According to Hugh Burnett, even years after the Racial Discrimination Act became law, "Three children, whose ages ranged from five to seven, went to a restaurant for ice-cream and the waiters not only refused to serve them; they just stood there looking at them . . . School children learn about Jim Crow before they learn to read and write."[1]

In her article for the *Southern Journal of Canadian Studies*, Karen Flynn explains how children in the town formed their identity, "Whether white or Black, living in Dresden, Ontario involved some form of racial consciousness. For whites it was reveling in their superior position in the racial order, and having the power to deploy racial labels as a means of reinforcing social distinctions, and for Blacks, it was the constant reminder of their marginality."[2]

Virginia Travis, who grew up in Dresden during this period, said. "I was allowed to go outside the boundaries of my home to play with other children, but there were differences as to who would play with me and who wouldn't. That was the first time I observed being different. White children separated themselves from Black children."

Nonetheless, Black athletes continued to represent the town on the field. The Junior B baseball champion during these years was the Dresden Athletic Club, an integrated club that included Black athletes Hugh McCorkle and Gerald "Elmer" Cook. The team won four consecutive Ontario championships from 1945 to 1948.

"My older brother, Gerald, was a great ballplayer," said Jarvis Cook. "He played semi-pro ball in the Intercounty League in St. Thomas in the late 40s . . . primarily as a pitcher but also third base. He was scouted by the New York Yankees but did not pursue a career in ball as his wife was in very poor health. This was around the time that Jackie Robinson broke the colour barrier in baseball. There were very few opportunities for a man of colour at this time."

Jackie Robinson broke Major League Baseball's colour barrier in 1947, aided in large part by Wendell Smith, whose father had grown up in Chatham-Kent. A talented pitcher who was denied a contract because of his race, Smith would become a sports journalist and outspoken advocate for integration. "It was then that I made the vow that I would dedicate myself and do something on behalf of the Negro ballplayers," Smith said, recalling the moment he was denied entry to baseball's upper echelons.[3]

Smith became the first Black sportswriter in America to work for a "white" newspaper when he was hired by the *Chicago Herald American*, and the first Black sportswriter to gain entry to the Baseball Writers' Association of America. As promised, he dedicated himself to fighting Jim Crow. Writing in the *Pittsburgh Courier* on July 25, 1942, Smith highlighted the hypocrisy of Black soldiers fighting for freedom abroad while many freedoms were still denied at home, mentioning baseball specifically. "Major League Baseball is perpetuating the very things thousands of Americans are overseas fighting to end, namely, racial discrimination and segregation."

In 1945, Smith helped orchestrate the attendance of Black ballplayers, including Jackie Robinson, at tryouts for the Brooklyn Dodgers and Boston Red Sox. The following year, he recommended Robinson to Brooklyn Dodgers general manager Branch Rickey, not because he was the best player in the Negro Leagues at the time, but because he believed Robinson had the character that would be necessary to integrate baseball. Rickey touted Smith as the man who orchestrated the integration of Major League Baseball, saying "This whole program was more or less your suggestion."[4]

Robinson played for the Dodgers minor league affiliate in Montreal during the 1946 season and Black Canadians travelled to see him play, including fans from Chatham-Kent. One of those fans who recalls seeing Robinson play was Beulah Cuzzens, Boomer Harding's sister:

"When Jackie Robinson joined the International League, and would come to Toronto, I would always go and see him play. That was an experience because, mostly, I'd go alone, and I would sit and listen to them—I think they called him every name you could think of that any Black had been called like 'n-----,' 'black boy,' 'eight ball,' 'coon.' And you would sit there and burn up."

In 1947, Robinson made his Major League Baseball debut for

the Brooklyn Dodgers. Jackie Robinson slowly became a household name, as did baseball's second Black Major Leaguer, Larry Doby, who followed Robinson to the big leagues three months later.

The colour barrier may have fallen in baseball, but it held firm in Dresden. According to historian James Walker, "not a single pool room would allow Black people . . . not a single restaurant, not a single barber shop where they could get their hair cut."[5]

On November 1, 1949, Sidney Katz published an article in *Maclean's* magazine entitled "Jim Crow Lives in Dresden," quoting Mayor Walter Weese, "The colored people here are given the same rights and privileges as anyone else. But this is a democratic country . . . You can't force anyone to serve Negroes. Perhaps you can get away with that sort of thing under Communism."

Earlier that year, the city council had asked residents "Do you approve the passing of legislation compelling restaurant owners to serve, regardless of race, creed, or colour?" The people of Dresden voted against the resolution 517-108, an outcome that prompted a sharp rebuke from *The Globe and Mail*: "The decision brings shame to Dresden and to all Ontario."[6]

Jarvis Cook remembers what it felt like to share the same struggles as others in town, but also to be different. "Most residents were economically equal and of lower middle class in Dresden, whether they were Black or white. I can remember a lot of uncomfortable situations growing up, like when your friends are going to a restaurant, and you can't go with them."

Dresden continued to represent "the height of expression of Jim Crow in Canada"[7] into the 1950s. Hugh Burnett continued his push, making Dresden the centre of Canada's human rights movement. In 1951, this resulted in the passing of the Fair Employment Practices Act that ended overt signs of discrimination. But Stephanie Simpson, Director of Queen's University Human Rights and Equity Office, observes that, "People were working alongside each other and it felt like to the outside world that everything was fine in Dresden. Even in this small place where everyone smiled at each other and was cordial, there was in fact, de facto segregation happening. [Blacks] were charged higher insurance premiums, they were denied loans and jobs, and were subject to curfews."[8]

As it had in the past, athleticism unlocked spaces for Black people. A move to a new ball diamond at Kinsmen's Park ushered in an Intermediate baseball dynasty. The Dresden National Hardware team captured the Ontario Intermediate B championship in 1951 and 1952 and won the Western Counties Baseball League title season after season. Two of the mainstays of the team were again Gerald Cook and Hugh McCorkle, now joined by Elmer's younger brother, Jarvis. The 1953 Dresden Legionnaires juvenile team continued the town's success, winning an OBA championship with both Black and white baseball players on the team.

Despite segregation in town, commonality began to emerge on the field. Wearing the same uniform and uniting against a common foe fostered camaraderie and support. Even from the stands, the heckles and jeers subsided as hometown fans called out words of support for a diving catch or a mighty swing, regardless of the skin colour hiding beneath a ball cap.

Trips to neighbouring towns like Wallaceburg, Petrolia and Sarnia were markedly different. "Dad never talked about it so much, but we all knew it was there," recalls Shelley McCorkle Clark, daughter of Floyd McCorkle. "His teammates seemed to be very protective of them. One story I remember hearing: they were with the junior team, playing in Sarnia and obviously people in the stands back in those days would holler and all that stuff. Someone was hollering negative racial stuff, and one of dad's white teammates, he said to dad, 'Are you going to do anything about it or do I need to do something about it?' Anyway, it ended up in a brawl and it wasn't even my dad who started it, it was somebody else. But my dad got a hold of someone . . . my dad is quite strong and his uncle came out of the stands and had to get my dad to let go of this guy."

In 1954, the National Film Board of Canada released *Dresden Story*, a documentary that interviewed a panel of Black residents and a panel of white residents about discrimination. According to Albert Ohayon, the National Film Board's curator, "The white panel felt that racial discrimination was only a recent phenomenon, while the Black panel relate how they've lived with it their entire lives." White residents blamed communists and Jews, and reported "the problem was caused by local Blacks who did not 'know their place" and who also "wanted to marry local, white women."[9]

Even as the film was being released, Hugh Burnett, the NUA, and other groups were working to pass the Ontario Fair Accommodation Practices Act, which forbade discrimination on the basis of race, creed, colour, nationality, ancestry, or place of origin. When the Fair Accommodations Act passed in 1954, outlawing discrimination in services, facilities, and accommodations in public spaces, local establishments in Dresden continued their now illegal segregation, prompting sit-ins and complaints, culminating in Canada's first racial discrimination trial. During the trial, Morley McKay, owner of Kay's Café, argued he was only protecting his business because "my customers have told me if we serve Negroes, they won't come in." In 1956, a Canadian court for the first time deemed that racial equality was a civil right. Black residents were finally served at Dresden restaurants.

Jarvis Cook took advantage of a more accepting environment to break more colour barriers in sport. In addition to baseball, he was the only Black athlete on the 1957–58 Dresden Lumberkings Intermediate A hockey team and was also part of Dresden's inaugural entry into the Western Ontario Senior Lacrosse League.

A lifetime later, Cook would be perched on top of D.A. Gordon Public School, retrieving lost dodgeballs, footballs, and baseballs for a crowd of kids below. Their cheers, reminiscent of those of the 1950s, would echo off the tall brownstone building and into the streets of Wallaceburg. With a weathered baseball in his hands,

Cook stood atop the three-storey brick building and picked his target—a patch of dirt in the field that, if you squinted, could look like home plate. From the ground, in the shadow cast by this man, you could see hints of a young baseball star as his arm pulled back and threw. Necks of children craned to watch the ball cut through the sky above before hitting its target with surprising force.

## Chapter 12

# DOUBLE PLAY

I've been a sport lover my entire life. I've devoured it on television, in magazines, and on fields and rinks with my friends. But my world of sport almost never involved women. As a spectator, women's sport was only available once every four years during the Olympic Games.

During the Tokyo Olympics held in 2021, I set an alarm to watch Canada's Rugby Sevens team in its final game of the tournament. Entering as medal contenders, the team was now playing a disappointing placement game against Brazil. The field was filled with women of colour, but I was awake to watch one Canadian in particular.

I'd been following Breanne Nicholas since her first season of rugby. In Chatham-Kent, it was easy to pick Nicholas out on the field, not only for her talent, which surpassed that of her teammates and opponents, but also because she was a multiracial athlete—Black and Indigenous—in a predominantly white community. An incredible athlete with explosive speed, Breanne grew up in Blenheim and played her earliest seasons of club rugby in Chatham, the latest athlete in a long line of exceptional women of colour.

In 1926, a group of Black women stood in a pasture in North Buxton wearing navy bloomers and white middies their mothers had made. With broomsticks for bats and a ball that had been patched and sewn so many times it would be unrecognizable as a baseball, the Buxton Bloomers played ball. While the first recorded participation of women in sport locally is an 1865 reference to figure skating, and records of women's hockey in Chatham appear in 1895, the Buxton Bloomers were the first women's team in the area.

The Robbins sisters—Alma, Lola, and Vera—had seen male family members and other boys in the community playing and decided they deserved an opportunity as well. In the Robbins household, baseball was a family activity and brothers Hyle and Stanton would go on to play for the Chatham Coloured All-Stars. According to Alma's daughter, Pauline Williams, "The girls always played ball with the boys . . . Even my mother, she would be out there too, and she was a left-hander, so she would be up there fighting too. The whole family, really. Even the other brothers."[1]

As Cleata Morris, a long-time teacher and Buxton resident recalled, "[The Robbins sisters] heard of these games that [the boys] were playing and said, 'Oh, well, we can do it too.' The whole family would be out there playing. It wasn't just the boys. The girls would be out there too, just fighting along with all the men. Didn't matter."[2]

In her book, *Legacy to Buxton* (1983), the sisters' descendant Arlie Robbins said, "how the folks looked askance at these 'tomboys' wearing bloomers no less." Soon, however, "the coming of the Buxton girls wearing bloomers caused only a mild ripple especially when they found out the type of rough and ready ball these girls were playing."[3] Indeed, the Bloomers were a tough team to beat, going undefeated against women's teams in the area, and even defeating the Buxton boys' team.

Women of all races struggled for acceptance in the "unladylike" world of sport, with sport participation from Black women in Chatham remaining largely informal until the Taylorettes, later known as the Maple City Jets, an all-Black women's team, formed in the 1950s. Even for white participants in fastball and softball, it wasn't until 1935 that women started to gain prominence in sport.

That year, twelve-year-old Marion Watson first suited up for the city's top women's team, the Chatham Silverwoods. A few seasons later, she joined Maple City Laundry and led the team to an Ontario championship in 1939, batting .513. Maple City, like all women's teams in Chatham, played at Tecumseh Park, often drawing up to 2,000 fans per game, especially after World War II suspended most of the men's leagues. Watson was the star of the region throughout the war and, in 1946, joined the All-American Girls Professional Baseball League memorialized in the movie, *A League of Their Own.* Now 23, Watson played professionally in 1946 and 1947 for the Peoria Redwings and Muskegon Lassies before breaking her leg sliding into home plate, an injury that ended her career.

The war was a springboard to popularity for both white and racialized women in fastball. Following World War II, the dominant team in the region was the Florence Chicks who played home games in small towns across Chatham-Kent including Wabash, Thamesville, and Bothwell. The team easily defeated opponents from larger cities that included Detroit, Toronto, Windsor, and Stratford, and won championships, including All-Ontario titles, in 1950, 1952, 1954, 1956, and 1959.

Calling those championship games from the public address box was a voice that became synonymous with women's softball in the area, that of Deo Suzuki. Originally from Sunbury, British Columbia, Suzuki had been interned at the Ontario Farm Service Force camp at the Dresden Fairgrounds where baseball was a popular pastime. Officially classified as a threat, Deo Suzuki was nonetheless recruited by the Canadian Army to serve as a Japanese interpreter. He served in the Intelligence Corps in India before being discharged in 1945 when the family moved to Florence where he worked at the post office and general store.

As soon as he was settled, Suzuki took up the microphone for the Chicks. He also volunteered with the Boy Scouts, Florence Community Centre, local school and church groups, and with St. John Ambulance. In addition, Suzuki maintained several community gardens and the local cenotaph. For his many contributions, Suzuki was awarded the Ontario Medal for Good Citizenship in 1980.

Chatham's Rosetta Alliet, who was born in 1937, was invited to play for the Florence Chicks as a young teenager. She recalled her experiences in an interview with the University of Windsor. "There were girls' baseball teams in Dresden, there were girls' baseball teams in Florence," she recalled. "We used to go there and play. At one point, they asked me to come and play with them, they were semi-pros. I was really tempted but my mother wouldn't let me go. I was only 15 so I couldn't make the decision for myself. And she said, 'no no no.' She didn't let us too far out of her sight for one thing. And I think that was a big mistake because I would have really enjoyed it."

Alliet caught the eye of the Chicks while playing for Chatham's Maple City Jets, an all-Black women's team that succeeded the Taylorettes. The Jets would bring large crowds of supporters to Tecumseh Park, located just outside the East End where most of the city's Black community lived. "When we were playing, when our team was playing in Tecumseh Park under the lights, we could hear the people from the neighbourhood, they were rooting us on," Alliet remembers. "And it made you feel so good. You know, it was great. Not only were we having a ball, they were having a ball, and it was something to pull the people out of the neighbourhood. We didn't win too many games, but we sure had a lot of fun."

For Alliet and women in the Black community of Chatham's East End, baseball provided a connection, an outlet and, at times, a lifeline. "I remember this community down here, it was like a real community. We were always into each other's homes. If one was in trouble, the other one was there to help." [4]

As it had for the men, sport also created opportunities for integration. During the 1950s, when integrated men's teams were now the norm, a few Black women, including Thursal Wallace and Paula Lambkin (the great-great-granddaughter of Josiah Henson), began playing for Dresden's predominantly white women's fastball team in the Lambton-Kent Girls Softball League. Wanda Milburn, a member of the Harding clan, recalls the impact of sport, "Being in sports, lots of times I found that I had a little bit of companionship with some of the kids. And I was on the basketball team. And then I went to school with my coloured friends and we played basketball together and then we just came home and forgot about it."[5]

Murray Scott, a noted Dresden ballplayer himself, watched his wife, Belva Wright, play baseball on the all-Black Taylorettes and Maple City Jets many times. He recalls that the intersectional issues of race and gender combined to create hostile environments for the women wherever they played.

"They'd run into a little more of the prejudice than our team did because they were playing out farther, Thamesville and Florence, in areas where they weren't known, and so they'd get heckled quite a bit. I remember one night we were playing up east, it was really hot, and there were mosquitos all over. They were playing at night with lights, and they were hollering from the stands, 'Them mosquitos won't like you Black people.'"

By the 1950s, the local Japanese Canadian community had formed the Kent Nisei Athletic Club that offered women's bowling, basketball, and softball teams. The women's Kent Nisei softball teams often competed at Tecumseh Park facing white and all-Black rosters. Eddie Wright recalls going to these games where he watched his sister Belva competing against his best friend's sister.

"Herb's sister Shirley Wakabayashi, she was quite the softball player. My sister Belva, she was a catcher, a very vocal catcher," Eddie recalls. "The families and the communities, the Japanese community would come out and support the Japanese team, and for the Taylorettes of course . . . all the people from down in the East End of Chatham would come."

By 1948, Japanese Canadian women in the area were competing in bowling competitions, primarily against other Japanese Canadians from nearby London. Even though bowling was popular for Black and Japanese residents in Chatham-Kent, alleys would not allow Black and white patrons to bowl at the same time until laws changed in the mid-1950s.

"Our youth group from church, if we wanted to have a bowling night, they had to rent the bowling alley so that we could go bowling alone," recalls Ruth Dudley. "My children and grandchildren played in bowling leagues here and were quite welcomed, but not when I was growing up."

Bowling was an entry point for many Japanese Canadian and Black women into sport. It also provided an opportunity for racialized families to come together and create cross-cultural bonds.

Another Chatham-Kent woman, Delores Shadd, had forged similar bonds a few years earlier when she coached racialized teams in Detroit. Ornella Nzindukiyimana, an expert on the Black athletic experience, says "it is suggested that Shadd and the [Red] Dragons represented a solidarity against racial prejudice through community creation. Whether done directly or indirectly through sport, it was a way to combat [racism] through sport."[6]

Born in Detroit, Delores Shadd's mother was from Dresden, and would later raise her daughter in North Buxton. The Shadds had roots in the area that dated to 1855 when Delores' great-great-aunt, Mary Ann Shadd, arrived in Chatham.

An early activist inspired by Josiah Henson, Mary Ann Shadd opened a racially integrated school in Windsor in 1851. In this she was emulating the Buxton Mission School at the Elgin Settlement, which had become the first racially integrated school in North America the year before. At a time when white residents were using schools to exclude Black children and assimilate Indigenous youth, the area's Black settlers were doing the opposite.

White students attended the Buxton Mission School at the Elgin Settlement because the quality of the education was so high. In 1908, another school was opened with Black leadership, this time in Chatham. When the Woodstock Industrial Institute was organized to "supplement the waning skilled labour force in the Chatham area," the Black organizers proposed that white and Indigenous youth be included.[7]

According to Mary Ann Shadd, "[T]he colored common schools have more of a complexional character than the private, which, with no exception I have heard of, are open to all." When her refusal to segregate her school cost her the necessary funding, Mary Ann Shadd moved to Buxton and became the first Black woman in North America to publish a newspaper. Committed to equity, she also joined Lucy Stanton, the first Black woman to complete a university degree, and Martin Delany to found the Chatham Vigilance Committee, which aimed to save people from being sold into slavery. Following the Civil War, Mary Ann Shadd would attend Howard University, where she became one of the first Black women to obtain a law degree in 1883.

Like Mary Ann, Delores was a fighter who pushed the boundaries and succeeded in roles dominated by white males. In the 1940s, she coached and officiated baseball, soccer, and volleyball in Buxton before attending Detroit's Wayne State University to become a teacher. While there, she coached five women's basketball teams including the Red Dragons, a team composed of Chinese Americans, and the Mexican Spitfire, a team of Mexican American athletes.

The Red Dragons, who Shadd coached in 1945, played out of the Neighborhood House, a centre in Detroit's Chinatown aimed at supporting underprivileged youth. Every Friday, Shadd and her Red Dragons team would challenge other teams of Chinese immigrants and descendants from cities that included Cincinnati, Toronto, and Chicago. A 1989 National Film Board documentary, *Older Stronger Wiser*, maintained that "Dolores and the Red Dragons withstood the colour bar, their friendship given strength by overcoming injustice."

Shadd also served as a baseball umpire for the Buxton men's baseball team and seemed to revel in pushing back against the sexist ideas of those in sport: "I remember we went off to Charing Cross and I could hear this man fussing something about us, but I couldn't hear it. It didn't sound nice anyhow. We got the team lined up and I said 'OK, batter up.' And wow, he hit the ceiling. Buxton was supposed to send an umpire; they had their rules. And they didn't send an umpire. So, one guy said, 'Miss Shadd now—' [the first man interrupted] 'No! I don't want no woman umpire.' The [one guy] said 'she teaches in [ . . . ] high school, I think you better stay out of her way.' And I said, 'Please let me in so that I can pull him out and kick him out of the park!' Because he was swearing, and I didn't— you know—I didn't allow that in the park. So anyhow, he got back. So, after that game, when the boys went anyplace, they had a female umpire; and that was fun."[8]

Outside sport, Shadd was passionate about farming. She served with the Associated Country Women of the World and as Women's Director (District 6) of the National Farmers Union, roles that saw her inducted into the Kent Agricultural Hall of Fame. On a trip to Kenya in 1977, Shadd managed to combine her passions of sport, agriculture, and education.

"I went to a village and I thought, 'now what in the world am I going to talk about, what am I going to say, I don't know. I don't know what to do'," she explained in a video about the National Farmers Union.

"So I said, you know what, take those sandals off and come on out here. And I drew a line. I taught physical education and health so we're going to learn how to run, we're going to learn how to win a race. On your mark, get set, get those hips up!

"So we spent the day in physical education and health, and they thought, how in the heck is she going to work that into farming? Well, that's easy. I'll call the government and ask them to send the last Olympic film that I saw to me, so I can show the children in Africa that they can make the Olympics. They're farmers, but they have something to offer. Yes, I'm using my physical education to help the people learn farming."[9]

In 1988, Delores Shadd became the first recipient of the Chatham-Kent YMCA International Peace Medallion and was one of the first five women to be recognized as local Women of Excellence. Shadd fought for women and for the Black community, two identities that Ornella Nzindukiyimana believes are inseparable, "For Black women, racial and gender constructs are not separate. They are connected and interwoven."[10]

Dolores Shadd passed away in 2013. While her legacy of creating opportunities for Black, Chinese American, and Mexican American women in sport remains, so do some of the barriers.

Buxton's Shannon Prince grew up playing softball with predominantly Black teammates. Playing in Chatham in the 1990s in a predominantly white league, she discovered that racist attitudes persist: "I was playing, and as we were leaving, this one girl made the N-comment. I was just stunned. I'm standing there thinking, 'Do you realize what you just said?' I just looked at her and then she repeated it like I hadn't heard her. 'Oh, you didn't hear what I said?' I said, 'That is a very derogatory word, and I don't want to hear you saying it again.' I gave her my tirade history lesson and walked away. And I didn't play for the next couple of games."

As a multiracial athlete, Breanne Nicholas, was largely spared from such overt racism. She was one of the region's top athletes throughout the 2010s, earning a spot on Canada's Rugby Sevens team, being promoted to captain in 2021. "Because the town I grew up in was predominantly white, I often found myself identifying as white even though I have Black, Indigenous, and white roots. In most spaces, I can pass as white because I am racially ambiguous, and I never really questioned my background growing up. I never noticed or experienced any blatant racism growing up, because while I was immersed in the community, it was all I knew. It wasn't until I visited other communities outside of our small town and grew up that I could identify the microaggressions that did take place. For example, others crediting my athletic ability for being Black, ignoring my full racial identity and the hard work I put into sport."

Even so, Nicholas has witnessed racism directed at teammates, and also knows the challenges of being a woman in sport. "When you are BIPOC but also a woman you are already having to fight stereotypes and being viewed through certain lenses before even being seen for what you have to offer and can provide.

"It is very important to have representation of BIPOC women athletes on our team and in sport in general. When youth, and in particular BIPOC youth, watch the Olympics and other international competitions and see BIPOC women athletes, it shows them that they too can represent in sport, and that can empower them to pursue sport on all levels."

Watching Breanne step onto the field at the Tokyo Olympics, her first Olympic Games, I celebrated her and every other Black or Indigenous woman playing at the highest level.

# Chapter 13

# SUNDOWN TOWN

In Wallaceburg, sunset can be a beautiful time, especially along the Sydenham River. A town of roughly 10,000 people, Wallaceburg was built on manufacturing. The famous Louisville Slugger baseball bats and Louisville hockey sticks were both made here; Hall of Famers like Mark Messier, Steve Yzerman, and Brett Hull would all visit to test their new hockey sticks.

Wallaceburg is connected by waterways to the Great Lakes. On summer days, the brown water slowly meanders through town and long shadows creep out from poplar trees, the quiet interrupted only by the sound of car tires rumbling across the four main bridges. Light shimmers on the wake of small boats driven by town teenagers, and kids sneak onto the old train bridge to drink cheap beer and swim in the turbid water. There's almost certainly a father and son standing behind the local library fishing from the boardwalk. In the centre of town is the walking bridge, where pedestrians can wave at boaters, and teens can steal a kiss in the fading light. And where a Black taxi driver was threatened with lynching if he dared stay overnight in the town.

I lived in Wallaceburg for more than two decades. In that time, I had only one Black classmate. Her name was Dawana. She had a wide smile, a tiny frame and at lunch she drank milk from a jar. Dawana left town before high school when her father, a minister, was reassigned to a new church. In my lifetime, Wallaceburg was a town where Black people both worked and lived—but I am the first generation who can make this claim. Since the 1880s, Wallaceburg had been a sundown town, a place where Black people could not stay after dark. In his 2018 book *Sundown Towns,* James Loewen uses census data to identify sundown towns across North America, comparing the Black population of towns to that of nearby communities and state or provincial averages. Wallaceburg was far from alone. The nearby towns of Ridgetown, Tilbury, and Blenheim also had unspoken sundown rules.

Similar to Black curfews, Indigenous people across Canada were subject to a pass system intended to keep them on reserves and out of white-dominated towns. Beginning in 1885, anyone leaving the reserve required a pass that could only be issued by an Indian agent. The law restricted economic ventures, including the outside sale of goods, prevented cultural and spiritual activities, and separated families, particularly when it came to opportunities for Indigenous parents to visit their children at residential schools.[1] White society did its best to restrict the movement of racialized populations until mobility became protected under Canada's Charter of Rights and Freedoms.

The sundown law in Wallaceburg purportedly started with a baseball rivalry between Wallaceburg and neighbouring Dresden. Whenever the two teams met in Wallaceburg, the game was followed by fights between fans and players. In Wallaceburg, the larger of the two towns, the Dresden contingent was almost always outnumbered and found itself on the losing end of these encounters. Soon, Dresden started recruiting Black boxers and wrestlers, most of whom had arrived as residents of Josiah Henson's Dawn Settlement. When these Black men arrived in Wallaceburg with the Dresden team, the tide changed in the post-game brawls, and Wallaceburg residents began recruiting their own reinforcements, white ship and lumber workers who were said to be the toughest of the tough. The rule for baseball games, and eventually the town, became that any Black person entering the town would have to fight one of these white town guardians. Black bodies were no longer safe in Wallaceburg, and a sundown town was born.

For decades after the baseball brawls subsided, Wallaceburg remained a quiet white sanctuary. But when a circus came to town in the early 1920s, a taxi driver from Chatham decided to take advantage of the demand for transportation and booked a room at the Tecumseh Hotel. Local taxi drivers resented the competition, especially because he was Black, and his presence after sunset offended other citizens. Angry residents told him to leave and, when he refused, broke into his hotel room and dragged him down McDougal Street to the river. The men placed a noose around the driver's neck and told him that if he didn't get out and stay out, he'd find himself hanging from the swing bridge. The man left his car and travelled by foot back to Chatham.[2]

It was unspoken but understood that Wallaceburg was for whites only. There was a complacent superiority, a belief that the white residents of Wallaceburg had earned their land and privilege, while their "lazy" neighbours, who "drank too much" and "chose" to stay in poverty were lesser. People of colour needed to leave before sundown, so the white residents could sleep safely, tucked in with their flannels and prejudice. One woman, June Robbins, described her experiences in Wallaceburg in the 1940s in *No Burden to Carry: Narratives of Black Working Women in Ontario, 1920s-1950s* "I was living in Chatham and working in Wallaceburg. Thirty-four miles a day; it was seventeen miles out there and seventeen miles back. Black people couldn't stay there after dark. They were prejudiced."[3]

For a blue-collar town built on agriculture and manufacturing, sundown has always been a time of rest, but for Black workers or visitors, it remained a time of fear.

In a town that owed much of its prosperity to team sports, an evening with superstar guest Rollie Miles was going to be a major event.

Rollie Miles was one of the undisputed stars of the Canadian Football League. Born in Washington, DC in 1927, Miles came to Canada to pursue a baseball career. An exceptionally gifted athlete,

Miles had signed a Major League Baseball contract with the Boston Braves and moved to Canada in 1951 to play for their farm team, the Regina Caps. When Rollie and the Caps were in Edmonton for a tournament, sportswriter Don Fleming spotted Miles at second base. He'd stolen seven bases in the game, and Fleming heard that he'd been a football star at an all-Black college in the United States. Following the game, and after a call to Annis Stukus, the Edmonton Eskimos head coach at the time, Fleming convinced Miles to stay in town to attend an Eskimos practice. Miles made an immediate impression and was signed to a three-year contract. Rollie Miles was now a football player. During that 1951 season, alongside Jim Chambers, Miles was one of only two Black players on the Edmonton roster, and he was often the only Black player on the field.

By 1957, Rollie Miles was a hero on the field and throughout Edmonton. As a running back and special teams player, Miles moved the chains forward. Ball in hands, he was fearless as he bounced off defenders and sped through gaps to find the open field ahead. On the other side of the ball, Miles was an accomplished defender. He could spot the threat, read the play a step ahead and lunge into the lane to make a tackle or intercept a pass. He had been a CFL All-Star for four consecutive seasons and had led Edmonton to three consecutive Grey Cup titles. Still considered one of the all-time greats of the CFL, Miles was a future Hall of Fame inductee, beloved and respected across the country.

Civic leaders in Wallaceburg were thrilled when Miles agreed to attend Brotherhood Week, an annual event planned to showcase the welcoming side of Chatham-Kent, as their keynote speaker. On February 21, 1957, Rollie Miles took the stage and faced an audience of nearly 200 white politicians, businessmen, and service club members. Everyone edged forward to hear their entertainer tell football stories and expound on the theme of brotherhood.

Then he spoke. "Throughout my life I have always tried to be a law-abiding citizen and up to now I've always succeeded. But I understand that just by being here at this hour, I'm a lawbreaker. So I think it would be best if, rather than making the law-breaking worse, I should just leave."[4]

The air left the room.

"This town has on its books a statute which says no Negroes are allowed to be on the streets after sundown," Miles continued. "Gentlemen, I'm a Negro and proud of it. If you're interested in brotherhood, then I'd suggest you scratch this law from your books."[5]

To either side of Miles sat white men, their faces even paler than usual. Two seats over from the podium, at the head table, one of the town leaders glared. Behind Miles, another man crossed his arms, his expression one of disbelief. After all, they had paid this man to come here. They'd brought him across the country to sign autographs, tell them stories about professional football, and to prove their inclusivity.

Rollie kept a photo of this moment: a silver microphone in front of him, his striped tie receding into his grey suit. The photo sat undisturbed for years until Rollie's youngest son, Brett, found it. He told me he stared at the photo of his father for a long time, bewildered. "I asked him, 'Why is that guy looking at you like that?' I was fascinated by this guy, the hate in this picture, and in that guy's eyes. It was the first person I'd ever seen in my whole life who wasn't smiling at my dad, so the photo fascinated me. I was like, wow, that guy doesn't like my dad. This guy in the picture had so much hate, he was cutting his eyes at him."

The Miles family knew this feeling, what it meant to be seen as lesser. While living in Raleigh, North Carolina, even their church singled them out. In a 2009 interview, Miles' wife Marianne explained that, "If you wanted to go to confession, you went after the white people went. If you wanted to take communion, you went after they had communion. My sister and I decided we weren't going anymore. I thought, 'If I'm going to die and go straight to hell, I don't care. I'm not going to go there to be humiliated like that.'"[6]

It had taken time for Edmonton to accept Rollie as a football player and a man, as well. During the family's first days in Edmonton, a director of the football team had shown Rollie, his wife Marianne, and their two children an apartment located above a store near the stadium.

"It was like an attic when you got up there," recalled Dr. Marianne Miles. "I just looked at my husband and I said, 'I'm not putting my babies in here.' Then I overheard this director say, 'I don't know what she's in such a snit about. She's never had anything better than this.' That's still in my head, because he had no idea how we lived, where we lived."[7]

The Miles family, which grew to include seven children, continued to encounter racial barriers. The Edmonton Eskimos were invited to dine at one of Edmonton's most luxurious hotels, as long as the handful of Black team members stayed home. When the family found a house to buy, a local radio station reported that a petition had been drawn up to stop the purchase; other citizens were outraged and spoke out in support of the Miles family until they were safely settled in their new home.

In the community, Miles proved a hard-working community volunteer, fundraiser, and leader who projected an air of confidence. In private he was strict, very religious, but abundantly kind. His daughter, Monica, maintains that when he said, "Stop, enough," all seven children would stop; his words meant something. Monica remembers: "He was that guy who wouldn't stand for people being treated wrong. This was his story, he was never afraid to stand up. He wasn't boastful, but he was a man of few words, and when he said something, it was important. I think he was strong enough in who he was as a person, there was no tolerance for hate, particularly if it was directed against his children.

"When I was in Grade 1 walking home from school, some older boys cornered me and called me the N-word. I was crying. When I got home and told my dad, he just flipped. He didn't stand racism, especially against his children. He went marching to the school, talked to the principal, and the two boys got expelled."

Her brother Brett has a similar story. "I was in Grade 1, and these guys in Grade 9 kept calling me 'Little Black Sambo.' My dad called the school and they marched every person in middle school in front of me until I picked out the guys who did it."

Monica believes it would be exactly like her father to step into a room of strangers and call out injustice where he saw it, no matter the circumstance.

After all, on his first day in Edmonton, Miles and his wife saw a billboard using a racist caricature of a Black youth on a rooftop billboard. Instead of driving on in his new town, Rollie marched into the office of the company responsible for putting up the billboard. Shortly thereafter, it was taken down and an apology was issued.

Entering Wallaceburg, it was the same for Miles. He was not prepared to let the racism that existed remain.

"I can see him going in there as a guest speaker and being very confident in the job he was about to do," Rollie's daughter Monica explained. "Who cares who he was talking to? They could all have had hoods on, and I don't think he would have felt threatened by that, because, 'I'm here to speak, and that's what I'm going to do.' I never saw my dad cower; I don't think him standing in front of a room of mostly white people would phase him."

Rollie Miles was not phased that night in Wallaceburg. "If you gentlemen knew about this law, why did you give me an invitation to break it?"

He had their attention now.

"Was it because I'm Rollie Miles, the football player who gets his name on all the sports pages? Or was it because you're really interested in brotherhood? It must be one or the other. If it's the first, I'll gladly write in your autograph books. If it's the second, why not write off that law if it exists?"[8]

Following another hostile silence, Wallaceburg Mayor Jack

Thompson rose from his seat to assure Miles that no such law existed. The mayor, Miles, and a group of volunteers then drove to the town hall to complete a feverish search for any such ordinance in Wallaceburg's by-laws, a search that came up empty.

In the eyes of the townspeople, the absence of a written rule was exoneration. Miles knew better. He knew that sundown laws were built on restrictive covenants, implied threats, bank redlining, realtor steering, and the demeanour of white citizens that, taken together, were more effective than written laws or physical signage.

In an interview published in *Maclean's* magazine, Miles defined six types of racist Canadians. He spoke of "loudmouths" who made comments to others, intending a Black person in their vicinity to overhear, and "'inhibited bigots"—people who said, "We sure treat you good up here, eh, Rollie?" He identified "thoughtless people," those who perpetuate racist expressions and stereotypical phrases, "race-baiters" who directly confront racialized people with slurs and the "social conscious whites who feared embarrassment or ostracism from associating with Black people." Worst of all, in his opinion, were the "do-gooders" who patronized Miles by declaring their tolerance.[9]

It was just such a group of "do-gooders" that Miles faced down in Wallaceburg—men celebrating Brotherhood Week and social inclusion in a town that did not count a single Black citizen—and the town blinked first. The following day, for the first time in town history, Mayor Jack Thompson spoke to newspapers and proclaimed, "Let it be known that everyone, regardless of race, colour, or creed is as welcome as the sun in Wallaceburg."

Sport had played a critical role in entrenching racism in Wallaceburg; now it proved equally important in combating it. In the early 1960s, William and Faye Highgate, a Black husband and wife, moved their family within the town limits. As Wallaceburg's first Black residents, they found community in the town, and their children found success. Decades later, a Black track star named

Jaime Gittens would find herself standing in front of a Wallaceburg crowd. Gittens, who had immigrated to Canada from Grenada, won multiple Ontario Federation of School Athletic Associations (OFSAA) gold medals in long jump and triple jump at the high school level, as well as Legion Provincial and National junior gold medals in long jump and triple jump during her teenage years. Eventually she accepted an NCAA Division I scholarship to the University of Toledo. The crowd before her was still largely white, but she was a resident of the town, being inducted into the Wallaceburg Sports Hall of Fame.

If only Rollie could have been there.

## Chapter 14

# FROM ARCHIE TO GENE

In his 1972 autobiography, *I Never Had It Made,* Jackie Robinson reflected on entering the game, and what had changed in sport and society since. He was not an optimist.

"There I was, the black grandson of a slave, the son of a black sharecropper, part of a historic occasion, a symbolic hero to my people. The air was sparkling. The sunlight was warm. The band struck up the national anthem. The flag billowed in the wind. It should have been a glorious moment for me as the stirring words of the national anthem poured from the stands . . . As I write this twenty years later, I cannot stand and sing the anthem. I cannot salute the flag; I know that I am a black man in a white world."[1]

In his final preseason game of 2016, San Francisco 49ers quarterback Colin Kaepernick took a knee during the American national anthem to protest anti-Black racism and police brutality against Black Americans. The following week, eleven more Black National Football League players joined him.

Police brutality and discrimination against Black and Indigenous citizens is not only an American issue. It happened in Chatham-Kent and continues today. Lorne Foster, York University's Research Chair in Black Canadian Studies and Human Rights, and Director at the Institute for Social Research, remembers his childhood in the city of Chatham: "The police in Chatham when I was young, they didn't see racialized, in particular Black men, young Black males, as significant at all, and by that I mean, they felt they could do anything that they wanted to me in Chatham and there would be no repercussions, and I always felt that in the presence of the police when I was a teenager."

It was something I never had to consider.

It wasn't only in the 1950s and 1960s, it's today as well. In 2015, Chatham-Kent was featured in a CBC *Fifth Estate* story looking at the use of body cameras by police officers after a Black teen, Jake Anderson, a successful football player in the community, was arrested. The charges against Anderson were only dropped after a security video of the event surfaced showing Chatham-Kent Police Service officers punching and tasering Anderson, who was not resisting.[2] After an internal review, the Police Service cleared their officers of wrongdoing in 2016, the same year Kaepernick started his protest. Both officers involved went on to internal promotions and accolades.

As Black NFL players continued to take a knee, something struck me—the sidelines began to look like the keys of my mother's piano. White men stood with Black men kneeling between them. As teammates, we're trained to be allies for each other, to have each other's back. But that alliance has historically extended only to the game itself, not the people who play it. Only a few have been true allies—activists who used their privilege to improve conditions for athletes of colour.

The first glimpse of fall had arrived. Stray leaves were dancing across the streets of Chatham's East End, catching in uncut grass or hiding under bushes, finding a spot to rest. The boys from a few roads over were arriving, hockey sticks in hand, passing a tennis ball back and forth as they walked. The rattle of wood on cement as each stick swept across the pavement is a sound Canadian youth know well. In the middle of Lansdowne Street, a pair of beaten hockey nets were waiting, along with three other boys. In the 1960s, the streets of Chatham were alive with children playing games.

It was a neighbourhood thing. Games would pop up pitting street against street, or friend group against friend group. Drew Robinson was the only Black person on the street that day. He scored his share of goals, but near the end of the game, Robinson got in an argument with a white boy from the opposing team who used the N-word.

Robinson's friend, who had invited him to the game, stood in shock. He had a moment, an instant to act, but his only action was silence. Drew looked around at his white friends, waiting until the words had settled and been carried by the breeze like the falling leaves. The dispute was over. Drew knew he could fight, but he was tired of fighting. Instead, the game ended there, the players heading home for dinner. Robinson walked home with his stick in his hands, the word—and the silence—ringing in his ears.

Drew had heard the word a thousand times, sometimes directed at him, sometimes at others, like when his father took him to watch his cousin, Jim, play baseball.

Jim Dudley played for Green Valley, and later Tupperville, against other small farming communities in the area. The all-Black Green Valley team, like most predominantly or all-Black teams of the era, faced its share of racism when it travelled away from the farming families who knew the players.

"I can remember one really appalling experience," recalls another of Jim's cousins, Ruth Dudley. "I can remember getting to Edys Mills. The name-calling, it was just absolutely brutal. So they weren't going to play ball, but finally did. They couldn't finish the game because people were throwing balls at them. That would have been around 1956."

In his teenage years, Jim attended high school in Dresden, and would help the predominantly white Tupperville team win a provincial championship. During our conversation, he recalled being the only Black player on the team. "I can remember a time when I was going to high school and met some of the guys. One day we were downtown walking along the main street and the guys said, 'Why don't we go and get something to eat?' I was the only person of colour; as we were walking down the street, they were talking about going to Kay's. I knew the history there, so I said, 'No, I'm not going to go in there.' One of my Tupperville teammates knew why I said that, so he said, 'Well let's go across the street to the Dairy Bar'."

By the time the Tupperville team reached the 1964 Ontario Baseball Association playoffs, Dudley was a star. In a home game against Dorchester, he pounded two home runs over the fence. The next day, he had his first chance at the plate in the second inning. "I walked behind the umpire, and there was a man that was standing behind the screen and he obviously knew what I had done in Tupperville the day before. As I walked by him, he said, 'What are you going to do now, black boy?' It caught me off guard, because that was one of the first times as a player I had experienced anything like that. I turned and looked at him, but before I could get to him, Kingsley—he was coaching third base—he ran down the line because he could hear it. He went in behind the screen and grabbed the man, and one thing led to another. Once things got settled down, I stepped into the batter's box and I hit another home run. As I stepped on home plate, I looked at this man, and said, 'That's what I'm going to do.'"

Kingsley Simpson, the coach who had recruited Dudley, was an ally. So was Jim Moore, a coach in a different sport who would have a similar impact on a young player.

In 1961, as happened every season, Chatham chose the best hockey players from each age category to perform as All-Stars in larger competitions. That year, a lone Black twelve-year-old made the roster for the Peewee All-Stars. Gerry Binga, a descendant of 19th-century baseball great William H. Binga, was used to being one of the only Black athletes on a team and was already accustomed to facing racism. Not only was he a top hockey player, he was an exceptional swimmer. But that year, his hockey coach, Jim Moore, changed his understanding of how others could and should face racism.

"We were playing in Detroit, and when you're the only Black

person out there, a lot of people in the stands have a lot to say. They were saying a whole lot of nasty things but I shut it out; if I let it bother me, I'd never play the game. Sure, it hurts when they call it to you, you're a little embarrassed. But you know what? I'm here to play and I'm going to show you how good I am and that I belong here."

After the first period, Moore put his hand on Gerry's shoulder and looked him in the eyes. "Would you mind sitting here on the bench, Gerry?"

No, he didn't mind. Another member of their coaching staff, Mr. Shackleton, was on the bench and patted a spot beside him.

"Just sit here, you'll be all right. Mr. Shackleton will sit with you," Moore added, before retiring to the dressing room with the rest of the team.

In the dressing room, Coach Moore explained to a group of eleven- and twelve-year-old boys what was happening to Gerry. He told them about racism and explained that what people were hollering from the stands was wrong and would hurt Gerry.

Thinking back, Binga says, "I got my first education of what it meant to have allies and it really impacted me. I think the coaches were so stunned that something so derogatory was going on—it was just unreal—they wanted the kids to know what was going on. I couldn't believe it. They all came out and patted me on the back and slapped me on the shin pads and everything else, and really supported me."

Gerry Binga went on to become the first Black player to suit up for the newly formed Blenheim Golden Blades. He was the Blades' first Black captain and, at the time, the only Black player in the Border Cities Junior Hockey League. He was recruited by the team's founder, Dave Baldwin, who, in 1971, signed Pat and Bob Cosby, the sons of Toky Sugiyama Cosby, to join a pair of Black players: Mike Robbins and Buddy Wright, whose Uncle Eddie was already a local hockey star. Pat, who had learned to play hockey by skating on frozen gravel pits with catalogues taped to his shins, would lead the team in scoring in consecutive seasons while Robbins became known for his strength.

"Back then it was a tough go, you get the calls, the racial slurs. Not so much from the players, but from the fans. It didn't matter what town you went to, you heard it," said Robbins.

One event in Petrolia stands out. "Petrolia was pretty bad. I remember we went to Petrolia; we were in the playoffs, and we had to wear a shirt and tie. I was on the ice and back then they had a metal screen around the ice, they didn't have the plexiglass. I remember it was near the end of the game. We had a face-off and froze the puck. And so a guy in the stands stood up, he called me a name and then he spit on me. When he stood up and leaned over the screen, I took my stick and kind of knocked him in the head. Well, that started a riot. And the guys, my teammates, they were right there. Wayne Cowell grabbed him and tried to pull him over the screen. He couldn't quite make it.

"When we were leaving, we had to go through the lobby, and some of the fans were trying to get at us. Our coach, Dave Baldwin, came into the dressing room and told us that when we went out, to make sure our ties were off. He didn't want anybody to wear a tie so they couldn't use it to choke us or anything. We got out, we got on the bus, and they were rocking the bus. So, the police had to come and get us an escort out of Petrolia."

Baldwin had learned that trick many years before during a fight in Port Huron, Michigan. From that day forward, he always wore a clip-on tie. And he knew when it was time for his players to take their ties off.

Baldwin was a hard man to play for. On his teams, the rules were the rules. There were no exceptions. He ran his programs, and pushed his athletes, with an iron fist, whether it was on the ice or the baseball diamond. He also repeatedly opened doors for local Black and Japanese Canadian athletes, judging them solely on their playing ability and potential. The history of Black and Japanese Canadian sport in Chatham-Kent is littered with references to Baldwin as a coach, manager, and teammate. He would invite prospects to visit his home on Lake Erie and recruit them to play for him while pulling them water-skiing or taking them out on his sailboat for the day.

It could have gone the other way. Growing up in Detroit, a city riddled with the Ku Klux Klan and white supremacists, there were machine guns stationed on the front lawn of Dave's school during the 1943 race riots that erupted in response to racism, poverty, and inequality during World War II. Violent mobs wandered the city until 6,000 armed military members arrived to bring an end to the violence. In total, nine white and twenty-five Black people were killed in the conflict. Seventeen of those Black deaths were at the hands of police. Baldwin appears to have been the kind of youth who, faced with racism and discrimination, develops an "awareness of power and privilege," which inevitably "allows them to reflect on what they see in their families and communities and strengthen their commitments toward a just, equitable, and empathetic society."[3]

On the baseball field, Baldwin suited up with the greatest Chatham had to offer. In the 1950s, he played for the Kent Panthers alongside Boomer Harding and Flat Chase. Before the game, he would drop his wife Margaret off at the Harding house, where she'd share a cup of tea with Boomer's wife, Joy, while their husbands went to the field to warm up. The Panthers, successors to the Chatham Coloured All-Stars, were now an integrated team, and won back-to-back Western Counties Baseball Association championships, with the 1957 Panthers narrowly falling in the Ontario championships.

When he moved to Blenheim, Baldwin played for the Blenheim Braves. At times, he'd also be recruited as a ringer for local Indigenous teams. The team would send a chauffeur to pick him up and bring him back after games. A pitcher, Baldwin would earn tryouts with the Detroit Tigers, although he turned down an opportunity to sign with the team.

By the 1960s, Baldwin was managing the Chatham Maroons hockey team and playing baseball for the Kent Asphalt Seniors in the Michigan-Ontario league. His teammates included a young Ferguson "Fergie" Jenkins.

At Chatham's Turner Park in 1959, a gangly Fergie Jenkins stood next to a slight Mel Wakabayashi. At fifteen, Jenkins hadn't yet found his stride. He'd been on provincial championship teams, playing with older players, but hadn't played a starring role. Mel, diminutive next to Fergie, was a star on the ice and field.

The pair had been asked to work out for a Major League Baseball scout, Gene Dziadura. Gene was born in Windsor and advanced to play minor league baseball in the Philadelphia Phillies organization. While playing in Iowa, however, Dziadura suffered a fluke spinal injury that ended his baseball career. He returned to Ontario and accepted a teaching position in Chatham from H.A. Tanser, who offered him the job on the spot when he said he could coach rugby. Tanser had unwittingly allowed an anti-racist into his midst.

Dziadura would become familiar with many young local athletes, including Jenkins and Wakabayashi. When a friend in the Phillies organization suggested Dziadura become a scout, he set to work. He watched Wakabayashi and Jenkins carefully and immediately saw Fergie's potential. Wakabayashi would play NCAA baseball but eventually choose hockey as his primary sport. Jenkins would become a Major League star and the first Canadian member of the Major League Baseball Hall of Fame.

Dziadura committed himself to helping Fergie. For the next three years, the pair would work out together three to four times per week on local diamonds. In the winter, Jenkins would pitch to Dziadura in the gymnasium of a local high school. "Gene was the first person who saw me as an athlete, and then he saw me from a different viewpoint as not being a first baseman, but being a pitcher," recalls Jenkins.

Not only did Dziadura prepare Jenkins to become an all-star pitcher, he tried to prepare him for the racist animosity he would face in the United States. Dziadura had toiled in the minors for a few seasons in Louisiana where he witnessed the abuse delivered by white fans and athletes. He had seen Black youth being barred from using "white only" drinking fountains and other public facilities.

He had also become a target himself for supporting a Black teammate named Sammy Drake, who would go on to play in the major leagues. Playing for the Lafayette Oilers in 1956, Dziadura, who was followed in the batting order by Drake, called out, "Come on, Sammy!" A group of white spectators started yelling at him, telling him not to speak to "that n------" anymore. A few innings later, Dziadura cheered for Drake again and celebrated with him as he crossed the plate, at which point the crowd again yelled at Dziadura, threatening to stab him if he continued talking to his Black teammate. Following that game Dziadura retreated to the clubhouse quickly, afraid of what might happen.

Not surprisingly, the Black community in Louisiana took to Dziadura. When boarding the local bus to make his way to the stadium, Black fans, forced to sit in the back, would call out to him and he would often cross the colour line painted on the floor to visit with them, ignoring the looks he'd receive from white people in the front.

Dziadura's son, Chris, remembers those stories clearly, and how these incidents impacted Gene as a person: "With his friendship with the Drakes, it would also be, being in a city and my dad saying, 'Come on let's go in for a bite to eat here,' and they'd say, 'Gene, we're not allowed here.' And Dad had a hard time with that because, like many people, he was just a good person. He really had to learn and adjust about how to act around teammates."

Dziadura understood Jenkins would have far more to contend

with. He told Jenkins, "See this skin, it's white and if I played behind you, if I make an error they won't get on me too much. If you make too many errors you'll experience much more criticism."[4]

Jenkins recalls, "He was the first one to tap me on the head and say, 'Ferguson, let me tell you one thing, when you sign, and when you play in the south, things are going to be totally different than how you've been brought up in Chatham.' And he was right. He gave me an insight for what I basically had to see on a personal level. You can read about it in the paper, but until you're there and actually are a part of it, and seeing it, it's different."

According to Chris Dziadura, the Chicago Cubs tried to hire his father to stay with Jenkins, and mentor him during his first pro season with Chicago's farm team, the Buffalo Bison. "In the spring of 1962, Fergie was going to play in Buffalo. Tony Lucadello, who was the scout who signed my dad and then asked him to be a scout, actually asked my dad if he wouldn't mind signing a contract for the summer to go with Fergie, because Tony was aware that Fergie was going to have issues."

Gene had to turn down the offer as he was getting married that summer, but the two remained close, each recognizing the contribution of the other. After his first Major League Baseball season in 1966, Fergie Jenkins, now twenty-four and removed from his own minor league torments, returned home for the winter. He was stronger and more confident as he walked back into the gymnasium where he'd spent so many winters; his throws made a louder smack as they connected with a glove. Across the gym, shaking the sting of catching Fergie's pitch out of his hand, almost a decade after their first game of catch, was Gene Dziadura.

More than fifty years after being the target of a racist taunt during a game of road hockey, Drew Robinson was finishing a career as an assistant district attorney in Tennessee. After university, he had attended law school at the University of Tennessee, where he played club hockey; he later joined a team called the Chattanooga Choo-Choos. "I was of course the only Black player. Hockey was new down south, and there was an awful lot of racial animosity. When people would see me out there, it wasn't a good thing," he remembers.

He'd since faced racism from judges, other attorneys, and on the streets. Thinking back to that game on Lansdowne Avenue, Robinson doesn't blame his friends for not speaking up. "A lot of people feel guilty when they're placed in that situation, when you have to make a split-second decision, as a young person, to act," said Robinson.

In Nelson, Dunn, and Paradies' 2011 paper, "Bystander Anti-Racism: A Review of the Literature" in the journal *Analyses of Social Issues and Public Policy*, the researchers observed that, "bystanders are most likely to help those they see as similar to themselves" but also consider "perceived personal risk," particularly when that risk was "perceived to potentially impact interpersonal relations." Other studies point to the fact that bystanders are less likely to act when others, including the perpetrator, are present.[5]

Although difficult, the benefits of intervention, or allyship, are clear. "[B]ystander anti-racism can establish social norms that will constrain racist behavior in the short term but also affect attitudes in the long term."[6]

In 2016, bystanders remained silent for an entire season of the National Football League. No white NFL player knelt alongside their Black teammates. It wasn't until the 2017 preseason that the Cleveland Browns' Seth DeValve took a knee. DeValve, a second-year player, is married to a Black woman, and wanted to raise his children in a better country and environment than the one that existed.[7]

In the days and weeks that followed, DeValve was celebrated in the media. Meanwhile, Colin Kaepernick had been blackballed and would never play again. To DeValve's wife, Erica Harris DeValve, this was not right. In an August 24, 2017 article for *The Root,* she wrote: "I am grateful for the widespread support and praise that Seth is getting for his actions, but I would like to offer a humble reminder that a man—a Black man—literally lost his job for taking a knee, week after week, on his own. Colin Kaepernick bravely took a step and began a movement throughout the NFL, and he suffered a ridiculous amount of hate and threats and ultimately lost his life's work in the sport he loves . . . We should not see Seth's participation as legitimizing this movement. Rather, he chose to be an ally of his Black teammates. To center the focus . . . solely on Seth is to distract from what our real focus should be: listening to the experiences and the voices of the Black people who are using their platforms to continue to bring the issue of racism . . . to the forefront."

The silence that looms after a racial slur, or an act of anti-Black or anti-Indigenous racism provides an opening for someone to speak, to become an ally. Archie McKellar and Reverend William King did this when they stood against Edwin Larwill and his mob. So did Archie Stirling when he paved the way for the Chatham Coloured All-Stars. Kingsley Simpson, Bob Moore, Dave Baldwin, and Gene Dziadura all chose to act, demonstrating that stakeholders—coaches, athletes, fans—can fracture the lines of racism from within.

But they did not steal the stage or stand on the field for applause. Each acted and then retreated to the background, while the marginalized athletes and citizens they acted with and for took the spotlight. They amplified the abilities and opportunities of others. It's what Harris DeValve hopes all white allies will do. "Listen to the voices of the Black people in your life, and choose to support them as they seek to make their voices heard."

# Chapter 15

# THE INTERNATIONAL LINE

I lived my hockey dreams on a cement pad in my father's barn. He tacked layers of plywood against the walls that would splinter and crumble as I pounded puck after puck. When friends came over, we'd trade the puck for a tennis ball, road hockey goalie pads, a baseball glove and blocker, and a helmet. My best friend would choose players from his favourite team, the Boston Bruins. I'd choose Detroit Red Wings. We were our heroes. I had the slapshot of Al MacInnis and the finishing touch of Steve Yzerman. In net, we would sprawl like Dominik Hasek.

From time to time, we'd throw in our local favourites, not always those who went on to stardom. I might pick a player from the Chatham Wheels, a local semi-pro team that played from 1992 to 1994. But when I was in net, I would typically morph into a goalie who left a lasting impression on me—Fred Braithwaite.

I saw Braithwaite play when my dad, uncle, and I visited the London Ice House to watch the London Knights of the Ontario Hockey League. Although his stint with the Knights was brief, less than half a season in 1991–1992, Fred Braithwaite electrified the crowd on a nightly basis. Donning London's green and yellow, Braithwaite was small, standing only five-foot-seven, but what he lacked in size, he made up for in reaction time, reflexes, and competitiveness. He would stretch and dive, making miraculous saves, stopping shots that appeared to be sure-fire goals. Each time he did, I'd leap from my seat with thousands of Knights fans, and we would collectively chant, "Freddy, Freddy, Freddy," until the action drew our attention back to the other end of the rink.

At the first game I attended, I was shocked when Freddy took off his helmet for "O Canada." I'd never seen a Black person play hockey, much less in person. Freddy was a game changer, not only on the ice for the London Knights, but in my mind. Braithwaite would go on to play 250 games in the NHL and represented Team Canada at the World Championships on multiple occasions. I avidly followed his hockey career until he retired following the 2012 season.

Our heroes take the form of what we see, and who we know. Seeing only white hockey players on my television and on the local teams I watched, they were all I could imagine. That is until Fred Braithwaite took off his helmet for our national anthem.

Howe is flying down the wing, he's going one-on-one with Doug Harvey. Harvey is fighting him off, the puck slips loose. Howe has it in the clear, Johnny Bower comes out to cut off the angle. Howe fakes, he shoots, he scores! And the crowd goes wild!

In a long driveway off Degge Street in the 1950s, three boys were pretending to be their hockey heroes, although none looked like them. The competitors were brothers Herb and Mel Wakabayashi and their friend, Eddie Wright. They'd been at it for hours, using a net placed in front of the Wakabayashi's garage.

Tokuzo and Hatsuye Wakabayashi had relocated to Chatham in 1950, settling on Degge Street in the East End. Alongside thousands of other Canadians, the Wakabayashis and their three children had been forcefully removed from Vancouver during World War II and initially sent to the Slocan City internment camp in British Columbia, where they welcomed another son, Mel, in 1943. By the time Herb was born the following year, the family had been moved again, this time to Northern Ontario's Neys Camp 100. Following the war, the Wakabayashis came to Chatham because they knew other Japanese Canadian families who had settled in the city. Here, Tokuzo, or Tom as people would call him, worked at a cosmetics factory, and later as a custodian at Union Gas. The family cooked daikon and made tofu in their garage, producing smells the neighbours would come to know well. When they needed extra money, Tom would sell vegetables from his garden.

The East End was multicultural, a landing point for immigrants, refugees, and Black settlers. While it was impoverished, it was also a model of inclusion. Chatham's white community had corralled the people who did not look or sound like them in this neighbourhood, but in doing so, they'd inadvertently created a community filled with pride. Professor Lorne Foster grew up playing with friends on Princess Street: "There was a sort of multicultural fabric to the East End, that didn't necessarily live by the same kinds of fault lines, racial fault lines, that existed outside of it. It wasn't a Shangri-la by any means because of the socioeconomic situation. It was very downtrodden economically, but we didn't know any better as young kids, not until we got to be teenagers and we could stretch regularly beyond the boundaries." At school on Mondays, his teacher would smile at the younger Lorne as he entered the room, saying, "there's my A student." Foster's chest would fill with pride; no one in his family had finished high school.

In the years following the war, Japanese Canadian families, including the Wakabayashis, became prominent members of the East End sports community, producing local athletes who excelled at basketball, baseball, softball, hockey, and bowling either on Nikkei teams formed as part of the Kent Nisei Athletic Club, or on community teams.

Japanese Canadian athletes were also making their mark in nearby Blenheim. The Cosby brothers both played Junior hockey for the Blenheim Golden Blades, while Dave and Phil Sunohara became successful multi-sport athletes. Before the war, Junichi Sunohara had been a prominent garden planner in Vancouver, specializing in miniature Japanese gardens. Like the Wakabayashis, the Sunoharas were initially interned at Slocan City, then later were part of a forced uprooting bringing the family to Cedar Springs, just outside Blenheim, to work on local farms.

The four oldest Sunohara brothers—John, Dave, Phil, and Paul—all loved hockey and shared one pair of skates, each patiently waiting their turn, playing in their boots in the meantime. Eventually the family could afford to enrol them in minor hockey and every team Dave and Phil played for became a top contender. They were the only non-white players on the Blenheim Midget hockey team; Dave was also the captain of the Blenheim High School hockey team and county pole vault champion. While still in their teens, Dave and Phil joined a men's league, suiting up for the Cedar Springs Rockets where Dave became the league's leading scorer, notching forty-six points in only twenty games. Following high school, Dave enrolled at Ryerson University where he played for the Ryerson Rams. Living in Toronto, Dave soon found another team, an all-Japanese Canadian hockey club known as Double S. Tile, nicknamed the Nisei Flyers.

Like the Sunoharas and the Cosbys, the Wakabayashi brothers were obsessed with hockey. "We were out there every day; it was Herb, Mel, and me," says Eddie Wright, a smile in his voice. "There was one goaltender, and it was one-on-one. We took turns. After school we were there with the rubber ball, and we were going at it until we lost the ball in the dark. It was competitive. Those were real dreams we were living when we were going through that, and we were hard at it." When it got too dark to play, they'd move inside and play euchre, with the eldest Wakabayashi brother, Don, joining in. Eddie was the weak link when it came to cards.

"Then of course in the baseball season it was the same thing—we had a catcher, a pitcher, and a batter. I can remember when Mel was pitching and I was batting, that ball was coming toward my head. Those were hard-core daily lessons. We were living the dream; it was a dream going through that, trying to outdo one another. Herb and Mel had high standards, they forced me to be better. With their skill level, they forced me to be good. I developed a philosophy through that—I would never be outworked."

As the oldest of the trio, Mel Wakabayashi was the leader. Where one went, so did the others. When Mel made the Chatham Maroons, Herb and Eddie would take turns carrying his bag for him. After a peewee tournament in Goderich, the newspapers dubbed them the International Line, a name that stuck from that day on, even after Mel, then Herb and Eddie, joined on the Chatham Maroons. They were each born in Canada and raised in Chatham, but the colour of their skin made them "international." Canadians were white.

The Maroons played at Chatham's Memorial Arena, a cathedral to hockey constructed on the grounds of Basic Training No. 12 in 1949. Thick beams still span the arching roof. Cold and beaten wooden benches surround the smaller-than-average ice surface. Wires are tacked to the outside of the boards, trying to catch up to advancing technology.

In the 1960s, the crowds at Memorial Arena were wowed by the skill and chemistry developed during those hours in the Wakabayashis' driveway. Mel and Herb were offensive dynamos. They were consistently league leaders in scoring, while Wright, no offensive slouch himself, took on a defensive role on the line. Together, none standing taller than five-foot-five, they darted and dashed through and around opponents, infuriating defenders. From the ice, voices could be heard raining down both cheers and slurs.

While they all faced taunting, Wright took the brunt of the racist abuse from the stands and opponents. Perhaps, as Frank Cosentino argues in his book, *Afros, Aboriginals and Amateur Sport in Pre-World War One Canada* (1998), the Wakabayashis were insulated by Wright in Canada's racial hierarchy: "In Canada a racial and ethnic hierarchy was established (reflected in immigration and Indian policies) that relegated Blacks and First Nations to the bottom of the ladder. Although also regarded as inferior and unassimilable, Orientals and South Asians occupied a higher rung."[1]

"I think I got it worse because skill-wise, they were just

unbelievably fantastic athletes," Wright said. "Myself, being Black, and being five-foot-three-and-a-half and 138 pounds, I had to be tough, physically and mentally."

While his white teammates prepared for a game, Eddie Wright prepared for battle. That's what he called it. To him, the game, and what it took to play, was serious. It didn't matter what town he went to—Leamington, Detroit, London, or his hometown of Chatham—Wright had opponents on the ice and opponents in the stands. "It was whatever it takes to win, and the fans certainly threw the insults at me left, right, and centre. The players on the ice were worse. I pretty much fought all throughout Junior. It really was something else and I actually ended up with an ulcer in my last year from some of the stress of that time."

For Eddie, the Wakabayashis were like family. Herb, in particular, was like a brother. Wright had a large and loving family of his own, but they weren't at the arena. He didn't want his mother or his sisters to have to witness what he went through game in and game out. "I didn't really want anybody who I thought really cared about me and loved me—family—there to see what I was going through, because it wasn't easy."

Eddie's sister Dorothy felt bad about not supporting him. She recalls, "I felt guilty, and went to my brother and said, 'Eddie I'm sorry that I didn't go and see you play hockey,' and his answer really kind of took me aback. He said, 'I'm glad you didn't.' He said, 'I had a job to do on the ice, and I'm glad I didn't have to worry about putting up a fight and getting you out of something up in the stands. I couldn't have handled that.' I felt better hearing that, because I would have started trouble. There were a lot of racial slurs thrown at him."

Eventually, his older brother Allan did go see his Eddie play, and trouble did result. Lorne Foster remembers the incident well. He was ten in 1963 when he was invited to accompany his best friend, Russell Wright, and Russell's father, Allan, to watch the International Line play in Windsor.

"As a young kid, I didn't quite understand and wasn't able to internalize the racial epithets and things said from the stands and all of that. I know that my first recollection of the racism in hockey was in Windsor with my friend Russell Wright. His father, Allan Wright, was a boxer, and he heard this guy in the stands saying the N-word about his brother Eddie. I can remember it, he was tenacious about those kinds of issues, and he wouldn't back down.

"He wasn't a huge guy, but he was tremendously talented as a fighter. I remember in Windsor, he took this guy who was a head bigger than he was . . . he would not tolerate that kind of racial slur against his brother, and he just started fighting the guy in the stands. It was so memorable for me. He was such a character, Allan Wright for me, it just sticks in my mind to this day. That was my first entry into sport and racism."

Despite the hardships, sport created opportunities for Mel, Herb, and Eddie. They won provincial baseball championships, cracked the lineup of the top hockey team in town, became a generation of idols for East End youth, and earned athletic scholarships to top American universities.

Mel was the first to leave town. He accepted a scholarship to play with the University of Michigan Wolverines hockey team. Mel was dynamic on the ice and charismatic off. He ended up captaining the Wolverines and was named the Western College Hockey Association's Player of the Year. He was an All-American during his time with Michigan and, in 2018, was named the twenty-first best player in Wolverine history. Following his NCAA career, Mel signed with the Detroit Red Wings. Although he never suited up for the Red Wings, he played professionally in Detroit's farm system with the Johnstown Jets and Memphis Wings.

Herb Wakabayashi was the next to go. He left Chatham to play in the NCAA with Boston University. At Boston, Herb earned multiple All-American honours, and was named team MVP and Boston University's Athlete of the Year following the 1966–67 season.

Much like at home in their driveway, the boys changed sports with the seasons. Both Wakabayashi brothers also played baseball at the NCAA level, and Mel earned an invitation to attend spring training with the Detroit Tigers. Their timing of entering the NCAA coincided with civil rights movements across college sports in the United States, a time when change was occurring, particularly for Black athletes in the American south. While significant barriers remained, "the years 1963 through 1966 represent a turning point in the levelling of the playing field; integration efforts in collegiate athletics would start picking up momentum."[2]

A year later, Herb and Eddie, inseparable in their youth, were reunited on a line at Boston University. Here, they were unstoppable, feeding off one another. They are particularly remembered as one of hockey's best penalty killing duos. They'd collect the puck, and pass it back and forth, protecting it from their opponents. If they lost control, they'd pin the opposing power-play unit deep in its own end. At one point, Herb and Eddie killed thirty-six consecutive minutes of penalty time without allowing a shot on goal.

At full strength, Herb and Eddie were joined by a French Canadian, Serge Boily. Now three Canadian boys were dubbed the United Nations Line, even though they didn't always play together. Wright would again face barriers that the Wakabayashis did not. In his sophomore season, Wright was replaced as Herb's winger, and he knew why.

When we spoke, Wright admitted, "that was a devastating time for me. I wasn't playing, I wasn't dressing for games, in practice I was on the fourth line. It was quite evident I should have been in the lineup. I kind of thought that it had something to do with the colour of my skin, I thought the colour of my skin was overshadowing my skill as a hockey player. I was very, very angry. I was an angry man for a whole year."

Living with Herb, Eddie thought regularly about bringing up the issue with his coach, but instead he silently endured. "It was certainly on my mind to bring that up," he said. "I hung in there. In the long run it was good for me, a very valuable lesson, not only about my skill as a hockey player, but as a Black man in the world that I was dealing with."

That season, Boston lost in the national championships to Cornell, who were backstopped by a future Hall of Fame netminder named Ken Dryden. Despite the fact Wright could have helped Boston, he remained sidelined.

The following season he finally got his chance. "I managed to get in the lineup in my junior year, and I was very successful. I was very productive, a productive member of the team. At the end of my career, Jack Kelly, my coach, openly admitted to me that I was one of the biggest mistakes that he ever made. I finally came to the realization, after going through all this, that I was probably a very important member of the team pushing everyone on the lineup. I deserved to be there."

At the completion of their college careers, the childhood trio took different paths. Professional hockey was never a goal for Eddie Wright. He wanted to be a physical educator, a teacher. In 1970, just as he was finishing his Master of Education degree at Boston University, he received a call from the state university of New York at Buffalo. At the time, the campus, especially the athletics program, was embroiled in racial turmoil resulting from discriminatory actions by the school's basketball coach. Buffalo had a hockey team but wanted to take it to the varsity level; if the school could find a Black hockey coach, the costs would be covered by affirmative action funding. Overnight, Wright became the first Black coach in men's NCAA hockey history.

According to Wright, serving as a coach did not protect him from the same abuse he had experienced as a player. "Racist taunts and gestures occurred at road games" and he also recalls fans "chanting a racist and homophobic slur" at him.[3]

The racism Wright faced throughout his career left its mark.

"Hearing the crowds chanting, it wasn't easy," Wright told *The Buffalo News.* "It wasn't easy. To this day I think it has an everlasting effect on the type of individual I am and how careful I am about where I go and how I deal with things."[4]

In 2022, Eddie Wright is retired and happy. He doesn't hold grudges or house any anger. In 2010, New York State University at Buffalo opened the *Edward L. Wright Practice Facility* to honour their famed coach. Every Sunday, Eddie sits down at his home in Arizona to speak to his sister. Growing up and while he was coaching in Buffalo, he was required to call his mother to give her a full account of his week. Now, he does the same with his sister, Dorothy. They are sharing their stories, keeping them alive within one another.

Following their NCAA careers, Mel and Herb Wakabayashi's hockey careers seemed to be coming to a close. They were small, and the hockey world was still dominated by white players. The game was fading around them until Father Bob Moran, a missionary priest who had become involved in hockey in Japan, set out to improve his Japanese club. He sent a message to his friend John "Peanuts" O'Flaherty, a former NHL player who was now a scout for the Vancouver Canucks. When O'Flaherty received a request from Moran to "get some Japanese Canadian hockey players," he knew exactly who to call.

Moran's first recruit was Mel Wakabayashi who, after some persuasion, joined the Seibu Railway Hockey Team in 1969. Each team in the league was allowed two non-Japanese players, or imports, so when Herb graduated from Boston University the following year, Mel suggested Herb join him. In an interview with the *Hartford Courant* in 1972, Herb explained, "My brother Mel was playing here when I finished at B.U. and suggested I might give it a try. Well, I always had wanted to see the country, so I came. But all I planned on doing was to play for a couple of years, stay through the Olympics just to see them, then go home."[5]

The 1972 Olympics were being hosted in Japan and provided an opportunity neither brother would have received in North America. In order to play on the Japanese hockey team, Herb had to become a Japanese citizen, which he did only five months before the games began. Mel chose not to become a Japanese citizen, so his future with the Japanese National team would be confined to coaching. Once in Japan, both began using the Japanese names they had been given at birth—Mel became Hitoshi and Herb became Osamu.

Following the Olympics, the brothers stayed in Japan, working and playing for Seibu. The Japanese league they played in was a company league, meaning players were hired to work for the company that owned the team. For the Wakabayashis, that meant jobs at the Prince Hotel. But their real career was hockey, where Herb was quickly becoming one of Japan's biggest sporting stars, prominently featured on Japanese television. When his team played, whether it was Seibu or the National team, Herb would stay behind in the locker room answering media requests while everyone else waited on the bus. On these occasions, he relied on an interpreter because he could not speak the language.

Success in Japan was not without struggle. In Canada and the United States, the brothers had been seen as outsiders, infant enemies born in internment camps who grew up to play hockey on the International Line and United Nations Line. In Japan, the struggle to be accepted continued. Here, they were still seen as outsiders, albeit celebrities, due to cultural differences and language barriers.

As the *Hartford Courant* article put it, "Both brothers agree it can be difficult having an oriental face in Japan and not speaking much of the language."

Mel said, "People would come up to me and start talking Japanese and they were surprised I couldn't answer them." His brother echoed the sentiment. "They think I'm lying when I tell them I can't speak it." Herb took to carrying a placard that stated he could not speak Japanese. Both men eventually picked up a working knowledge of the spoken language, but neither could read or write Japanese.

While language seemed the main barrier for Herb, Mel saw his Canadian roots clashing with Japanese expectations. In a February 4, 1972 interview with the *Montreal Gazette*, Mel said, "My wife is Japanese from Tokyo, but I've been brought up in the Canadian style. Here, a wife is a servant to her husband and they never heard of women's lib. A man doesn't lift a finger at home, the woman does everything. But I can't get used to that," explained Mel. "Well, other Japanese are very unhappy with me. They think I'm starting a bad trend. They fear I'm going to start a women's revolution here."

By 1978, *The Boston Globe* was reporting that "He [Herb] is a big hockey star. Everybody knows him." Eddie Wright, visiting Herb in Japan just prior to the 1980 Olympic Games, noticed the same thing. "Herb was kind of regarded almost like a God. When I was with him over in Japan, he was so highly respected by the players."

By the time the 1980 Winter Olympics rolled around in Lake Placid, New York, Hitoshi and Osamu Wakabayashi had lived in Japan for more than a decade and had accepted their stardom in the country's hockey world. Herb was set to captain Japan's hockey entry and to serve as the country's flag bearer during the opening ceremonies. Mel was also in a leading role, serving as head coach for Team Japan.

Back on North American soil, the Wakabayashis appeared suspended between two nationalities and two identities. An article in the *Dayton Daily News* on February 20, 1980 read: "As they say, Hitoshi Wakabayashi *looks* Japanese. And well he might since he is the coach of the Japanese Olympic hockey team competing here in the XIII Winter Games. But when he talks, he's pure Canadian right down to the long O in about and out."

The same day, Eddie MacCabe wrote about Mel's coaching for the *Ottawa Citizen*, "When something untoward happens, he is no part of the unflappable Oriental. There is no mild "ah so" in a car-load. He is as animated as any Canadian. In fact, he is a Canadian."

The 1980 Games were a swan song of sorts for the brothers. Mel would soon retire from his role coaching Japan's National team, although he would return to coach Japanese teams intermittently in the following decades. Herb would spend two more seasons playing for Japan before he left the game as well. Both settled permanently in Japan, although they each made several trips to Canada in the years that followed their hockey careers.

Herb died of cancer in 2015, a great loss to his family and his best friend Eddie. The inscription on the massive headstone that marks his grave in Japan reads, "A Great Hockey Player Lies Here." His skates are there, bronzed, and there are hockey sticks resting against his headstone. While primarily remembered in Japan, Herb was also a trailblazer for Canadian hockey. He, along with Mel and their contemporary Dave Sunohara, paved the way for the next generation.

When Dave Sunohara died of a heart attack in 1978 at age forty-two, his seven-year-old daughter Vicky was already a burgeoning hockey star. At their home in Scarborough, Ontario, she shared her father's passion from the moment she could walk and talk.

"Everything was hockey. My dad built a rink in our backyard, we played hockey in the basement. My first words were 'shoot score, shoot score.' I was just two, and he'd always ask, 'Are you going to be a hockey player?' I always wanted to be a hockey player. Whether it was the basement or the rink outside, I remember always wanting to play hockey with him. He'd make the rink at our public school too, and he'd flood it at night, and I remember begging to go with him. I'd be there all the time playing with the boys.

"My mom always told me that I was just two-and-a-half when he brought me to the rink. When he brought me home, he told my mom, 'You're not going to believe this, Vicky can skate.' My mom said, 'Awesome. She can be a figure skater.' My dad said, 'Not a chance. She's going to play hockey.' When he put me on skates, that was pretty exciting for him, and I just loved it. I don't remember loving anything more than hockey. Whether it be at our school or in our backyard on the rink that he made me, it was all about hockey."

Dave Sunohara enrolled his daughter Vicky, at the age of five, in a boys' hockey league where she became the top scorer, with thirty-six goals that season. After she was banned from boys' hockey because of her gender, she made the switch to the women's game. Following her father's death, she would arrive at the rink with her Ukrainian mother and people would say, "you must be adopted."

Despite her passion and her immense talent, there were times when she wanted to quit. "I was being called 'chink,'" recalls Sunohara. "I wondered why can't I be like everyone else, why am I being called names? I didn't want to be called names. I thought sometimes, maybe I didn't want to play anymore. My mom really helped me out in that. She always said to me if people were calling me names, it was because they just wanted me to stop scoring. She'd say, 'Just go play harder, go score more.'

"I'd go to hockey if I had a bad day, or things going on in my life, and it would be my place of freedom, a place to get away and forget about anything bad. I'd go and step on the ice and it would be my outlet, my happy place."

Sunohara joined Canada's national team and, at age seventeen, played in the first IIHF sanctioned World Championships in 1990. In total, she would win seven World Champion titles, with her uncles in the stands at almost every game of each tournament. At the 1990 World Championships, Sunohara played alongside Black hockey legend and Hockey Hall of Fame member Angela James, who would later become her teammate in the Central Ontario Women's Hockey League. By then, the media had evolved enough that they were not characterized as the International Line.

During the 1998 Winter Olympics held in Nagano, however,

Sunohara's ancestry became the subject of media interest just as it had for the Wakabayashis. Her status as a Japanese Canadian who was the star of Team Canada at the first women's Olympic hockey tournament meant that she was flooded with interview requests from Canadian and Japanese media.

"I didn't feel different," she explained. "I just thought of myself as being Canadian." But her grandparents, Junichi and Mei, had grown up less than thirty kilometers south of Nagano, and distant relatives and friends of her grandparents packed the stands to see her play. When she stepped on the ice in her Team Canada jersey, Japanese fans showered her with love.

"When I got there and got on the ice for the first game, my hockey card was blown up into a life size poster, and there were banners saying 'Vicky Sunohara, we are your relatives.' It was amazing. My teammates were like 'oh my gosh, this is unbelievable.' I really had no idea. It was pretty special." She scored six goals and nine points in five games, ultimately losing a heartbreaking gold medal game to the United States.

Following the tournament, a local reporter who was serving as Sunohara's translator took her to Ueda, the town where her grandparents were born. There, a group of more than eighty distant relatives and family friends threw her a banquet. She was a hero viewing familiar faces in an unfamiliar land.

"They had pictures of my mom and dad on their wedding day. My grandmother's relatives were there. A couple of the women looked so much like my grandmother, it was unbelievable. It was all a surprise. It wasn't like, 'I'm going to Japan to get to meet some relatives,' I had no idea they'd be there. It was all such a shock."

Vicky Sunohara would become one of the most decorated hockey players in Canadian history. She and Team Canada rebounded from their silver medal performance in Nagano to win Olympic gold in Salt Lake City in 2002, and again in Turin in 2006. TSN named Sunohara to their All-Time Women's Team Canada in 2020. That same year, she was named the Ontario University Athletics Coach of the Year, and the USports Women's Ice Hockey Coach of the Year after guiding the University of Toronto Varsity Blues women's team, whom she'd coached for a decade, to an Ontario title. Also in 2020, Sunohara received the Sakura Award, an honour bestowed by the Japanese Canadian Cultural Centre on an individual who has helped to promote Japanese culture and enhance awareness of Japanese heritage in Canada and abroad. After fifty years of hockey excellence, Sunohara had certainly done that and more. She'd come a long way from her father's backyard rink.

Once, while walking through the old Maple Leaf Gardens to address her Toronto Varsity Blues team, Sunohara paused to look at a display case. The historic arena had become the home of the Ryerson Rams, her father's former team. There, through the glass, between trophies and plaques, was a photo of her father, alongside his Ryerson teammates, staring back at her.

"I looked in this big display, and there was his photo. I was about to coach and it was just so emotional. I had to keep it together because I was coaching a big game, but inside, I just wished I could have had a conversation with him. I wish he could have seen it, that he could have seen me playing and now coaching."

Sunohara hopes the next generation of athletes will be able to play the games they love regardless of race. "I hope they don't have to think about racism. To think that kids, or any person going to do something that they love, that it could be turned into something they hate because they face racism is hard to think about. I hope they can just play hockey and think, 'This is amazing. I'm a person of colour and I can just play.'" If they do, they will have athletes like her, her father, Eddie Wright, and Mel and Herb Wakabayashi to thank.

## Chapter 16

# A PARADE FOR FERGIE

For years I would follow the same truck on my way to work. The driver and I likely woke at almost the same time, checked the same weather reports. Maybe we sat down at similar tables and drank our coffee, and then stood to gather our coats and shoes.

The darkest hours seemed to be those just prior to sunrise, my turn signal illuminating the world in intervals. As I pulled onto the highway, the man in his truck would pull out ahead of me like clockwork. I could see his eyes in the glow of my headlights on his rearview mirror. There in the darkness on the road in front of me, he'd accelerate. My beams would strike the tailgate of his truck and bring to life the Confederate flag painted there. Each morning I wondered about that man. We were in Canada after all. This flag had no geographic origin here, but it did have meaning.

Eventually, the driver of that truck would pass a sign reading "Welcome to Chatham—Home of Fergie Jenkins."

By 1968, Fergie's status as a local hero had long been established. He was Chatham's son. Dressed in an expensive suit, he stepped down onto the ice at Blenheim's Memorial Arena, one hand on the boards, the other holding a hockey puck. Fergie Jenkins strode confidently to centre ice and stood at the face-off dot as the Blenheim Blades announcer boomed his praises to the crowd. Accolades and accomplishments. There was a pause for applause, then a wave from Fergie.

The announcer asked team captains to join Jenkins at centre ice for the ceremonial puck drop. Gerry Binga stepped over the boards from the hometown bench and set up at centre ice across from his Detroit counterpart. Binga was used to being the only Black man on the ice, but on this occasion he was joined by his childhood idol, only a few years his senior.

"I skated up to Fergie and said, 'What, you come to the arena and you don't bring your skates?' I was proud of that moment I got to stand there with him. I was proud of him," said Binga. "I really loved the guy."

Walking home from school, Gerry Binga would break into a sprint every time he returned to Chatham's East End. As he approached the Jenkins' home, he'd pause, look through their picture window and wave. Many days, he would see his mother, Klaassiena, standing with Delores Jenkins. Klaassiena would wave back. Delores didn't—she had lost most of her eyesight giving birth to Fergie, her only child, when her optic nerves were damaged during labour.

Klaassiena was a war bride who immigrated to Canada from Holland following World War II. She was white, so her marriage to Bethune Binga caused a scandal. As author Charmaine Nelson wrote in a January 29, 2021 article for *The Walrus*, interracial marriages in Canada were often "seen as threatening to white male power," and for Canada's white population, "signalled the demise of the so-called purity of the white race."

Despite what some said in the neighbourhood, Klaassiena and Delores formed a strong bond. Delores helped Klaassiena with her English and Klaasseina would read news stories to Delores. As Klaasseina's English improved, she also helped Delores learn how to read and create braille.

"She was a good woman. I just loved her to death," Binga recalls of Delores Jenkins. "She had the greatest laugh. Well, it was because of my mother and his mother's relationship that I got into sports. She's the one that kept telling my mom, get him in sports, get him in sports, and my mom did. She always told me, be like Ferg."

Binga was a lean athlete with a defined chest and arms that looked like a rolling mountain range. He became a swimming champion and a strong track and field athlete. He also loved hockey.

So did Fergie. An athlete from the moment he could stand, Fergie gravitated to basketball, baseball, and hockey. He got his first pair of skates around the age of five, and played hockey more than any other sport, dreaming of some day joining the Chatham Maroons, and being like his NHL idol, Doug Harvey.

As a teenager, Fergie and his father, Ferguson Jenkins Sr., travelled to an NHL exhibition game between the Toronto Maple Leafs and Boston Bruins. On the ice was Willie O'Ree. Jenkins was inspired and believed hockey was his path until, later that year, he and his father took in a baseball game between the Detroit Tigers and the Cleveland Indians. Playing for Cleveland was Larry Doby, Major League Baseball's second Black player, and the first in the American League. Doby hit a pair of home runs, and despite being on the visiting team, the Detroit fans cheered his success. Jenkins turned to his father and said, "You know, Dad, I think I want to play baseball."

After signing a professional contract at eighteen, Jenkins began playing in Florida in 1962. He remembers receiving a lecture as soon as he arrived, explaining where he could go and where he could eat. During one of his first road games in Florida, he walked into a restaurant with his teammates. "We can't serve you," the woman behind the counter told him. Fergie returned to the bus to find his Black teammates had not left their seats. They explained he needed to give a white teammate his money so that teammate could bring him back some food.

The civil rights movement, and the words of Dr. Martin Luther King, were ringing in the ears of Black youth in America. Black protestors were marching for their rights, only to be pelted with rotten fruit and eggs. White men were attacking Black people in the streets and policemen turned dogs on them.

Back in Miami, that same group of Black athletes lived in a different hotel from their white teammates and spent hours travelling between the stadium, where their talents were required, and a Black neighbourhood, where their identity was accepted. On the road, the Black players slept in funeral homes and brothels. If they were lucky, they'd be served behind restaurants, out of sight of the white patrons inside.

As Fergie climbed the ranks, things did not improve. Two years after turning pro, Jenkins was playing in Little Rock, Arkansas. After practice, Jenkins and his Black teammates would return to the parking lot to find their vehicles defaced: "We don't want you n------s. Go home."

The Little Rock ball diamond was no sanctuary. Walking into the stadium, Jenkins had to pass under signs that read, "No Black ball players on the team." He had to use separate washrooms, and drink from Black-only water fountains. But when the game started, he was expected to strike out his opponents.

In 1964, the same year the Civil Rights Act was passed, and a year after Martin Luther King stood on the steps of the Lincoln Memorial in Washington and proclaimed, "I have a dream," Fergie Jenkins still stepped onto the field to a chorus of boos and slurs.

With her vision gone, Delores never got to see Fergie pitch. She would attend his games, as she loved sitting outside, and when articles highlighting his success made their way into the town newspaper, Klaasseina and others would read them aloud. After Fergie made it to the Majors, his mother would sit in their kitchen, listening to his games on an old transistor radio her husband had bought her.

In the years that followed that puck drop in Blenheim, Klaassiena Binga would take on an even larger role, staying by Delores' side as she battled stomach cancer, a fight that would end only two years after that faceoff, when Delores was fifty-four.

1967 was Fergie's first twenty-win season in the Majors, a performance that landed him a spot in the All-Star game. He had escaped the Jim Crow racism of the minor leagues, and today, Fergie was a hero. His hometown decided to throw him a parade.

Sitting at his desk in Cleveland, Tennessee, Drew Robinson remembers that day. Growing up in Chatham, Robinson had played any sport he could. With five kids in the house, no one had good equipment, except when it came to baseball. As soon as Fergie Jenkins signed with the Chicago Cubs, he started sending his old spikes, along with gloves and bats, to kids in the neighbourhood, including the Robinsons. Fergie's father and Drew's father were friends, and the younger Jenkins had been taught to take care of those around him. Robinson quite literally grew up playing in Fergie shoes.

Later, after finishing law school in Tennessee, Robinson would take in an occasional Chattanooga Lookouts game. On the walls of Engel Stadium, Fergie's photo was prominently displayed, no longer a second-class citizen.

Robinson was there on Fergie Jenkins Day. So was a teenage Gerry Binga, a star athlete still trying to be like Fergie Jenkins. Like many in Chatham's Black community, he crossed the tracks to honour his sporting hero with some anxiety. "I remember when we used to go uptown here, my mother took me into the Sunshine Restaurant," recalls Binga. "We sat there an hour and they wouldn't serve us before they finally came over and said to my mom that they couldn't serve her because I was there. She blew up. I didn't understand what she said because she spoke Dutch."

Ferguson Jenkins Sr. had worked as a chef at the William Pitt Hotel in downtown Chatham. The finest establishment in town, the hotel employed dozens of Black residents, who served as elevator operators, bellhops, dishwashers, shoe-shiners, cleaners, labourers, and cooks. Fergie prepared each dish with pride, even though the William Pitt, like almost every other restaurant in town, was segregated.

Although precedent had been set in 1956 by Hugh Burnett in Dresden, instances of discrimination still occurred. The William Pitt Hotel was not integrated until 1963, after a local Black man, Alvin Ladd, complained that he and five friends had entered the Esquire room in the William Pitt and were told, "It is not the hotel's policy to serve Negroes."[1] The last segregated school in Ontario, located only a few kilometers outside Chatham in the town of Merlin, was not closed until 1965.

On a fall day in 1967, Fergie Jenkins was driven down King Street along the same route his father had travelled as a member of the Chatham Coloured All-Stars thirty-three years before. Children held signs cut into the shape of baseballs, each with the score of one of Fergie's twenty wins. People hung out windows to catch a glimpse of Fergie; adoring fans waved as the North Buxton marching band passed. As they passed 6th Street, the William Pitt Hotel loomed. It was the same, and it was different—if he had wished, Fergie could have stopped the parade, walked in and ordered a meal. After all, it was Fergie Jenkins Day.

Sitting beside Fergie on the parade route that day was his first wife, Kathy Williams. The pair married in 1965 and had three daughters—Kelly, Delores, and Kimberly—before divorcing in 1987, four years after his Major League career ended.

The next year, Jenkins married Maryanne Miller and bought a 160-acre ranch in Oklahoma. In December 1990, Maryanne was in a serious car accident, suffering a broken neck, a punctured lung, and several other injuries. A month into her hospitalization, Fergie received the call they'd both been waiting for. After being passed over twice, he was to be inducted into the Baseball Hall of Fame. Maryanne and Fergie had dreamed of this day, and when he told her, reading her clippings from New York and Chicago newspapers, she smiled, unable to speak, her face filled with pride. She died four days later. In a February 17, 1991 interview with *The Baltimore Sun*, Jenkins said, "My mother always wanted me to excel. Maryanne wanted me in the Hall of Fame. I'm going to be happy because my dad will be there with me, and my mother and Maryanne will be there spiritually."

At his Hall of Fame induction, Fergie Jenkins spoke of loss. The loss of his mother, who died of cancer when Fergie was only twenty-six years old. The loss of his wife Maryanne. The loss of his friend Tony Lucadello, the scout who had signed him to a professional contract, who had taken his own life two years prior. He also spoke of triumph. His daughters were there, as was his father, a member of the Chatham Coloured All-Stars who had been denied access to baseball's professional levels by the colour of his skin.

"He didn't make the major leagues because he was limited by history," Jenkins said in his induction speech. "But he has outlived that history. I always told him that anything I do in baseball, I do for the two of us, and so now I feel I'm being inducted into the Hall of Fame with my father."[2]

Jenkins was the first Canadian inducted to the Major League Baseball Hall of Fame. His likeness has appeared on a Canadian postage stamp and he is a member of the Order of Canada. Outside Wrigley Field in Chicago, there is a statue in his honour. In a life filled with both triumph and tragedy, he was also the Canadian Press athlete of the year four times and won the Lou Marsh Award in 1974.

The Lou Marsh Award has recognized Canada's top athlete since 1936, but the honour is tainted by the racist views of its namesake, a sport journalist who wrote for *The Toronto Star* for forty-three years. Janice Forsyth, Western University's Director of Indigenous Studies, was tasked with conducting a review of Marsh's legacy for award organizers in 2021. Her conclusion was that Marsh "spent his career energizing racist sports journalism."[3] In the years leading up to World War II, Marsh described the Nazi treatment of the Jewish people as "an internal German matter," and maintained that the mistreatment of Jewish people was "overblown." His descriptions of Black, Indigenous, and other athletes of colour are littered with similar slurs and stereotypes. Forsyth believes that "his journalistic style no doubt influenced generations of readers and reporters, which helped to normalize practices we see in sport today."[4]

More than fifty years after Chatham decided that a Black man would be the face of the community, I sat in the dark, holding a cup of coffee, watching my television screen fill with the flash of fireworks over the Olympic Stadium in Tokyo. A new generation of athletic stars was being paraded into the stadium for the opening ceremonies of the 2020 Tokyo Olympics.

A wave of Canadians wearing white pants and red jackets with "Canada" stretching down the right sleeve entered the stadium. In the midst of a global pandemic, all were wearing masks. Leading the parade of athletes was Nathan Hirayama, a Japanese Canadian rugby player, and Miranda Ayim, a bi-racial basketball player.

Ayim, whose father is Black, was born and raised in Chatham, moving to London during high school. She was born the same year Fergie Jenkins married Maryanne Miller. Ayim earned an NCAA scholarship to play for California's Pepperdine University and then played in the Women's National Basketball Association and several international leagues. She had been representing Canada on basketball courts around the world since 2006.

Now the thirty-three-year-old Ayim was representing her nation and women of colour, who perhaps had not seen prominence of this magnitude. "It's important for young women and men to see someone who looks like them perform and succeed at a high level. It challenges preconceived limitations and societal norms," Ayim told me. "If you don't see it, you often don't imagine it as a possibility. And if other people don't see you there, they assume you can't. It's a vicious cycle."

Media coverage of Ayim's selection marked a long-overdue change in sports journalism, and a departure from the racist depictions of writers like Lou Marsh. I was watching, as were thousands across Canada, as Miranda Ayim broke the cycle. I couldn't help but think of Fergie Jenkins, and his parade, of Ferguson Sr. and Delores Jenkins, and what they had experienced, to arrive at the possibility of Ayim's moment at the head of the parade.

# Chapter 17

# NOT YOUR MASCOT

On my first day of kindergarten, I waited by the window until I could see the lights of the school bus barreling down our gravel road. Then I grabbed my green frog backpack, ran outside and stepped onto the bus. Two stops later another boy, a few years older than me, got on with his sister. His name was Shaun. I would get to know him well riding that bus and later, in high school, we spent a season on the same junior hockey team. Shaun loved hockey, but he could kick a football farther than anyone our little town of Wallaceburg had ever seen. In his senior year, playing for the county football championship, he kicked two field goals on a rain-soaked and muddy field, both from beyond fifty yards, to score the only points of the game. A few years later, while I was in university, I watched him kick his first field goal for the Dallas Cowboys.

In total, Shaun Suisham spent ten seasons as a kicker in the NFL. I still see his autographed photos in local restaurants and there is a display in the local museum. Seeing this memorabilia evokes mixed emotions. While I am proud of the player, the kid I'd grown up with who made his career in professional sport, I am disturbed by some of the images because, in addition to the Dallas Cowboys and the Pittsburgh Steelers, Shaun Suisham played for the Washington Redskins.

Responding to public pressure and disgruntled sponsors, Washington dropped their team name in 2020, the same year the Edmonton Eskimos began their transformation to the Edmonton Elks. But other North American sports teams still cling to names based on racist stereotypes: football has the Kansas City Chiefs while baseball has the Atlanta Braves, and the Chicago Blackhawks are members of the National Hockey League.

All of these teams, and countless others at the amateur and semi-professional level, appropriated Indigenous culture and symbols to identify their sports as uniquely North American, a tendency that is not confined to sport. While football is considered an American invention, many of the modern-day rules were developed in Canada, and the Lenape game of *Pahsahëman* may have combined with soccer and rugby to influence this evolution.

The first recorded game of American football, which still bore a strong resemblance to soccer, took place between Rutgers and Princeton universities in 1869. By the time Harvard played McGill in 1874, the game featured an elliptical ball instead of a round one and included the forward pass and tackling. Five years later, Yale player Walter Camp solidified new rules, earning him recognition as the "Father of American Football."

Football was emerging just as teams and leagues were proliferating in other sports, many of them with names derived from Indigenous culture or images. In Chatham-Kent and surrounding communities, this manifested in names such as the Petrolia Redmen, Leamington Indians and Blenheim Braves. By far the most popular reference, however, was to Chief Tecumseh.

Tecumseh was a Shawnee chief who resisted American expansion into Indigenous lands, a cause that had claimed his father and brother. A noted orator, Tecumseh travelled through the United States and Canada promoting traditional Indigenous culture and calling upon Indigenous peoples to reject European influence. During the War of 1812, Tecumseh aided the British in capturing Detroit, only to be killed during the subsequent Battle of the Thames near the Lenape settlement of Eelünaapéewi Lahkéewiit, Delaware Nation, that became known as Moraviantown.

A monument to Tecumseh stands near the site of his death

outside Chatham and his bones rest in the Highbanks Cemetery on Walpole Island. By 1922, the earliest documented Eelünaapéewi Lahkéewiit baseball team proudly called itself the Moraviantown Tecumseh.

But Tecumseh's legacy was more often erased by overwhelmingly white teams who appropriated his name even as they ignored his message. One of the earliest examples was the London Tecumsehs, a professional baseball team founded in 1875 that became Canadian champions in 1876 and International Association champions in 1877, defeating the Chicago White Stockings for the title. The team played out of Tecumseh Park in London, which still stands as the oldest continually operating baseball grounds in the world, now known as Labatt Memorial Park. In the 1930s, the London Tecumsehs were reborn as a semi-professional hockey team playing in the International Hockey League.

In Chatham, the Barracks Grounds, where Chief Tecumseh fought a skirmish to delay the advance of American forces in early 1813, were renamed Tecumseh Park in 1880, part of the transition from military use to a baseball and cricket facility. By the 1890s, a semi-professional lacrosse team, the Chatham Tecumsehs, played at Tecumseh Park. Further afield, the Tecumseh Lacrosse Club was founded in Toronto in 1910 and, in 1911, a professional hockey team known as the Toronto Tecumsehs played in the National Hockey Association, a direct predecessor of the NHL.

Chief Tecumseh was not the only Indigenous leader of the War of 1812 to have his legacy appropriated. The name of Sauk leader Black Hawk, who fought alongside Tecumseh at the Battle of the Thames in what is now Chatham-Kent, has been utilized by the NHL's Chicago Blackhawks and NBA's Atlanta Hawks. In Chatham-Kent, the Tilbury Hawks played from 1993 to 1995 until the team was disbanded after a case of criminal hazing.

The Tilbury Hawks' logo was a caricature of Black Hawk, modelled after the version still used by Chicago's hockey team. Similarly, the Tecumseh Soccer Club still uses a depiction of Chief Tecumseh as their logo. The team is based in Tecumseh, Ontario, a town founded by French settlers but named after an Indigenous resister.

The use of Indigenous images as logos went hand-in-hand with the naming of teams and reflected a more general trend toward mascots, which began appearing in North American sport in the 1880s. Derived from the French *mascotte*, or good luck charm, the first mascots were either children or pets who evoked feelings of paternalism in players and fans alike. The same complacent sense of superiority allowed teams to co-opt First Nations' culture under the guise of "honouring" Indigenous people. In reality, as McLean, Wilson and Lee point out in *The Whiteness of Redmen: Indigenous Mascots, Social media and an Antiracist Intervention*, this practice upholds "stock tropes of Indigeneity and masculinity that freeze Indigenous people in the colonial era."[1]

They go on to say: "The ongoing racialisation and dehumanisation of Indigenous peoples through texts such as mascots is necessary for normalising white supremacy. White settlers come to rely on Indigenous mascots as a way to both understand themselves as superior and regulate representations of Indigeneity. In this way, white settlers maintain control over representations of Indigeneity as a technique for continuous self-constitution."

Researchers Gammage and Hanna have called the use of Indigenous people as mascots an "epidemic" in regions of North America, particularly on the traditional lands of the Lenape people. As recently as 2020, they found more than sixty schools in Pennsylvania still using Indigenous-themed mascots and names including Red Raiders, Little Indians, Big Reds, Indians and Redskins.[2] At the professional level, Major League Baseball Commissioner Rob Manfred continues to defend both the Atlanta Braves and the "tomahawk chop."

Such steadfast commitment to team symbols has proven to be more difficult to overcome than more tangible racial barriers. All

professional sports leagues have long been integrated, at least officially, and people of colour are slowly making inroads in the ranks
of managers and coaches. The same season Shaun Suisham joined
the Washington Redskins, Tony Dungy, whose grandmother was
born and raised in Chatham-Kent and met his grandfather in
Dresden, became the first Black coach in NFL history to win a
Superbowl title.

The move away from racist depictions in sport is happening
primarily on a grassroots, case-by-case level. In 1995, the Chatham
MicMacs stopped using the Blackhawks logo and reverted to their
earlier name, the Chatham Maroons. In 2016, the Alvinston Indians
baseball organization, located less than twenty minutes north of
Chatham-Kent, decided to change their name and logo, which
mimicked that of the Cleveland Indians. On November 1, 2016,
*The National Post* quoted a twelve-year-old player in the Alvinston
organization. "It's disrespectful to First Nations people," he said.
"And if the pros won't do it, we'll lead the way."

When the chief and council of Delaware Nation at
Moraviantown heard the news of Alvinston's change, they sent
money to the organization to help offset the expense of new jerseys
and signs. Denise Stonefish, a former fastball player and future
chief, supported the organization's decision saying, "We're not
caricatures."

In 2019, Maine became the first jurisdiction in North America
to officially ban the use of Indigenous nicknames and mascots in
schools. State of Maine Governor Janet T. Mills passed LD 944
into law with a unanimous vote. State records confirm widespread
consensus: "While Indian mascots were often originally chosen
to recognize and honor a school's unique connection to Native
American communities in Maine, we have heard clearly and unequivocally from Maine tribes that they are a source of pain and anguish.
A mascot is a symbol of pride, but it is not the source of pride.
Our people, communities, and understanding and respect for one

another are Maine's source of pride and it is time our symbols reflect that," Governor Mills said in a statement at the time.[3]

Representative Benjamin Collings stated, "they are people, not mascots," a sentiment echoed by James Francis, Penobscot Nation's tribal historian. "The argument has always been that 'we are honoring you.' By passing this legislation the State of Maine is truly honoring Native Americans."[4]

"None of us are mascots anymore," said University of Maine Chair of Native American Programs, Darren Ranco. "Overwhelming research shows how harmful Native mascots are to children, especially to Native children, and LD 944 ensures that our children will not be harmed by the kind of disrespectful representations of Native people that always come with these mascots." [5]

The subsequent changes made by professional teams in Cleveland, Washington, and Edmonton have increased pressure on the holdouts in Atlanta, Kansas City, Chicago, and elsewhere, but residual harm remains. In 2014, I paid my first adult visit to William Allman Arena in Stratford, Ontario, as the coach of a minor hockey team. Built in 1924, the arena is a postcard to the past—a six-year-old Wayne Gretzky scored his first goal here and this is where future NHL All-Stars Chris Pronger and Rob Blake got their junior hockey starts. With time to kill before the game, I examined the trophy cases, looking at mementos from so many championship teams and future professional hockey players. I moved steadily through the exhibit until I came to the red and blue cover of a Stratford Cullitons game night program from the 1982–83 season.

Inside a blue and white outline of an Indigenous person in a headdress that matched their long-used logo was a cartoon of another Indigenous man with a bulbous nose and buck teeth. He had a ponytail with a feather sticking up from a headband, skates on his feet and a jersey that read "Stratford Cullitons." In one hand, he held a tomahawk; in the other he carried scalps emblazoned with the names of other junior hockey cities in the league.

When I got home that night, I emailed the City of Stratford. "It was great to visit historic Allman Arena, but I was incredibly disappointed to see such a racist display in the trophy case at the arena." I requested they work to remove any such display.

The mayor's administrative assistant replied, confirming a note had been sent to the Stratford junior hockey club, and that the program would be removed. When I returned to Allman Arena two years later, I found myself standing in front of the same trophy case. And there, staring back at me, was the same racist program. Nostalgia had apparently trumped empathy—and humanity.

## Chapter 18

# MAKING IT WORK

Pat Cosby walks from shelf to shelf until he finds the album he was looking for. He pulls down a neatly tied stack of pages, some photos now missing, their places marked with names. Dozens of photos remain glued to thick black construction paper, pictures of Pat's mother, Toky Sugiyama, as a smiling teenager, posing with her friends and siblings against a wooden fence, mountains in the background. Other photos are signed by her friends: a young girl on a bicycle, a handsome boy sitting on some steps with a guitar in his hands, a group of girls lying in the grass. They could be confused with photos of a typical childhood, except that the angles hide the shacks and fences that defined the Tashme internment camp in British Columbia's Fraser Valley.

Pat pushes the stack of photos across the table. "These are yours. Take them with you."

I didn't know what to say. It felt wrong. "Are you sure? These photos are beautiful," I said, hoping he would change his mind.

Pat had no children, a fact he called his greatest regret. "When I die, they'll go in the garbage. Maybe you can find someone who will want these. Maybe someone will find them interesting or important."

Pat and I live only a few hundred meters from each other. His family used to live across the street from my house; he shows me photos of what it looked like sixty years ago. I open the door and step out onto his porch, into the heat. Over my shoulder hangs my bag, heavier now, carrying photos of Toky and her friends. The weight of the past presses into my shoulder.

Sitting in a restaurant in Cedar Springs, surrounded by fruit orchards a mile from Lake Erie, Joe Izumi and his four children were ready for lunch. As was the case most weekends, they were greeted with a smile from their server, Toky Cosby. Sodas were ordered and hot beef sandwiches, with the promise of ice cream later.

Cedar Springs was home to a pocket of Japanese descendants who had either stayed in the area after their internment or arrived after the war. The Sugiyamas were in the latter category. Toky and her family were settled in Chatham-Kent by a local church and looked after by nuns. She was given a job blocking beets and picking peaches and apples at local orchards.

When Toky married a white Irishman named Richard Cosby, their union, unlike other interracial marriages of the time, was welcomed by both families with open arms. The couple moved to the village of Cedar Springs and raised three sons, who they would enrol in hockey and a local marching band, where they learned the bagpipes.

Joe Izumi, on the other hand, had been interned in Chatham-Kent and moved to Toronto after the war. His marriage to Margaret, an eighteen-year-old white woman from a well-to-do English family, was not well received. Riding the subway, the couple would hold hands, inviting taunts. "What are you doing with that Jap?" white men would yell.

Joe worked as a chef at the Royal York Hotel. He built elaborate ice and butter sculptures that were displayed in the Queen's Ballroom where the upper echelons of Toronto society danced and drank. In the kitchen, Izumi shook hands with Sammy Davis Jr., Frank Sinatra, and Dean Martin. He knew their favourite dishes by heart.

The couple soon had two children, Wayne and Lynn, but Joe couldn't see his family staying in the city. The walls were too close, the ceilings too low. He wanted to approximate the life that had been taken from him in Chemainus and Cowichan Bay. Joe convinced Margaret to move the family to a small house just outside Blenheim where his children would have open space to play and an opportunity to fish.

Before moving his family to Chatham-Kent however, Joe travelled to the community in search of work. "He went to the unemployment office, and the guy there said there's no jobs here, go back to Toronto," Joe's daughter Georgina recalls. "So my dad went out and immediately found three jobs as a cook. He comes back to the unemployment office and tells the guy, 'I don't need your help anymore, I just found three jobs: one at the William Pitt, one at a restaurant, and one is at St. Joseph's Hospital, but it's taken, because I start on Monday.' And the guy just sat there with his mouth open. He did encounter racism, but he turned it around, that was the way our father handled it."

Georgina was born soon after the family arrived. She was followed by their youngest child, Bob. A year and a half later, Margaret decided she was going to return to Toronto. Joe didn't argue, but he told her that he would be keeping the kids.

Now a single father of four, Joe Izumi had to work even harder. He took side jobs picking strawberries and tomatoes, working the tobacco fields and slinging beers at the Cadillac Hotel in Blenheim until 1:00 a.m. for minimum wage and penny tips, sneaking home in the middle of the night to steal a few hours of sleep before he woke at 5:00 a.m. for his primary job as head chef of St. Joseph's Hospital in Chatham.

At St. Joseph's, Izumi would sneak steaks and special dinners to patients to lift their spirits. He would also cook for the many events put on by the priests and nuns, including Joe's closest friend, Sister Mary James who, in another life, might have been more to Joe. If he had a moment, he might stop by the kitchen of the William Pitt Hotel to talk baseball with his friend, Ferguson Jenkins Sr.

At home, six-year-old Lynn was cooking for her siblings. After school, she would watch over the youngest, potty training and caring for Bob. While Joe was at work and the older kids were at school, their neighbour, Mary McTavish, would watch Bob, a generous gesture that was especially noteworthy given the times.

There were other acts of kindness as well. Walking to school on her first day at Ransom, a tiny one-room schoolhouse, Lynn was crying. As they approached the school, completing their three-kilometer walk, Joe looked at his daughter, tears falling onto her dress, soaking through to the crinoline beneath, and said, "You know you just have to do this. You have to make this work."

Standing at the end of the school lane was a white girl who approached and took Lynn's hand. Lynn stopped crying immediately and walked down the lane hand-in-hand with her new friend.

Bob wasn't so lucky. "I experienced a lot of prejudice growing up and for years after. It kind of knocks you back. It really knocks you back because you always wonder, well, am I not as good as everyone or what? In hindsight, a lot of people that were prejudiced, they only knew what they knew. My grandparents in some cases had probably been in Canada longer than their families or relatives. Prejudice was pretty normal. It wasn't one specific incident, it was hundreds. I'd be called 'Jap', or 'fucking Jap' so often."

As a teenager, Bob met a girl who he hoped to date, but her father, a prominent community member, told her that it would be better if Bob met a nice Japanese girl to marry. Bob couldn't understand. His family were the only Nikkei in town, and people made sure he knew it. "Her father didn't think he was being prejudiced. In his mind, he believed that's the way it should be. When I look back, that's almost Ku Klux Klan-like. It's like, stay with your own kind."

When Joe wasn't working, he was with his children, getting them involved in sports. During his years in Toronto, he played baseball with the Nisei League, a recreational Japanese Canadian team based in Christie Pits Park, a hub for Japanese Canadians in the late 1940s. He also became a star of the Toronto Bowling League and had a chance to turn professional, after his five-pin team won the Toronto League title in the early 1950s. By this point, however, Joe's family came first.

Once settled in Chatham-Kent, Joe became Blenheim's first bowling coach, and coached his daughter Lynn and her teammates to an Ontario championship in 1967. He also coached her softball team, and Wayne's baseball team and, on weekends, would load his four children and their friends into his Volkswagen Beetle to go fishing. With nine people in the car and rims almost scraping the road, Joe would drive to Rondeau Bay, Erieau, or the Thames River, where the kids would laugh, play, and compete to see who could catch the most fish. For the Izumi family, it was cheap entertainment.

Each year, Joe would enter his children into the Rondeau Rod and Gun Club Derby, which they'd almost always win. Wayne, Lynn, Georgina, and Bob took turns taking home top prize in their divisions. The kids would fish all day for sunfish and perch, and then they'd swim off the docks while the weights and winners were being calculated. Soon, one or more of the Izumi kids would be called up to accept their prize.

In 1975, Joe decided to start his own event, founding the Rondeau Bay Bass Fishing tournament, the first bass fishing tournament in Canada. Lynn would help her father set the anglers off in the morning, and then the two would eat eggs, bacon, home fries, and toast at a nearby diner before returning for the weigh-in. The first year of the tournament, it hailed so badly that Bob and his partner had to temporarily abandon their boat and hide beneath a picnic table on shore.

Bob was busy with his job working for the Ministry of Natural Resources, maintaining the same spaces in Rondeau Provincial Park that his father had worked to construct while interned during World War II. He cut the grass along the roads his father helped build, spread mulch on trails, chopped wood, and—his favourite job— netted fish for display in the park's museum. "For me at the time, it was absolutely a dream job," Bob recalls but, as seasonal work, it could not be his career.

At nineteen, Bob still didn't know where he was headed in life so he went to work at the International Harvester factory in Chatham building transport trucks. When he was laid off by the company, Bob made a decision that changed his life forever. Through his many fishing connections developed through his dad and the Rondeau Bass Fishing tournament, Bob heard that Mercury Marine Canada was looking for someone to do fishing seminars at the Toronto International Boat Show. They'd tried to get noted American television and radio fishing personality Al Lindner, but he was already booked. So Bob and his father drove to Mississauga to pitch his services to Mercury. Bob was hired to do ten days of seminars, earning $25 a day. Here, he created the connections and gained the sponsors that would help him launch his career.

Around the same time, 1977, Bob and his childhood friend George McTavish bought their first bass boat together and won his father's Rondeau Bay tournament. A few months later, Bob and George found themselves sitting in their boat, fishing off Long Point in Lake Erie with Fergie Jenkins. Even though their fathers were friends, the two had not grown up together.

"When I met Fergie for the first time, the thing I noticed first was how tall he was compared to me. I mean I was five-seven and he was six-five. Here's this tall, wiry guy, he was just so nice and gracious," Bob remembers of their day on the lake. "Fergie was a good bass fisherman. He was very good, his hand-eye was good, his baseball talent helped him to be a great caster. He was a good angler." At his farm outside of Blenheim, Fergie, his father and daughters, would often fish at a pond on their property, which Fergie had stocked with fish.

In the late 1970s and early 1980s, Bob continued tournament fishing and speaking at seminars across Canada. In a 1981 *Maclean's* article, the magazine called Bob "Canada's first professional sports fisherman."[1] He wasn't getting rich, but he was doing what he loved. "I didn't starve to death, but I certainly didn't make a lot of money during those years. I made enough to get by."

At a family picnic, Izumi met Bob McGuigan, Lynn's husband's uncle, who owned Memory Bank Advertising. By the end of the day, Bob and Bob had decided to shoot a pilot episode for what would become *Bob Izumi's Real Fishing Show*. In 1983, McGuigan pitched the show to twelve television networks across Ontario; all twelve, plus a thirteenth, signed on to air *Real Fishing*.

"The next year it went across Canada, and subsequently into the States, and a few other countries like France and China," Izumi explains. Locally, his fame skyrocketed in the late 1980s when CBC Windsor decided to run the show in primetime on Saturdays, immediately preceding *Hockey Night in Canada*.

"I asked the program director why he did that, and he said, 'Well, we have *Hockey Night in Canada* that comes on, and *Don Cherry's Grapevine*, and we were competing against the big three networks in Detroit, and we just wanted something different to put in there.'" At the time, television was antenna-based; there were no digital networks, no cable or satellite networks and Bob Izumi had a captive audience. "In those days I'd cross the border and the border agents would recognize me, and I'd go into a K-Mart and people would recognize me."

As Ron MacLean, host of *Hockey Night in Canada's Coach's Corner* recalled in an interview with the *Globe and Mail* , Izumi wasn't just competing with Canada's quintessential broadcast, at times, he was beating it. "We once were nominated for a Gemini and lost to Bob Izumi's fishing show. And that was the end of Don [Cherry] allowing his name to be put up for awards."[2]

Izumi's newfound fame was an insulator against the racism he faced as a youth. "Very rarely did I see it once I got involved in the media. It was almost like it puts you on some kind of weird pedestal where all of a sudden you don't see it or hear it or it isn't as prevalent. That could have been the changing of the guard or the changing of the times, where the prejudice started to wane."

Shortly after the show launched, Izumi's brother Wayne joined the production. According to Bob, it was Wayne, working behind the scenes, who was often the innovator of what audiences were learning. "Wayne was, after my dad, who was the initiator, Wayne was definitely the one who influenced me the most on bass fishing techniques. Wayne was always reading. He's well read, he absorbs it, and he was always very in tune with the latest fishing techniques. Him being nine years older than me, he was very much an influence on how I got hooked on fishing as I got older. He was always the innovator in trying new techniques."

Soon, *Bob Izumi's Real Fishing Show* added a magazine and a nationally syndicated radio show. When it ceased filming at the end of 2021, it was the end of an era. One of the longest running syndicated television shows in Canadian broadcast history, it was on the air for thirty-eight years.

The end of *Bob Izumi's Real Fishing Show* is also a beginning, as Bob won't sit still for long. "I like doing multiple things, and I think that came from Dad. He didn't have a lot of idle time, and I find idle time boring. It must be from him, he was go go go. He had this saying, it was 'give it with all the gusto.' Even though it is kind of old-fashioned, that's kind of how I live my life, I love going hard and giving it with all the gusto. I'm going to work and fish until I die."

So far, Bob has won over seventy professional bass fishing tournaments, including Joe Izumi's Rondeau Bay Tournament multiple times. He won the Canadian Open, Classic Championship, and several Angler of the Year titles. In 2019, he captained Team Canada to a gold medal at the Pan American Sportfishing Bass Championships.

Joe Izumi was a single father of four at a time men were expected to do little domestically. On weekends, when he should have been exhausted from working multiple jobs, Joe would pile a carload of children into his vehicle for a day of fishing. Bob recalls his father saying, "if it's for the kids, do it." Wayne and Bob have lived by that motto, developing the Bob Izumi's Kids and Cops Fishing Days program which introduces tens of thousands of Canadian youth to fishing each year. They've also worked to preserve ecosystems and provide outdoor education to youth through their Fishing Forever not-for-profit.

Because of people like the Izumis, competitive fishing in Canada remains relevant. In 2021, Bob welcomed his first grandchild to the world. Perhaps there will be a spot for him in the family business, without the barriers his grandpa, and great-grandpa faced.

Bob Izumi overcame poverty and racism to turn his passion into a successful media career. He made it work and so did Trevor Thompson, a Black kid from Dresden who loved sports.

Thompson's father was a long-time police officer in Dresden. Growing up in the 1970s, he worked with his uncle, DeWayne Guest, at Dresden Raceway. Guest was one of the harness racing's most successful Black drivers, his career highlighted by a second-place finish in Macau at the 1983 World Driving Championships. When he wasn't in the stables, Thompson was working outside the gates, parking cars for track-goers. Like most kids in Dresden, he grew up playing hockey and baseball and visiting the raceway.

After college, Thompson worked as a social worker, then selling insurance. "I was making a bunch of money and was never more miserable," he recalls. Then he saw a Black sportscaster on television. Fred Hickman worked for Turner Broadcasting System (TBS) as a co-anchor for CNN/Sports Illustrated, on NFL and NBA pre-game shows and co-hosting at the Lillehammer and Albertville Olympic Games.

"I saw him and thought, that guy is sitting in my chair. If I can do anything, I want to do that." Thompson decided to pursue a career in sports broadcasting and called Scott North, another

Dresden man who was working for the Hockey Hall of Fame as the keeper of the Stanley Cup. North set up a lunch meeting between Thompson and *Hockey Night in Canada* host Ron MacLean. The meeting went well.

"Ron said, 'When you get to Toronto, give me a call.' So when I got to Toronto, I called Ron, and he said, 'Come on down to Maple Leaf Gardens on Saturday and we'll have a job for you as a runner.' So I got a job with *Hockey Night in Canada* working with Ron and Don. From there I took some courses at Ryerson and got a job behind the scenes at TSN."

Thompson was working with one of sports most controversial personas, hearing Don Cherry pontificate on a nightly basis. "He absolutely is 100% the same on the camera as he is off," Thompson said of Cherry. "He's just as obnoxious and bombastic as he is on the air."

Growing up Black in Dresden and playing hockey and baseball in Southwestern Ontario, Thompson was prepared for a hostile environment. "The kids were fine, but when you'd go to Wallaceburg, Petrolia, Sarnia, the racism was next level and really in your face. My parents had to really explain it to me because I would fight. They would explain to me you can't fight every time something like this happens, because you'll be fighting every day of your life. You have to learn to play through it, roll with it, and understand it's their problem not yours. There's nothing wrong with you, it's their issue. So I just looked at it that way, accepted it for what it was, and learned to rise above it. But absolutely racism was there. On the field of play, and in the community, and in other communities around, it was definitely a thing."

Thompson rolled with it until his effusive personality and booming voice earned him an opportunity as the sideline reporter for the NBA's newest franchise, the Vancouver Grizzlies. When the airline lost his luggage, Thompson arrived at the interview in cut-off shorts and flip-flops, and still got the job.

The Grizzlies, however, were short-lived, and Thompson jumped at an opportunity to work closer to home for Fox Sports in Detroit. Since then, he's stood on the field at Comerica Park covering the Detroit Tigers, he's interviewed Michael Jordan and Jack Nicklaus, and he's been on the ice and court for three Detroit championships: one with the NBA's Detroit Pistons and two with the Detroit Red Wings.

He considers the Red Wings' 2002 Stanley Cup win the highlight of his career. "I was hosting intermissions and post games. It was surreal: it was the biggest stage I'd been on, being in the winning dressing room, being part of the champagne celebrations. I couldn't believe that that's where I found myself at that point."

Thompson has accumulated four Emmy Awards for his sportscasting in Detroit, his first coming in 2007 for his work hosting *Red Wings Weekly*.

Behind the scenes, Thompson continued playing men's hockey, and returns to Dresden regularly. In the sports world, including the business of sport, he sees change, but not enough.

"I don't really know if you can change it, I think the more things change—interracial marriages, immigration—the more you get to see not just Black or white, but people from other countries, other religions and nationalities, people start to look different. Things change naturally as populations change, but changing people's attitudes, as long as people are passing this down to their kids, and racism is going to be tolerated in certain circles, I don't know if it's ever going to change.

"If you're going to be raised that way and it's accepted in your household, or taught in your household, then you're going to continue to pass it down. The more communities change and people start to move in, and people's faces start to change, that might be the only way. Other than that, unless people's hearts start to change, I don't know if it will ever stop."

Racism is generational and it's ingrained. Still, his presence in sport, like that of broadcaster Fred Hickman, is an invitation for more Black sportscasters in the future.

Lynn Izumi made a promise to her father. They would return to Chemainus and Cowichan Bay, to finally revisit where he'd grown up. It was a pilgrimage her sister, Georgina, had made with their father years before. Lynn thought there was time. She'd become a doctor and was just establishing her practice when Joe Izumi died of a heart attack.

With her father gone, Lynn went alone. She found Cowichan Bay without a map, following the stories her father had told her. In Chemainus, Lynn walked down the streets admiring the murals painted on businesses and buildings in the town. She stood in front of a painting of the annual parade in Chemainus. The image depicted a float filled with Japanese Canadians. On the float, painted larger than life, were two of her aunts, dressed in kimonos.

Just outside the town, Lynn walked through the Japanese Canadian cemetery. During the war, the graves were toppled and desecrated. The Izumi family had been in Canada since 1899, but they had still been seen as enemy aliens. Now a large monument stands to remember these people, including Joe Izumi's mother. Lynn hopes this stone is too large to topple.

Pat Cosby also travelled to British Columbia. He flew to Vancouver with an uncle and two cousins who had settled in Toronto after the war. They rented a car and drove along the Fraser River, through Surrey and Abbotsford, through Chilliwack to Hope, tucked beneath the Cascade Mountains climbing 8,000 feet into the sky. From Hope, they turned southeast and travelled along the Crowsnest Highway until they reached Sunshine Valley, where Tashme was located.

Pat, his uncle, and two cousins stepped out of the car. There were no buildings on the site, which once held almost 3,000 Japanese Canadians. It was only trees and mountains now, with the odd home speckled along the road. They stood in silence, the minutes ticking by, until Pat's uncle declared it was time to leave.

In sport, time is measured by seasons: hockey season or fishing season. During his bowling days in Toronto, Joe Izumi once won a gold watch. Joe could have sold it—he needed the money. Instead, that watch marked the progress of a lifetime. After he passed away, it slipped off his son Wayne's wrist and into the calm water of Rondeau Bay. To Wayne, it was a devastating loss. By now, the hands have stopped, frozen on a single moment.

I packaged up the photos Pat Cosby had given me. Moments of another kind, also frozen. A piece of history he did not want lost when he died. After a few emails, I'd found where the photos belonged. They were to become part of the collection at the Nikkei National Museum & Cultural Centre in British Columbia. Here, others would see them, and know the history, and perhaps in time, hearts would change.

# Chapter 19

# STICKS AND STONES

The first Indigenous teammate I had was Isaiah Kicknosway. His father, Bryan Loucks, would drop him off at the arena in Chatham and, as he walked back to the lobby, I'd look at Bryan's ponytail dividing his shoulders. In my first year of junior hockey, I played with Isaiah's brother, Gabriel, as well.

In Junior, no one messed with Gabe, but that hadn't always been the case. When he was ten years old, Gabriel Kicknosway was playing in Strathroy as his grandparents and parents watched from the stands. As he exited the ice, a Strathroy fan, displeased with his dominant performance, entered the hallway and, in front of the team, physically assaulted Gabe. His assailant was charged and convicted. When the judge asked him if racism was behind his actions, he said he could not possibly be racist, as he had a Portuguese friend.

It's a common argument, but as Tyler Parry wrote in an article for the *Black Perspectives* blog, "A Brief History of the 'Black Friend,'" the claim of having racialized friends, family, or coworkers is often used as a "cover for racist statements or actions."[1] Parry references Daniel Effron's 2018 paper that stated "white people who are accused of racism overestimate how much their past decisions might 'convince an observer of their non-prejudiced character.' In other words, they have built a form of 'racial credit' through their intimate associations with a person of another race, and such interactions satisfy a personal need to call upon these credentials when contesting accusations of racism."[2]

The Kicknosways were a family of athletes. Brothers Gabe and Stacey played hockey while Jacob, and eventually Isaiah, preferred lacrosse. Each fall, Isaiah and Jacob would spend hours in their front yard on Walpole Island scooping up fallen apples with their lacrosse sticks, throwing them into the St. Clair River. Only the darkness stopped them. There weren't many kids playing lacrosse on Walpole Island in the 1990s, so the brothers crossed the bridge to join the minor lacrosse system in Wallaceburg.

Wallaceburg's lacrosse program, which features players from Walpole Island and across Chatham-Kent, plays in the Ontario Lacrosse Association alongside teams from Six Nations of the Grand River, the only Indigenous community in North America that has people of all six Haudenosaunee nations living together. Many Wallaceburg players have competed with and against Six Nations athletes at the junior and senior levels, while many Six Nations players have travelled the opposite direction to play with the Wallaceburg Red Devils. Jacob Kicknosway played Junior A lacrosse and won a Minto Cup as a member of Six Nations, while Isaiah played for the Wallaceburg Red Devils Junior B team and represented Team Iroquois internationally.

Another of these athletes is Marshall Powless, who hails from Six Nations. His older brother Johnny spent over a decade playing in the National Lacrosse League, winning numerous championships, and being honoured as the league's Most Sportsmanlike Player. The younger Powless, who made his National Lacrosse League debut in 2021, played Junior B lacrosse for the Wallaceburg Red Devils in 2018 and spoke out about the racism he faced there: "I experienced racism in both minor and junior levels. In minor . . . this kid came up to me and called me a wagon burner. At the time, I didn't know what that meant until I asked my mom. In Junior, I was playing against Hamilton, and this guy came up to me in between the whistles and said, 'You're nothing but a dirty native.' I replied with 'what was that?' and he said, 'you heard me.' I said, 'no I didn't' and he said, 'are you going to steal my truck after the game?' He began to go on about how we don't pay taxes and other stuff."[3]

Such incidents are not new. In the 1960s, former Ontario Lacrosse Association executive member Jim Naish recalled defamatory comments based on colour and race, and discrimination toward all-Indigenous lacrosse teams when they played in Wallaceburg. Author Allan Downey, in his 2018 book *The Creator's Game: Lacrosse, Identity, and Indigenous Nationhood*, uses Naish's recollection as one of several examples of "evidence of exclusion, racism, discrimination, and injustice" in lacrosse, and across Canada.[4]

In 2020, the Ontario Human Rights Commission announced an investigation into racism in the sport of lacrosse "in the face of troubling reports of racial slurs and mistreatment in games involving Six Nations lacrosse players."[5]

From the perspective of Six Nations of the Grand River Chief Mark Hill, the game is "a gift from the Creator. Lacrosse is the bridge that is meant to be shared with the world, in friendship, peace and unity."[6]

But the connection between lacrosse and Indigenous communities was fractured during colonization and through the residential school system. As Ontario Human Rights Commission Chief Commissioner Ena Chadha stated at the time, "Lacrosse has long been a way for Indigenous communities to connect with each other in a spirit of trust, respect, and honour, but connections with non-Indigenous communities are quickly broken and trust is destroyed when they are fraught with harassment and abuse."

Isaiah Kicknosway is a driving force behind a key initiative by Indigenous people to reclaim lacrosse. He is the founder of Anishinabe Baagaadowewin, a non-profit lacrosse organization that represents the Anishinaabe Nation. Says Kicknowsay, "I thought that there was no infrastructure for that development either on reservation or off, other than the Iroquois Nationals. I'm not Iroquois, so there was no mechanism for that development. That's the idea with Anishinaabe Baagaadowewin—to play lacrosse whether it's the wooden stick game, Anishinaabe-style, or modern-style. It brings the culture forward into present day, it's an avenue for developing cultural connection for Indigenous youth. It's a social development tool that can be used. It brings Indigenous communities together and creates a sense of pride for First Nations players."

Anishinabe Baagaadowewin, along with the Iroquois Nationals, has been recognized by lacrosse's governing bodies as a sovereign nation, and is now part of international competition. The team will compete under its own flag in international tournaments with the mission to "awaken (the spirit), educate (the people), develop (the game) and unite (the fires)."[7] The presence of two Indigenous teams competing as independent nations is a source of pride, and an important symbol of reclaimed autonomy. Through Anishinabe Baagaadowewin, Kicknosway is laying the foundation for lacrosse to again become prevalent on Walpole Island and in other Anishinaabe Nations.

Bryan Loucks told me you can see the transformative power of the game in nearby Six Nations. "They give their babies lacrosse sticks to play with and chew on. You drive around Six Nations and almost every kid is running around with a lacrosse stick in their hands. And I look forward to the same thing here, kids with a lacrosse stick and ball."

He hopes his son's program will help other Indigenous children to again feel that intrinsic bond with the game of lacrosse. "If we can get people running around and chasing a ball, and feel what it's like to fall down and get up, and then fall down and get up again, with the support and guidance and caring of uncles and aunts and family, it lifts all of us up when a kid gets up, or a team gets up."

The reclamation of lacrosse is part of a larger movement to help Indigenous communities recover from the ravages of residential schools. Isaiah's maternal grandmother, Ida Mae Blackbird, was taken to Shingwauk Residential School at age four. Both his parents, faculty members at the University of Windsor and Western University specializing in Indigenous law, value the culture that was lost. Bryan Loucks explains, "In terms of intergenerational ripples, it's very much a part of our family, not only as individuals, but as a blended family system."

Even though it was originally introduced as a tool of assimilation, hockey became a bright spot for victims of residential schools. When they returned home, the hockey, along with the trauma, came with them, supplanting earlier versions of the game. These Indigenous games were present as early as the mid-1600s, including the Mi'kmaw game called *Duwarken*, which translates to "a ball played on ice." The first record of local all-Indigenous teams playing organized hockey dates to January of 1928, when the Ojibway-Cree Barnstorming Tour stopped in Chatham-Kent and beat a local Blenheim team. Hockey existed outdoors on Walpole Island and at Delaware Nation before this, but no record of teams competing in local leagues exists from these communities.

As neither Walpole Island nor Delaware Nation at Moraviantown had arenas, most Indigenous players were dependent on neighbouring white communities, primarily Wallaceburg and Ridgetown. The name that built hockey on Walpole Island, and the leader in the development of Indigenous hockey in the area, was Cecil Jacobs. "He was a hockey guy," recalls Delaware Nation historian Darryl Stonefish. "He got his hockey from the residential school in Shingwauk, Sault Ste. Marie; it was ingrained in his mind. He even died in an arena, going to a hockey tournament in Sudbury."

In the 1950s and 60s, Cecil Jacobs was a talented defender for the Walpole Island Hawks, one of the top teams in the Wallaceburg Town Hockey League that won the league title in 1960. He was also integral to the founding the All-Indian Hockey Tournament in 1957–1958. Intended to build connections between First Nations communities in Ontario, the tournament featured men's teams from Walpole Island, Kettle Point, Cape Croker, and Sarnia. Eventually it grew to include Indigenous teams from reserves surrounding Forest, Six Nations, Muncey, Oneida, and Christian Island. In addition to hockey, the tournament featured pow-wow celebrations including a beauty pageant, drumming, and dancing.

By 1961, white players from the top hockey programs in the

region were being recruited for all-Indigenous teams. On February 20, *The Windsor Star* published an article under a headline that read "Indians May Bar Whites from Tourney." Jacobs is quoted as saying, "There has been a lot of ill feeling about whites playing. We have a rule that three whites may play for each side so long as they are amateurs and are not OHA players . . . Everyone wants to win but this is taking it a bit too far . . . Reservation representatives believe that by the time the tournament is held next year . . . whites will be barred from competition. After all it is an Indian tournament. We should make it all-Indian."[8]

By 1970, a minor hockey version, the All-Ontario Indian Hockey Tournament, was launched and included a Walpole Island team. In March of that year, the tournament was opened by longtime Toronto Maple Leafs captain and Indigenous hockey player, George Armstrong. A month later, Walpole Island hosted their first minor hockey tournament. These tournaments were precursors to the Little Native Hockey League, also known as the Little NHL, which has featured boys' and girls' teams aged five to seventeen since 1971. All players in the Little NHL are required to be Indigenous, and the tournament draws hundreds of teams, and thousands of competitors annually.

Cecil Jacobs helped build the infrastructure that allowed other Indigenous hockey players to emerge from Southwestern Ontario. In the mid-1960s, Dan Miskokoman played OCAA hockey for St. Clair College, and NCAA hockey at Western Michigan before returning to Walpole Island, where he was later elected chief. In the same era, Walpole Island's Bob Peters played five seasons of professional hockey and earned a tryout with the NHL's New York Rangers.

Just as hockey was being developed on Walpole Island, Delaware Nation at Moraviantown was claiming baseball as their own. Provincially, the All-Ontario Native Fastball Tournament began in 1971, and was won multiple times by Delaware Nation teams. A group of volunteers, including Gordon Peters and his father Omer, built the community's own diamond, the kids levelling the ground with hoes and rakes while the adults pounded nails into benches and dugouts.

In 1962, Gordon helped his Thamesville team win an Ontario Peewee title. Playing Thornhill in the finals, this was his introduction to the world outside Chatham-Kent. At a time when the Peters home still didn't have indoor plumbing, he stayed in a hotel equipped with unfamiliar amenities. He and his dad arrived in a car loaded with spare tires and extra parts and made sure to park on a hill so they would be able to get started again.

Gord played baseball at a time when students from Delaware Nation were required to attend school in Ridgetown. "Ridgetown didn't want us, but Ridgetown took us," he recalls. "They used to threaten us with going to the Mush Hole (Mohawk Institute) if we didn't smarten up and behave. Even teachers would tell us that. 'You want to go to the Mush Hole?'"

Residential schools were still in operation and the Sixties Scoop was underway, so the threat of family division was ever present. "My grandmother and my grandfather on my dad's side both went to residential school. The threat was always there, all the Indian Agent had to do was to sign a letter saying he believed the child was being neglected, and that was it, he would sign it and they would take the kid. I knew a lot of kids my age who went."

Prejudice against Indigenous students was pervasive. Wallaceburg teachers of the time described Indigenous students as "generally more unruly and don't care; marks mean nothing." Indigenous students were "slower," "can't be reasoned with," are "quick to fight," and show a "lack of interest in everything."[9]

In 1972, after complaints surfaced regarding the treatment of Walpole Island residents at the hands of Wallaceburg police, a task force, led by Dennis Latten, the senior administrator of the Ontario Police Association, investigated and found that officers within Wallaceburg's police department were holding Indigenous youth as young as ten in jails cells, unattended, for truancy. The task force also found that officers allowed a white teenager to beat up a detained Indigenous youth, then moved him to another cell to do the same to another Indigenous boy. One police officer orchestrated the attacks while five other officers stood by and watched. In Latten's final report, he stated that Wallaceburg police officers were subjecting Walpole Island residents to treatment "as no other Canadians."[10]

Things were no better in the schoolyard. "It was always Indians versus whites on the playground, always," Gord recalls. But sport could also be an equalizer. One adversary, Paul Brown, started out an enemy but "We started getting along when we played baseball together."

When the seasons changed, Gord switched to hockey, which would become his sport of choice despite significant barriers to entry, specifically travel and money. "I never had equipment, I had some old junk equipment, really thin little shin pads," he explained. "My house league team was called the Moose. I just had a sweatshirt and every Saturday my sisters would sew on the 'M' for Moose, because I didn't have a jersey. We couldn't afford a jersey."

Racial tensions appeared on the ice. "I used to play on the pond, that's where I learned how to stickhandle. We used to have our own games on the pond all the time, and it was good, amongst ourselves. But eventually people started coming to the pond. There was this one white family, they lived near us. They were a hard-working family, and they asked if they could come to the pond. So they came to the pond, and then other people started coming, and pretty soon we were back to the same thing as the playground, playing Indians against whites on the pond and we'd end up fighting. I did experience discrimination playing hockey in Ridgetown, and that's when I left."

However, there were also some signs of change. Peters recalls one particularly memorable incident. "We got to the playoffs and the coach says, 'You know we're going to do this, we're going to play our best players, everybody has got to work doubly hard.' You know, he gives the big speech. And so, I got to ride the pine, he put me on the third line. I think it was after the first game we played that the players wouldn't go out, they wouldn't play. Lo and behold, Paul Brown says, 'The players have had a meeting, and if we're going to have our best players on the ice then Gord Peters has to be on the ice too.' Here one of the young guys on the second line stood up and said, 'Gord can take my place, he's a lot better hockey player than I am.' So he gave up his spot for me. And his dad was one of the coaches. But I would have never had a chance to play in the playoffs if the guys hadn't stood up for me. I would have ridden the pine."

The same attitude was missing from the spectators. "They called me different names from the stands. We were playing in the championship against Leamington, and they used to come and bring all kinds of signs about squaws, and they would drum and holler at me, throw crap at me. Blenheim was pretty bad too."

But Peters persevered and became the star of the Dresden Jr. Kings, where he filled the nets. When he scored a hat trick, caps would fly. In fact, when the NCAA's Ohio State arrived in town to scout another player, it was Peters who stole the show and was offered a scholarship.

Things became easier after he arrived at Ohio State in 1969. The hockey team, which included Peters' enemy turned ally, Paul Brown, treated Peters as an equal. During a career that spanned four years and eighty-four career games, he amassed an impressive 148 points while earning a Bachelor of Science degree in Public Administration. Following his NCAA career, Gord Peters played professionally in the International Hockey League for the Columbus Owls, and later played senior hockey in the United States Hockey League. After his hockey career, he became a nationally recognized spokesperson and advocate for Indigenous rights.

The year after Peters graduated from Ohio State, another Indigenous player, this time from Walpole Island arrived. Cecil Jacobs, son of the legendary father of the same name, would go on to lead the school in power-play goals, scoring twenty in his first season, a mark which still stands as a school record for most goals by a defender. In 1973, the younger Cecil Jacobs became the Southern Ontario recipient of the Tom Longboat Award that honours Canada's top Indigenous athletes.

The next Walpole Island hockey star to emerge was Cecil's nephew, Ian Jacobs. His experience would be markedly different— no longer a tool of assimilation, hockey was being reclaimed by Indigenous communities as a tool of health and freedom.

In 1987, when Ian Jacobs was seven years old, Walpole Island First Nation built its own arena, part of an initiative to recreate the sense of community that had been destroyed by residential schools. Researcher Madelaine Christine Jacobs describes residential schools as "acute sites of segregation and assimilation where children were sequestered from their parents and, often, subjected to abuse that caused lasting trauma to indigenous persons, families, and communities."[11] Survivors struggled to find a sense of place and to find employment. Unemployment became rampant on Walpole Island, reaching 60% by the 1970s. Many young adults migrated across the border to Detroit where they could get a regular paycheque. Even those who did not attend residential schools themselves felt the effects. Researcher Graham Trull quotes one Anishinaabe youth: "It affected my life like the rolling snowball builds and builds. My Gram was angry, that made her treat her kids rough, that made my mom angry and treat her kids rough . . . they had no help, but they are getting better now."[12]

Ian's grandfather, Rufus Jacobs Sr., survived Shingwauk, while his grandmother had been taken to Mohawk. When they returned, they carried the trauma with them but were able to overcome their hurt to create a supportive family structure for their children and grandchildren. Says Ian, "I worked really hard to get where I am. I had a lot of adversity, there was so much that could have dragged me down, but I really had that support system. The best thing about my playing time was the amount of support I had from my family. If I didn't have that support, it would have been pretty tough."

The new arena quickly became a community hub and a source of pride. Bill Tooshkenig, chief at the time, watched local children grow up on this ice. He maintains that social issues, including suicide rates, decreased as a result. Hockey was now their game too.

Ian Jacobs was part of a new generation of youth for whom the arena was a place of joy and freedom. "It was so awesome having our own minor hockey system, there were so many advantages for us Indigenous kids just to go and enjoy the game and not worry about anything else," recalls Jacobs, who now has children and grandchildren of his own. "Once we cross that bridge, once we leave the Island, we're in a whole new world. There's been a few negative things that have happened in Wallaceburg, but I never remembered that on Walpole. We were all the same."

Times were changing, but progress was slow. "Growing up, I never saw any racism or discrimination playing on our own reserve, but then playing in Sarnia, it was different," recalls Ian Jacobs, who played AAA hockey in Sarnia. "There were three or four other guys from Walpole, so that transition wasn't as tough, but I remember a few times my dad having a heated conversation with the coaches, and you never knew why. We were always taught to respect everyone, but now that I'm an adult and have a son in sports, I kind of know what my dad was doing, and it had to be pretty tough, because I know it was tough on me, understanding what my dad was standing up to."

In 1993, the Walpole Island Hawks became the first all-Indigenous hockey team to win an Ontario Minor Hockey Association championship. Coached by Stacey Kicknosway, the team clinched the victory in front of a large crowd at the Walpole Island Sports

Complex after travelling through "every little racist town in the province."

Luckily for the boys on this team, they travelled with the entire community behind them. "Whenever the boys were playing, the whole community came out, the whole community. Young and old," recalls Stacey's father Bryan. "It was a huge social moment to visit and to yell and encourage. In a sense the whole community followed that team through its journey. Buses were rented for those of us that didn't have transportation, and fundraising left and right in order to support the boys with jackets and identification. It was the community that was part of it, all of the families were connected in some manner or another with a hockey player on the ice. Going to those small towns, in some cases we outnumbered the local teams. When there was an incident, of course it went into the crowd."

By 1998, Ian Jacobs was sitting in the stands of Buffalo's Marine Midland Arena at the NHL Entry Draft. Surrounded by his grandparents, aunts, uncles, siblings, and parents, he watched another lanky six-foot-four forward, Vincent Lecavalier, descend to the stage, where he would don a Tampa Bay Lightning jersey for the first time as the number one draft pick overall.

At the time, eighteen-year-old Jacobs had just finished his first season in the Ontario Hockey League with the Ottawa 67s. Jacobs was not naive, he knew he would not hear his name immediately. He was rated to go in the fifth round. As the fifth round came and went, Jacobs began to feel frustrated and anxious. As the sixth round and then the seventh round passed, he turned to his support system. He returned to the hotel with most of his family to get some food and allow the anxiety of the day to fade away. Within an hour of returning to the hotel, the phone rang. It was Jacobs' agent informing him he'd been drafted by the Florida Panthers, 203rd overall. "The entire hotel went crazy celebrating. It was an unbelievable experience. The best part about it was you had your family there, the people who matter most to you." Jacobs was the first resident of Walpole Island First Nation drafted by an NHL team.

The following year, Jacobs was back on the ice with the Ottawa 67s. Ottawa was hosting the Memorial Cup, and again the Jacobs family, including his grandparents, were in the stands to witness another career highlight. Jacobs had a spectacular tournament, sitting in the top ten in scoring en route to helping his team win the Memorial Cup in front of 10,525 fans at the Ottawa Civic Centre.

Jacobs remembers one particular game when his line was firing on all cylinders. He'd scored the tying goal and assisted on another. When the buzzer sounded, the three stars were announced. The first star of the game, despite Jacobs' efforts, was his linemate Joe Talbot, a centerman who went on to a solid professional career. He was also an ally, willing to recognize when something was not right.

"After the game, they came up with the three stars. My centerman, Joe Talbot, came up to me after the game and looked at me and said, 'Hey, I don't know what you'd have to do to earn this, but here you go.' They gave out these golf putters for being named first star and he gave me the putter that he'd received. I just started crying. I don't know if it was because he thought people just weren't noticing my skill level that game, or if it was because of who I was. That just hit home for me and made me look at things a little different. I was asking myself, 'Do you want to be this Native teenager?' Because I was getting treated different.

"To this day that's one of those memories that I tell people, when it comes to racism and discrimination, to have someone come up to you and do that and say that, it's just unbelievable. There are really good people out there who care and understand and recognize."

Today, Jacobs has three children of his own, and still feels the support of his family. His grandparents, who survived so much, were his biggest fans. As time passes, and Jacobs learns more, he can see the tinges of trauma in the way he was raised. And with every new discovery, and every news story about the horrors of residential school, such as the 215 unmarked graves of children discovered near Kamloops, British Columbia in 2021, Jacobs sees things more clearly.

"I've heard the odd story about this and that at residential schools, but there never really was much discussion. You knew the situation, but you never knew how bad it really was. We never really talked about it. The first time I learned about the unmarked graves and the kids, that's the day it really hit home. Just non-stop thinking about what my grandparents went through. It brings tears to my eyes. Every time we saw more news, my wife would just start crying and crying, you know, being a mother, and imagining the feeling of having her child taken. It was really difficult, even to this day, knowing you had grandparents involved in that. It's hard to wrap your head around it. On Canada Day, I called my grandma and just said, thank you, thank you for surviving, and getting yourself out of there.

"There's so much history. To be honest, I'm still learning, and it's okay to be learning, I'm trying to know a little more, to find out more. I never knew why people would treat someone like that. It just hurts. When you have kids, your first instinct is to protect. We need to find a way to get along with everyone and take care of our families. A lot of people don't want to talk about it, but I hope now they do. There's a lot of hurt. My grandmother, hopefully this helps her deal and heal for the rest of her time here, and I think that's what everybody here needs, to heal."

Of the traditional way of life, Jacobs says, "It was lost to me. I can't remember, other than going to pow-wows, I can't remember too much about the traditional ways. It's kind of sad because I don't even know half the Island, it's just not as strong as I wish it was. As far as I can remember, there weren't too many traditional talks. We did the church, Christmas times, we were believers, one hundred percent. My wife's family is Christian, we're believers, but we do understand who we are, and where we come from, and this is only going to make us stronger in a lot of ways."

Jacobs is moving forward with his family behind him, healing and intact. But he knows it will take teammates like Joe Talbot, and a lot of conversation to continue the process of truth and reconciliation.

# Chapter 20

# BACK IN THE GAME

In high school, Cheryl Tooshkenig and I were on opposite sides of the hall. I didn't know her, but I knew people like her, people from Walpole Island. At the time, I had a preconceived notion of what "people like her" meant. I avoided the hall where Indigenous students stood just as I'd been instructed by older white students during orientation. As both Cheryl and I remember, it was called "naab corner" and in our town, "naab" was a slur.

We had more in common than we knew, Cheryl and I. We played all the same sports—hockey, golf, volleyball, badminton—and we were both observers of the turmoil that went on between our classmates, between our races.

"I know for a while when I went to high school, there was a lot of fights," Tooshkenig said. "It was like, 'those Indians always stand in that corner and they're looking at me.' And then it's like, 'ah they want to fight.' There were fights, but I was mostly an observer. I would watch people, watch their actions. I don't know if that was just growing up, the good and the bad."

I don't know either. In some ways, we're all stuck between worlds. For some, it is reckoning with past wrongs, the racism of our families and communities. For others, it's between reconciliation and reclamation, and the loss of language and culture. The good and the bad. Then and now.

The Indigenous game of *Pahsahëman* was played between men and women. In *Historie of Travaile into Virginia Britannia*, William Strachey, who visited North America in the 17th century, describes an Indigenous version of football played in the traditional territory of the Lenape as early as 1610.[1] The ball, typically oblong and made of deerskin stuffed with hair, would be thrown or kicked through two trees that served as goalposts.

Writing in the 1790s, Jacob Burnet provided a more complete description: "The men played against the women; and, to countervail the superiority of their strength, it was a rule of the game that they were not to touch the ball with their hands on the penalty of forfeiting the purse. The females had the privilege of using their hands as well as their feet. They were allowed to pick up the ball and run and throw it as far as their strength and activity would permit. When one of the women or girls succeeded in getting the ball, the men were allowed to seize her, whirl her around, and, if necessary, throw her on the grass for the purpose of disengaging the ball, taking care not to touch it except with their feet. The contending parties arranged themselves in the center of the lawn; the men on one side, the women on the other. Each party faced the goal of its opponent. The side which succeeded in driving the ball through the stakes at the goal of its adversary, was proclaimed victor, and received the purse."[2]

Following the demise of Pahsahëman, Indigenous women continued to find space in sport, despite the colonizing force of residential and day schools, which sought to instill specific gender roles on youth. Up to the 1940s women and men of Walpole Island competed head-to-head racing the wild ponies, the Ojibwe spirit horses that once roamed free. Sometimes called the Little Horses of the Big Woods, these were hardy animals able to survive the harsh winters and the mud of spring. The oaks would provide shelter from the scorching summer sun and, as the ground hardened, hooves beat the soil, reverberating across the Island like drumming in celebration of the foals born each year. Over time, the stewards of this land erected corrals for these Ojibwe spirit horses, which were slightly smaller than an average horse, with furry ears and a dorsal stripe running across their withers and back, and down each leg, a distinguishing feature of the breed. When the Walpole Island Fair approached each fall, riders would walk into the fields among the horses and choose one to be their partner in the annual pony races. The Ojibwe spirit horses were beautiful as they ran.

In the late 1920s and throughout the 1930s Eva Shipman and Ida Sampson raced their Ojibwe spirit horses at the annual Walpole Island Fair. Eva named her horse Silver. Silver was not tame—no one would tame this horse—but she could make him run, sometimes fast enough to win. Ida Sampson rode Jimmy. Jimmy was the colour of soil, and Ida wore a red shirt to race, beads in her hair. She wanted to wear a feather but knew it would fall out.

Ida had started riding horses when she was seven years old, while working at the local stable, and she joined her first pony race at twelve. "I wasn't even a little scared of a horse," Ida recalled. "I was raised with horses . . . I had to look after them." According to Ida, it was the older Eva who got her into the races. Despite her slight frame, Ida was fearless, using her heels and voice to urge Jimmy to run faster. "Just two of us girls riding with boys, racing with them . . . [Eva] was riding around there—she had a couple of ponies and she used to come with her dad. And she used to ask me, we'd be riding on the road . . . somebody asked us to ride in the fair."[3]

The fair had been running since the 1890s, moving from the Anglican Church grounds to a new fairground that sits near the river, where the Walpole Island Ferry to the United States operates today. The pony races were so popular that steamers would arrive along the rivers to bring spectators. To the cheers of fans from Detroit, Port Huron, Windsor, and all parts of Chatham-Kent, Shipman and Sampson, along with other regular racers, would coax on their horses.

A generation later, some remnants of gender parity remained. Growing up in Delaware Nation at Moraviantown after the war, Shirley Huff and her sisters, Gwen and Veronica, could keep up with anyone. If you put a target in front of them, they could hit it. "My dad was a sniper in the army, and at the age of twelve he taught me how to shoot," recalls Shirley. "He had this .22 and we'd have target practice; he taught me how to shoot a can, and I remember there was a bird on top of a barn, and he said, 'I want you to shoot at that.' And I did, I killed it." The Huffs were poor and hunting was their main source of food. Shirley and her siblings would help her parents hunt for squirrels and rabbits.

But colonization was steadily eroding Indigenous practice and replacing it with other gender norms. According to a 2010 report from the Native Women's Association of Canada: "Strategies of colonization were gendered purposefully to undermine and remove Indigenous women's traditional authority and agency. The Indian Act and residential school education were designed to destroy women's traditional roles within clan, kinship and governance systems, preparing them instead to become the 'property' of individual men as good 'Christian' wives and mothers, dependent upon and submissive to male authority, and isolated within nuclear families."[4]

As Robertson wrote in "Indigenous Women's Experiences of the Canadian Residential School System" for the *Journal of Multidisciplinary Research at Trent* (2018): "Female students spent much of their time cooking, cleaning and praying instead of receiving an education as it was believed that they were destined for lower-level employment such as domestic work and did not require the same amount of classroom learning that white students did.

"Female students suffered what is deemed as double-sided abuse, as they were not only punished for being Indigenous, but also for being women."

In sport, there were clear divides at residential schools. Boys were participants while girls were spectators, and the options presented during recreational time, including at Shingwauk Residential School, where the majority of Walpole Island youth were taken, was highly gendered. "The burden of inadequate equipment appears to have fallen more heavily on girls than on boys. If there was equipment, such as table-top hockey games, to go around, it would generally be the boys who would benefit . . . girls sat, held dolls, and talked in the dormitory; boys gathered around a hockey game in their recreation room."[5]

Born in 1947, Shirley Huff belonged to the first generation to avoid residential school. Her mother Retta and father Joseph would watch their kids and their neighbours play baseball in their yard. Retta's brother, Charlie Jacobs, would often be there. According to local historian Darryl Stonefish, whose father played with Jacobs, "he was bound for the big leagues" until a brain tumour took his life.

Uncle Charlie opened Shirley's eyes to what playing sport could look like. "Charlie was a ballplayer. He had all these books, and when I looked at them, I'd see pictures of these ladies in their uniforms. They weren't fancy uniforms, but I thought, one of these days I'm going to play baseball just like them."

Like most children from Delaware Nation, Shirley was sent off reserve for school and sport. And there, like most Indigenous youth, she saw first-hand how the world viewed her.

"My mother always taught us to turn the other cheek. I was always proud to be an Indian, always proud to be Native. When I played volleyball in school, some of the girls from the opposite team would call us Native girls 'Chinese.' I told the girls, don't say anything, just play hard, and when we win that's when you can tell them something."

In 1963, a teenage Shirley finally saw the chance to put on a baseball uniform like those she'd seen in her uncle's magazines. But it involved her driving from Delaware Nation at Moraviantown to Wallaceburg, a town known for presenting barriers to Indigenous peoples.

"I saw an advertisement in the paper, it said 'tryouts,' I was raised in Moraviantown, and Wallaceburg is probably a fifty-minute drive from Moraviantown Reserve. I asked my mother, 'Can I go over there and try out?' And she said, 'Sure, we'll take you.' I went to try out and the coach pulled me to one side. I thought uh oh, I must not have made the team. He said to me, 'You're a very good player, are there any more girls who can play like you?' And I said, 'Yes, my two sisters. My sister Gwen is a year older, and my other sister Veronica is two years younger.'"

The Huff sisters became a force for the Wallaceburg Sertomettes, helping the team win a league championship, with Gwen being named team MVP that season. Despite their success, the stands remained hostile.

"When we were in Wallaceburg playing a fastball game, I can remember we had a lot of people come to our games, a lot of Native people. Even my relatives from Algonac, Michigan, which is just a ten-minute ferry ride away. A fellow hollered at the coach, he said, 'Of all the girls in Wallaceburg you have to pick three Indian girls.' He was behind the fence, and my Gwen, she picked up a baseball and heaved it at him, and everybody laughed."

Humour was a common coping mechanism for the Huff sisters. "We were playing in a tournament and one of the girls complained to the umpire, saying Gwen had an illegal bat. So the umpire came over and checked it out. He said, 'I want to know where you got this bat,' and being Native, she said, 'I carved it myself.' Everybody cracked up, and the ump said, 'One more smart remark like that and you're out of the game.'"

When humour wouldn't suffice, Shirley attempted to use antagonism as motivation. "I could always handle it. I knew I was good, and I could always handle it, but it was good to have my sisters there. There was a song they'd sing, 'Catcher's bad, pitcher's worse, and look at the dope they've got on first,' and that was me. But people would say, 'She's no dope, she's a good player.' I had a fair complexion, light hair and skin. My sisters had darker complexions and dark hair, so I was kind of sticking up for them more than myself."

The Huff sisters were an anomaly in local sport. They were

Indigenous women playing integrated baseball and once had an opportunity to cross gender lines as well. "The men's fastball team were short of players, they needed a first baseman and they needed a shortstop. It was a tournament so, instead of forfeiting the game, they asked us to play. I went to first base, and we played . . . I'll tell you, the fellow who threw from third base to first, Gord Peters, he almost broke my hand. I was young and skinny, and I still caught it and got the out."

In 1967, Shirley joined the Wallaceburg Hornettes hockey team, and competed in the first Wallaceburg Lipstick Tournament, which was billed as the North American Girls Hockey Championship Tournament, the first women's hockey tournament in Ontario history and one of the first in Canada. This tournament would later become the Ontario championships. Detroit Red Wings general manager Jack Adams, for whom the NHL's Coach of the Year award is named, and Vezina Trophy and Stanley Cup winning goalie Johnny Mowers presided over the first tournament and a crew from *Hockey Night in Canada* was on hand to record the games. The TV crew played an exhibition game against the Hornettes before the tournament began and lost 6-2.[6]

Huff was the lone Indigenous player on the team, but she wasn't the only Indigenous hockey player in the tournament. The year prior, Six Nations of the Grand River had won a one-day event that was a predecessor to the Lipstick Tournament. The leader of that team was Bev Beaver, the Southern Ontario Tom Longboat Award winner for 1967. In the years to come, she would join the Burlington Canadettes, leading them to an A division title at the tournament in 1972, when Beaver was named MVP. In 1980, Bev Beaver became the national Tom Longboat Award recipient, Canada's top Indigenous athlete.

The Lipstick Tournament was a major stepping stone for the promotion of women's hockey in Ontario and Canada. It was the spark that women's hockey had been waiting for to push the game into the mainstream, to spawn more leagues and tournaments, and to establish a governing body for women's hockey. It became a mecca for players, including in 1982, when Angela James won the MVP award playing for Burlington. James, whose father was Black and moved to Mississauga, Ontario to escape racial segregation in the United States, would become a member of the first class of women inducted into the Hockey Hall of Fame after winning four World Championship gold medals with Team Canada.

The same year as the first Lipstick Tournament in 1967, the Walpole Island Hawks won their first All-Indian Hockey Tournament. Women from Walpole Island arranged a banquet where the team was feted and given championship jackets. But women did not participate in the tournament itself and were relegated to the associated beauty pageant. As Paraschak and Forsyth stated in their 2011 article for *Ethnologies* journal, "Aboriginal Women 'Working' at Play," this delineation of responsibility and access to sport was well understood by Indigenous women:

"Women consistently identified sport at the Aboriginal community level as a space shaped by gendered notions about women's work, whereby the women are there to support the men in an unpaid and unrecognized capacity.

"With fewer opportunities at their immediate disposal, and faced by both racism and sexism at times, the women have learned to make the best of what is available to them, all the while connecting those current boundaries to a broader critique of male power and privilege in sport."[7]

Even the equipment reflected traditional gender roles and stereotypes. "One thing about hockey, we had to use figure skates to play, and I was always tripping and falling all over with these little picks on the end, so I took them to a man who sharpened skates and I got them shaved off, so I played okay with it," Huff explained. "As the months went on I picked up a pair of boys skates from the Goodwill store and played hockey. I loved it."

Fran Rider, a founder of the Ontario Women's Hockey Association, and early participant in the Lipstick Tournament confirms the inequity of equipment: "The equipment on the market is mostly for a male body. Some of it gives protection to a female body, some of it doesn't. It's hit and miss for coverage. We need better protection in a smaller piece of equipment."[8]

Many of these antiquated gender roles—women cooking, cleaning, and caring for children—were ingrained in both Indigenous men and women through colonization and supplanted traditional norms that also included trapping, preparing hides, transmitting knowledge, and conducting ceremonies.

Shirley encountered the result of this indoctrination when she married Walpole Island's Bill Tooshkenig, "[Bill] didn't really want me to play hockey because that was a boys' sport, so I'd sneak out, and sneak around to play."

Bill, however, knew he was marrying an athlete. "He wanted to get married in July, and I knew I had a big baseball tournament coming up in August. I said nope, I'm not going to get married until after I finished my baseball tournament. That's how much I loved baseball."

While Shirley and Bill were part of the first generation to avoid residential school, generational trauma remained. "My mother had impacts from residential school, the whole community had impacts," Bill explains. "My mother would never hug me. Most mothers would hug their kids. Even when my brother died and his body was at our house—they did that in the old days—I felt this arm go around me and I thought it was my mother, but it was my aunt. My mother never ever hugged me like that, because of residential school impacts. They taught little boys and girls not to talk to their brothers and sisters, so they'd end up being aloof and distant from them. You can feel it on the reserve, but it's slowly changing."

Their children, Steven and Cheryl, grew up with supportive parents and a love of sport. They took turns clinging to their father's golf bag and drifting off to sleep in a golf cart pulled by their parents. Cheryl in particular was in the game immediately, any game she could play: golf, hockey, badminton, tennis, or volleyball. When the Walpole Island arena opened, thanks in large part to Bill's leadership as chief, they were among the first on the ice. When they weren't playing team sports, the two would spend hours on the makeshift green that they had created in their front yard, golf clubs in hand. Bill would spend mornings in the front yard, cutting the grass surrounding the golf holes his children had dug. Making sure no cars were passing, the Tooshkenigs would take careful, calculated swings, although they would occasionally need to apologize to their grandmother when a ball crashed through a window of her neighbouring house.

As the children aged, errant swings became a rarity. Both were accomplished golfers in their teenage and adult years. Cheryl would win an Ontario title and take silver at another provincial championship. She played NCAA golf for Kent State and Oakland University before becoming the first North American Indigenous golfer in history to play in an LPGA sanctioned event. Her brother, Steven, turned pro at twenty-two and would later be hired by the Canadian Junior Golf Association to teach the game to Indigenous youth.

Shirley and Bill taught their children to advocate for Indigenous rights, both in sport and the community. Cheryl recalls, "Both of my parents were very strong advocates of human rights. I would go with them when they would have marches. I was the observer and I would see how unfair things were. Hockey was a sport that I played and watched my brother play, and people would get really into the games. At that time there were a lot of brawls on the rink and off. I can remember one in Bothwell where everyone was arguing and fighting and I was getting caught up in it. I wanted to act out, to say things, but my mom gave me a look that said, 'Cheryl, drop it, don't even think of getting involved' and dragged me out of that arena. I've seen a lot of things and heard a lot of things—the Native

American Indian stereotypes of, 'you guys are drunks,' 'what's wrong with you, you're savages,' 'you're on welfare.' Those were standard and I thought okay, what else do you have? I've heard it all before."

Despite what she heard from the stands and her opponents, Cheryl was born in a generation where talent and skill had begun to supersede race. Leaving Walpole Island and Wallaceburg to play NCAA golf in the United States, Cheryl Tooshkenig was seen in a new light. She was no longer "just another Native" from the Island, or just a girl for that matter; she was going to be an athlete and an academic. Here, where athletes were treated with reverence, that's all that mattered.

"It felt like going in as a blank slate; nobody really knew me other than being a golfer. They had no concept of, 'oh you grew up on an Indian reservation, how was that?' It was just 'you're a player, you're my teammate.' I guess in a way that was good, it was just focused on sports."

Cheryl had stepped out of one world and into another. But in some ways she'd always lived two lives, two parallel existences—one as an athlete, another as an Indigenous person. One as a Christian, and one who knew where she was from. Her parents had been taught to turn away from traditional beliefs as children and struggled as adults to reconcile their faith with their commitment to equality and Indigenous rights. They tried to shield Cheryl from learning about Indigenous religious practices at school on Walpole Island.

"Growing up, one of my earliest memories is being taken out of the Indian traditions, anytime when we'd have presentations in the Walpole school that were geared toward traditional stories, that were geared toward anything from the culture I was removed from. A teacher would come and get me and say, 'Okay, Cheryl can't participate,' and I was like why? My parents are both religious, they're Christians, at that time I thought, 'What's so wrong?' I didn't understand. It felt like I was between two worlds."

Alyssa Sands, the daughter of Bill Sands, knows that feeling of being here and there, or neither here nor there. Girl, Indigenous, athlete, other. Growing up, she would be tasked with cleaning her father's hunting lodge but was not involved in guiding or hunting itself.

"In my family there were certain expectations of the girls. I remember going out to the cornfields with my dad, but I don't have any memories of being asked if I wanted to go hunting. I always wanted to go. I didn't want to stay home and cook, or do the dishes, or clean ducks, I wanted to be out there, having fun. Duck hunters, when I was younger, seemed bigger than life to me. They were these giants, and not because I was a small girl, or because a lot of times they were famous people. It was something about each person, they just had something. But I don't remember seeing a lot of women going hunting."

Bill Sands carried the lessons of the Mohawk Institute with him. "I know the gender roles that were placed on my sister and me weren't because our parents thought we were too fragile and delicate. The same gender roles were beaten into my dad and my maternal grandmother at residential school. It's just how things were."

"I was fourteen when I was finally allowed to go on my first duck hunt," explained Alyssa. "It was a huge day for me, I remember the excitement I felt the night before, it felt like Christmas! I begged for as long as I can remember to have the chance to go hunting with my dad. I knew it was work for him, but my brothers all got to go all the time, even my younger brother. I didn't know why I couldn't."

Even on this first hunt, Alyssa was not allowed to pull the trigger, only to observe. "I remember being so upset after the hunt that I wasn't allowed to shoot. I had to carry the duck strap, with a limit that I didn't even shoot."

Driving around Walpole Island, Alyssa tells story after story of hunts. "It's more than catching or killing. It's the hours spent out on the land and water. It's the quiet. It's watching the sun come up over the duck blind. Freezing your toes off in the most beautiful snowfall. It's helping to provide food for my family, the same way my dad and brothers have for years. There is a sense of accomplishment to it, being a woman."

Alyssa Sands is working to extend this opportunity to others by running land-based learning programs involving hunting. She is particularly focused on helping young women and girls reclaim their traditional place in Indigenous culture.

"My son, Brayden, was four years old when he went on his first turkey hunt with his Papa. I asked if I could go, and Brayden replied, 'Girls don't hunt! They cook the food the men bring back!' I laughed, but internally, I was pretty devastated. The same gender roles that I hated and that excluded me from doing things I really wanted to had now infiltrated my sweet boy's mind. Eleven years later, my son is my best hunting partner."

Hunting is helping Alyssa gain ground the same way Shirley and Cheryl Tooshkenig used their talent to open doors that otherwise would have remained closed for Indigenous women.

The Native Women's Association of Canada maintains that "traditional Indigenous gender roles and relations have been profoundly disrupted by colonialism and the residential school experience; contemporary relations are shaped by this legacy. Just as dismantling and destroying traditional gender balance was an essential strategy of colonization, gender justice must be an essential element in both the process and outcomes of reconciliation."[9]

The reclamation of culture and language is ongoing, and sport is a part of that.

During our Jeep tour of Walpole Island, Bill, Alyssa, and I talked about ceremonies, and traditional knowledge, managing the invasive species of the swamps, about snakes, and reconciliation. We talked about outdoor learning, about mental health, we talked about healing. We talked about God, the Creator.

When we found ourselves stuck in a muddy field, Alyssa shifted the Jeep in and out of gear, mud shooting out from the tires. She shifted into forward, then reverse, over and over. She was determined—after all, Alyssa has been stuck before.

Eventually, the car lurched a few feet backward and Alyssa slammed on the gas. We splashed through the spot that had held us, the Jeep drifting sideways as it slowed. The engine roared and a spattering of mud, buckshot from the tires, plastered the vehicle. Alyssa smiled, and we let out the breath we were holding. She had found her way out.

We moved forward, albeit slowly, together.

# Chapter 21

# HOMECOMINGS

It wasn't until my fifth year at Western University, while in teachers' college, that I first heard any details of residential schools. Here, in a First Nations education course, I was also taught about treaties, the Indian Act, and the loss of language and land. I sat there with tears in my eyes, struggling to understand the way white people, including me, had conveniently overlooked the barriers we'd built and the culture we'd attempted to erase.

In 2015, the Truth and Reconciliation Commission of Canada (TRC) released their report, which included ninety-four Calls to Action. Despite the creation of this report, Indigenous peoples in Canada have continued to go without access to clean drinking water, face disproportionate incarceration, struggle with mental health and high suicide rates often tied to generational trauma and poverty, and have not received government support to end emergencies such as the crisis of missing and murdered Indigenous women and girls.

It took the discovery of unmarked graves, those of Indigenous children, first hundreds and then thousands, in the spring and summer of 2021 at residential schools across Canada for the TRC's report to hold meaning for many Canadians. As Prime Minister Steven Harper stated in his 2008 apology to residential school survivors, Canada had profoundly failed Indigenous people. People like the Sands family.

Bill Sands pulled his car up behind the Mohawk Institute, the residential school he'd endured for four years as a child. His daughter Alyssa and son Dustin were in the back seat. They'd been in nearby Six Nations attending the Little NHL hockey tournament.

"My kids were small and I took them there. I never went back to the school until that time, and I pulled up at the back of the Mohawk Institute. I pulled up there, stopped the car and turned it off. The windows were down, and I had the most evil feeling I ever felt in my life. I turned around and looked at my kids and said, 'You guys feel okay?'"

They got out and looked for the spot where Bill had carved his name on a brick, but the visit was brief. Bill had spent enough time here.

Years after this cursory return, Bill Sands reluctantly accepted an invitation to return to the Mohawk Institute for an event. Children were running and there was singing, but there was no joy, no celebration. The former youth of the Mohawk Institute had gathered, upon invitation, more than thirty years after the facility closed its doors. Bill brought his youngest son, Dustin, to see the place that had impacted his life so profoundly. When the organizer invited those present to tour the building, the weight of the location—the walls and mortar, the hidden spaces, the boiler room, the darkness—encompassed them. It was a place of evil where children had been tormented by staff. It was a reunion, but definitely not a homecoming.

Back on Walpole Island, Bill sat with the Walpole Island Residential School *Gaa-Shaabwiijig* Committee. They drank coffee and listened. They talked when they were ready. It was a place of healing, a place of truth. A monument was erected on Walpole Island: shiny black granite with hundreds of engraved names, rows upon rows, including Bill's, of children who were taken. Constructed in 2002 by a group of survivors as a step toward healing, the monument stands as an unmovable reminder for all generations. It reads, "From inside those walls no one outside heard our cries; when we left, no one outside heard our cries from within."

Gord Peters is doing his best to make those cries heard. Through the telephone, I could hear nostalgia in his voice when he talked about those early days hitting stones with his father and skating on ponds. But he learned more from his father Omer than how to be a top athlete. He learned the importance of representing his people, the sovereignty of First Nations, and the need to advocate for Indigenous rights.

Sport helped create that opportunity. Now, there's strength in his words. He will not be swayed, and he is determined to move forward. "There is no truth and reconciliation. There's an attempt at reconciliation, but it's not even true reconciliation. We've left the truth out of the truth and reconciliation. The federal government doesn't address the fact that they unilaterally disposed of the treaty process. They don't talk about titles to land, of our governance process, everything that was there before the treaty process that was unilaterally abandoned by Canada. They choose not to talk about them because they are the key areas that would change the world for all of us."

He continues, his voice powerful. "It's not just residential schools that are the problem. The process started in 1876 with the Indian Act. There are four major things that changed our world. The first thing that happens is that they change our governments to this current chief and council system; second, they put us on reserves; third, they created disenfranchisement, particularly for women who they saw as the strength of our government; and then they created the Indian Agent to control everything in the community. The chiefs and council could not make any decisions without the Indian Agent.

"So that's already in place, that process they established to control absolutely everything. Residential schools come because they don't believe assimilation is happening fast enough. In the 1960s, they take our kids again, a second time, they called it the Sixties Scoop. They took our kids and fostered them out all over the world. And then the day schools. Some of those schools were like residential schools. All those things have a cumulative effect on our community, and the only way we're going to overcome that is making those choices for change by ourselves. I think our culture is what is required. We're doing our language right now, we're reviving it.

"What people are starting to recognize is that we have our own belief system, we have our own way of communicating with the one God that exists. And we have ceremonies. Our burials are different today.

"If you have signed a treaty with Canada, there's no way Canada should be able to settle a lot of legislation, like language legislation or child welfare legislation. It's part of the termination and assimilation process to ensure those final connections are broken. When we choose to follow those laws, we choose to draw down that power from Canada."

Like Indigenous peoples before them, Japanese Canadians were systematically disenfranchised—their property confiscated, their livelihoods destroyed, their culture obliterated. Following World War II, many Japanese Canadians were exiled to Japan, a country they'd never seen before. Most were banned from returning to British Columbia. It wasn't until 1949 that Japanese Canadians regained the right to freely move throughout Canada.

In 1947, the National Association of Japanese Canadians (NAJC) was formed and would become the organization responsible for igniting the push for redress in the 1980s. In 1984, the NAJC released a document titled "Democracy Betrayed: The Case for Redress," which called upon the government to "take such steps as are necessary to ensure that Canadians are never again subjected to such injustices," and that the "fundamental human rights and freedoms set forth in the Canadian Charter of Rights and Freedoms be considered sacrosanct, non-negotiable and beyond the reach of any arbitrary legislation."[1]

On September 22, 1988, more than four decades after World War II ended, Prime Minister Brian Mulroney officially apologized to

Japanese Canadians and promised to redress the wrongs done through dispossession and internment. Addressing the House of Commons, Mulroney said, "We cannot change the past. But we must, as a nation, have the courage to face up to these historical facts."

In addition to the apology, each survivor received compensation: a pittance of $21,000. A community fund was established, and $24 million was earmarked to establish a Canadian Race Relations Foundation. Japanese Canadians who had been deported to Japan, and their descendants, had their Canadian citizenship restored, and pardons were granted for Japanese Canadians who had been imprisoned during the war.

Some of those receiving redress were players and family members of the Vancouver Asahi baseball team, once the pride of British Columbia's Japanese community. Established in 1914, the Asahis, who played at Vancouver's Powell Street Grounds, were a collection of Japanese Canadian All-Stars in the Vancouver and Fraser Valley areas. Playing in the Vancouver Industrial League, the Asahi won successive championships beginning in 1922. From 1937 to 1941, the team won five consecutive Pacific Northwest Championships. As with all facets of life for Japanese Canadians, the war marked the end of the Asahi, which was disbanded in 1942.

In 2003, the Vancouver Asahi became the first racialized team inducted into the Canadian Baseball Hall of Fame, another small but significant step toward reparation. In 2021, residents of Chatham-Kent organized a Field of Honour game to encourage the Canadian Baseball Hall of Fame to extend the same recognition to the Chatham Coloured All-Stars.

As the fall leaves started to change in the midst of a global pandemic, two teams consisting entirely of descendants of the original All-Stars played at Fergie Jenkins Field. Ninety-nine-year-old John Olbey, the brother of Cliff Olbey, received an ovation as he stepped on the field, holding his walker.

It was obvious how much this team meant to the community on

that day. Several hundred fans arrived. Organizers moved through the crowd; I was one of them. Wearing yellow shirts with volunteer tags around our necks, we stood out. Members of the media swirled around the field and between dugouts collecting photos and video, documenting new stories. The day was a success, on and off the field. It was a moment of recognition. More than eighty years after the last iteration of the Chatham Coloured All-Stars played a game, their descendants formed two teams and gathered to play.

This team is not just representative of Chatham's Black community; it is representative of an entire city, or at least the city we want to be. During the previous summer, I had marched with thousands of others through Chatham's East End to show that Black Lives Matter, right past a white man sitting on a porch draped with a Confederate flag. In Dresden this summer, a white resident repeatedly took down a Black Lives Matter flag and threw it in a nearby dumpster. He was charged and convicted.

On Fergie Jenkins Field, there was no hate that day. People were buying All-Stars hats and jerseys; money was dropped into a donation box for the Chatham-Kent Black Historical Society. Without the stories, without the proof of the racism that followed their win, you'd think the men who played for that 1934 Chatham Coloured All-Stars team had remained heroes. You'd never know how quickly the town returned to a segregated existence.

The All-Stars have been in the Chatham Sports Hall of Fame since 2000. The local Hall of Fame donated a stone monument to the team, which was unveiled by the children of Flat Chase in a ceremony prior to the Field of Honour game. Perhaps it should have been in the East End's Stirling Park, where the team played. Several decades ago, Black people would not have been welcomed on the field now named for the town's most famous citizen. That field was for white people only; now a monument to Canada's first all-Black provincial champions will sit here forever. The city has changed and so have the games.

"I certainly have taken my love for the game for granted," said Rebecca Prince, who represented the Robbins family that afternoon. "I am forever thankful to be able to play the game of baseball that I love so much, and feel privileged that there will no longer be a game called 'on account of darkness.'"

The sun was shining as the game ended 3-2, the same score that should have secured the title for the 1934 All-Stars.

Rebecca's daughter Adalynn was there cheering on her mommy, while my daughter Ezra stood beside me on the steps of the dugout. Addy and Ezra were born only a few weeks apart. They met at the library, had playdates at the park, took music class together, swam, ate ice cream, and now, at not quite three years old, they are playing on the same baseball team. You can't really call it baseball at this point, but there are gloves and balls and running. They bounce across the field, both with long hair stretching to their backs, unabashed, open-mouthed smiles on their faces. With each successful swing, teeth emerge from behind lips, affirming the happiness these games can bring. After their final practice of the season, the girls sat on the ball diamond sweeping pebbles, drawing pictures in the dirt, their laughter breaking into a thousand little pieces that skipped across the grass. Their mothers snapped photos of them together.

Addy and Ezra don't know that Addy is Black and Ezra is white. At least they don't know there is meaning ascribed to these identities. Someday, I hope Adalynn and Ezra read this story and see their names together. And I hope their stories are different than mine, and different than those of Dorothy and Toky, Boomer and Bill. The opening pages of Addy and Ezra's story are full of hope.

Other pages, however, remain unturned. In early 2022, during Black History Month, the All-Stars were denied entry into the Canadian Baseball Hall of Fame for the fifth straight year. Thwarted again on the uneven playing field of history, this story remains a work in progress.

Stories are all we have. The many stories of racism in sport overlap like stacked pages, chapters in the same opus. They are retellings of folklore, creation stories where the setting and characters are different, but the narrative is the same. Today, the story is both more and less clear than it was throughout the last two hundred years. People of colour are on teams and in the stands. We tell ourselves that this is the end, that parity has arrived, ignoring the systemic barriers that remain intact.

There is a path forward. A way to write new chapters. Chapters that include families being reconnected and supported, chapters written in Indigenous languages, chapters in full colour where people of all ethnicities work together to ensure decolonization occurs, including in sport.

I've always loved sports. The murmur and expectation of a crowd. Skates cutting across a fresh sheet of ice. The path a golf ball makes across a dew-covered green. I remember what it was like to be at that stadium, or in that arena. Time on buses and in locker rooms with teammates; triumphs and failures. I know now that I was privileged while others weren't.

When athletes lose, or a disappointing season ends, we're taught to look forward, to set new goals. Coaches and scouts analyze what went wrong and develop ways to prevent these mistakes from reoccurring so that we do not repeat our failures. They teach and they train. They build. If only it were like that everywhere. If only we put the same care into the systems that bind and oppress as we do into the wins and losses of a game.

Walking through Wallaceburg or Chatham, or standing at the river on Walpole Island, I can place myself here, but it's hard to know if this is still the prologue, or if we're somewhere in the middle of this story. Racism and systems of oppression still exist and, in many ways, are getting worse. And yet, there is cause for hope.

One thing is for sure—we can see now. The truth of the racism in our past, and our present contributions to the oppression of others in sport and society is being told. Often, the truth is within us, held in a story. The same stories, told again, waiting for a new ending to be written for the next generation of athletes.

Behind the bench of the ball diamond, I watch Ezra and Adalynn. They are so small and fragile. I scoop up my daughter along the third base line, and hold her there, pausing for a moment as her chin pushes into the nape of my neck. Addy climbs the bleachers, where her grandparents sit watching. Her little sister is learning to walk, absorbing the evening. I set Ezra down and we walk across the field, her tiny hand in mine and her glove tucked under my arm. We wave goodbye to Addy. When we leave the field that evening, the sun is still shining. No one will call the game on account of darkness tonight.

# ACKNOWLEDGMENTS

This project would not have been possible without the gracious assistance of the Chatham-Kent Black Historical Society and Black Mecca Museum, as well as members of Walpole Island First Nation and Delaware Nation, and the Shingwauk Residential Schools Centre. It is my hope that the athletes and descendants of those included in this book will finally be recognized for their amazing accomplishments, and that the wrongs committed against Black, Indigenous, and Japanese Canadian people across Canada are reconciled, redressed, and never repeated.

This entire project came to be while sitting in the Chatham-Kent Black Historical Society and Black Mecca Museum. While there, an email came across the desk of Executive Director Sam Meredith from Tidewater Press, and a book was born. I appreciate Lynn and Kilmeny from Tidewater Press for putting their faith in me to preserve these stories.

Thank you to the following individuals who generously contributed their oral histories and recollections to this project. In alphabetical order, they are: Miranda Ayim, Marg Baldwin, Gerry Binga, Jarvis Cook, Valerie Cook, Pat Cosby, James Dudley, Ruth Dudley (Lambkin), Chris Dziadura, Janice Forsyth, Lorne Foster, Blake Harding, Bob Izumi, Georgina Izumi, Lynn Izumi, Ian Jacobs, Fergie Jenkins, Isaiah Kicknosway, Jenna Lemay, Monica Lipscombe (Miles), Fred List, Bryan Loucks, Samantha Meredith,

Brett Miles, Michelle Miles, Cheryl Mitchell (Tooshkenig), Terry McCorkle, Shelley McCorkle Clark, Breanne Nicholas, Gord Peters, Marshall Powless, Shannon Prince, Mike Robbins, Drew Robinson, Alyssa Sands, Bill Sands, Murray Scott, Rebecca Smyth (Prince), Vicky Sunohara, Darryl Stonefish, Trevor Thompson, Bill Tooshkenig, Shirey Tooshkenig (Huff), Dwight Wakabayashi, Eddie Wright, Dorothy Wright-Wallace.

# ABOUT THE AUTHOR

A resident of Erie Beach, Ontario, Ian Kennedy is an educator and journalist with a passion for sport and storytelling. In 2011, he founded CKSN (Chatham-Kent Sports Network), an online news outlet covering both amateur and professional athletes. His reporting has been featured on radio, in newspapers and in publications that include *The Hockey News, Yahoo Sports* and *Outdoor Canada* magazine. He holds degrees in Kinesiology and Education from the University of Western Ontario.

# ENDNOTES

## Introduction

1. Landon, "Canadian Negroes and the John Brown Raid," 174.

## Chapter 1: Under the Pear Tree

1. Ullman, *Look to the North Star*, 88.
2. McLaren, "'We had no desire to be set apart': Forced Segregation of Black Students in Canada West Public Schools and Myths of British Egalitarianism," 32.
3. Bonner, "This Tract of Land," 98.
4. Ibid, 32.
5. Ibid, 98.
6. Walker, "The day Jack Johnson became the first black world heavyweight champion," accessed November 2, 2021.
7. Legislative Assembly, *Journals of the Legislative Assembly of the Province of Canada*, 570.
8. Vinci, "A study of Race-relations Between Blacks and Whites Over Issues of Schooling in Upper Canada, 1840-1860," 35.
9. Griffith, "Sports in Shackles," 71.
10. Robidoux, "Imagining Canadian Identity through Sport," 210.
11. Gemmell, *Cricket, Race and the 2007 World Cup*, 26.
12. Day, "Impulse to Addiction," 185.
13. Gilmore, "Black Athletes in an Historical Context," 7.
14. Cosentino, *Afros, Aboriginals, and Amateur Sport in Pre World War One Canada*, 8.
15. *Chatham Tri-Weekly Planet*, May 12, 1876, 26.
16. Day, ibid, 185.
17. Ibid.
18. "Chatham Honors Dr. H. A. Tanser," *The Windsor Star*, October 19, 1962.
19. Tanser, *The Settlement of Negroes in Kent County*, Ontario, 162.
20. Ibid, 137
21. Victor Lauriston, *The Windsor Star*, October , 1939, 15.
22. Tanser, "Intelligence of Negroes of Mixed Blood in Canada," 650.
23. "Immigration Major Item," *The Windsor Star*, February 12, 1941.
24. Robinson and Robinson, *Seek The Truth*, 137.

## Chapter 2: It Was Never Our Game

1. Shanahan, "Chenail Ecarte Purchase: September 7, 1796," accessed December 16, 2021.
2. McDougall and Philips Valentine, "Treaty 29: Why Moore Became Less," 257.
3. Eamon and Marshall, (2018). "First Nations and Métis Peoples in the War of 1812," accessed January 20, 2022.
4. Jones, *History of the Ojebway Indians*, 42.
5. Jennessaux, "Letter from Walpole Island," History file 8-9, 5.
6. Ibid, 5.
7. Narraway, "Settler Colonial Power and Indigenous Survival," 15.

## Chapter 3: A Bible in My Hands

1. Biggar, *Anecdotal Life of Sir John Macdonald*, 177.
2. Canadian Parliament, *Official Report of Debates (1883)*, 1377
3. Nock, *A Victorian Missionary and Canadian Indian Policy*, 76.
4. Stephens, "Speaking the Pictures in my Head," 324.

5. Missionary Diocese of Algoma, (1897). *Twenty-Second Annual Report of the Shingwauk Wawanosh Homes*, 14.
6. Powers-Beck, "Chief," 512.
7. Adams, "More than a Game," 25.
8. Jenkins, *The Real All Americans,* 7.
9. Staurowsky, "An Act of Honor or Exploitation?", 299.
10. Harmon, "Blood Quantum," accessed December 18, 2021.
11. Molski, "Get to Know the History of Native Americans in Baseball," accessed December 7, 2021.
12. Kiyoshk, "Transcript of Interview," 3.
13. Nin.Da.Waab.Jig., *Walpole Island,* 66.

## Chapter 4: The Great White Hopes

1. McCafferty, "*Tommy Burns,*" back cover.
2. Walker, ibid.
3. Jeffries, Jim, "Tommy Burns' Price," *The Scone Advocate*, January 29, 1909, 3.
4. Walker, ibid.
5. Harris, "Looking Back at the Legacy of 'The Great White Hope'," accessed January 29, 2022.
6. Jack Johnson, "Final Statement of Jack Johnson," *Chicago Tribune*, July 4, 1910.
7. Fetter, "The Fight of the Century," accessed November 12, 2021.
8. "Arthur Pelkey Now Looms Up As Legitimate 'White Hope.'" *The North Adams Transcript*, March 30, 1912.
9. "Arthur Pelkey Wants to Meet Luther McCarty, New Champion," *The North Adams Transcript*, January 2, 1913.
10. "Arthur Pelkey's Father Offers Him a Farm to Give Up Boxing," *The North Adams Transcript*, April 16, 1912, 6.
11. Cosentino, ibid, 13.
12. George T. Pardy, "Jack's Retirement Looks Like A Bluff," *The Nebraska State Journal*, August 4, 1912.
13. Horn, "Two Champions and Enemies," 133
14. Brown, "Boxing Darwin's Shadow," 65.
15. Beal, "As 2011 dawns," accessed 23 November 23. 2021.
16. Walters, "Narratives of Canadian Identity," 41.

## Chapter 5: The Home Team Wears White

1. Howe, *The Refugees From Slavery in Canada West*, 44.
2. Poole, "Conspicuous Peripheries," 183.
3. Wiggins, "Wendell Smith, the Pittsburgh Courier-Journal and the Campaign," 9.
4. Harding, "Transcript of Interview," 0:38:02.8
5. Nzindukiyimana, "And, Needless to Say, I Was Athletic, Athletic, Too," 123.
6. Bill Reddick, "Chatham Colored All Stars: Reliving the winning 1934 OBA title drive," *Chatham Daily News*, October 5, 1994.
7. Olbey, "Transcript of Interview With John Olbey," 9–10.
8. Cartier, *Politics & Other Games*, 68–70.
9. Robbins, *Legacy To Buxton*, 149.
10. Harding, ibid, 0:39:27.3.
11. Ernie Miller, (1978). "Boomer Harding—One Great Guy," *The London Free Press*, September 7, 1978.

## Chapter 6: Learning to Play Ball

1. Sheffield, "Of Pure European Descent," 11.
2. Assembly of First Nations, "Heroes of Our Time Scholarships," accessed 20 December 20, 2021.

3. Peter Edwards, "Truth and Reconciliation report: Canadians should be taught about racist past, First Nations members say," *Toronto Star*. June 2, 2015.

4. Megan Stacey, ( "Gordon Peters wants to improve communication with Ottawa and the public," *The London Free Press*, June 5, 2014.

5. Hebscher, Mark. (2021). "Mark Hebscher on why Lou Marsh's name must be removed," accessed December 18, 2021.

6. Sheffield, ibid, 7.

## Chapter 7: The Home Stretch

1. Hanley, "Chatham's Early Musical Life," 55.

2. Henry, *Emancipation Day*, 70.

3. Jones, "The Greatest Negro Harness Horse Owner," 266.

4. Gilmore, "Black Athletes In An Historical Context," ibid, 7.

5. Gilligan, "The enslaved jockey," 18 December 18, 2021.]

6. "Negro Jockeys Shut Out," *The New York Times*, July 29, 1900.

7. Griffith, ibid, 72.

8. Day, ibid, 116.

9. Ibid, 130.

10. Waterstone, "Being Black in Harness Racing," 7.

11. Harness Racing Museum, "Hall of Fame: Lewis D. Williams," accessed December 18, 2021.

12. Waterstone, ibid.

## Chapter 8: Not Canadian Enough

1. Bailey, "Arrival of the Fittest," 59.

2. Bangarth, "The Long, Wet Summer of 1942," 47.

3. Ibid. 49.

4. Rhyno, "Internment, Racism and Baseball in Southwestern Ontario," 41.

5. Bangarth, ibid, 48.

6. Ibid, 48.

7. Ibid, 53.

8. Ibid, 53.

9. Bailey, ibid, 55.

10. van Waas, "The Grand Experiment," 99.

11. O'Hagan, "POWs and "the Good Ol' Hockey Game," accessed December 12, 2021.

12. Chandler, "The Happiest Prisoners," accessed January 20, 2022.

13. Lavoie, "Angler & Prisoners Of War," accessed December 15, 2021.

14. Chandler, ibid.

15. Chatham This Week, "Japanese-Canadian internment a less-than-glorious part of our history," *Chatham-Kent This Week*, December 15, 2021.

16. O'Hagan, "Beyond the Barbed Wire," 396.

17. Chandler, ibid.

18. Ibid.

19. Bailey, ibid, 58.

## Chapter 9: Turning the Tables

1. Titley, "Narrow Vision," 50.

2. Narraway, "Settler Colonial Power and Indigenous Survival," 35.

3. Jenkins, "Spirit Horses," accessed December 16, 2021.

## Chapter 10: Ragging the Puck

1. Kevin Shea, "Lucknow's Chin brothers and their moment in spotlight with Maple Leafs," Toronto Star, October 2, 2016.

2. Ibid

3. Ibid
4. Ibid
5. Ibid
6. Katz, "Larry Kwong, Gifted Athlete," accessed December 16, 2021.
7. White, "The Chin Brothers," accessed December 16, 2021.
8. Paikin, "Facing Racism, Finding Comfort," accessed December 12, 2021.
9. Scanlan, "Mike Marson on challenges he faced," accessed December 6, 2021
10. Harris, "Breaking the Ice," 62.

## Chapter 11: Jump Jim Crow

1. Flynn, "Beyond the Glass Wall," 138.
2. Flynn, "Who would play with me?" 112.
3. National Baseball Hall of Fame, "About Wendell Smith," cccessed 1February 10, 2022.
4. Washington, "Joe Louis and Jackie Robinson's Pittsburgh story," accessed December 19, 2021.
5. Macnab, "Hugh Burnett," accessed December 2, 2021.
6. "Dresden Voters Reject Equality for Negroes," *The Globe and Mail,* December 6, 1949.
7. Lambertson, "The Dresden Story," 70.
8. Queen's University, "Uncovering the Stories of Black Heroes," accessed October 20, 2021.
9. MacDowell, L. and Radforth, I. (2006). Canadian Working-Class History: Selected Readings. Toronto: Canadian Scholars' Press.

## Chapter 12: Double Play

1. Nzindukiyimana, "And, Needless to Say, I Was Athletic, Athletic, Too," 109.
2. Ibid.
3. Robbins, *Legacy to Buxton,* 138
4. Alliet, "Transcript of Interview with Rosetta (Rosie) Alliet," 4.
5. Nzindukiyimana, ibid, 106.
6. Ibid, 115.
7. Chatham-Kent Black Historical Society, "Chatham-Kent,"accessed February 9, 2022.
8. Nzindukiyimana, ibid, 116.
9. National Farmers Union. "NFU - In Union Is Strength," accessed 9 Feb. 2022.
10. Nzindukiyimana, ibid, 92.

## Chapter 13: Sundown Town

1. Nestor, "Pass System in Canada," accessed January 20, 2022.
2. Lyle Thackeray, "Brotherhood Year Round - Racial Tolerance In Wallaceburg," *The Windsor Star,* February 25, 1961.
3. Brand, *No Burden to Carry,* 151.
4. "Rollie's Negro 'Curfew' Speech Throws Town Fathers For Loss," *Edmonton Journal,* February 22, 1961, 1.
5. Ibid
6. John MacKinnon, "Black Athletes Survive Sport's Very Bumpy Road: Rollie Miles' wife experienced racism, looks forward to historic nauguration," *Edmonton Journal,* January 20, 2009. C2 .
7. Ibid.
8. "Rollie's Negro 'Curfew' Speech," Ibid.
9. Miles, "About Racial Prejudice," 4.

## Chapter 14: From Archie to Gene

1. Robinson and Duckett, *I Never Had It Made,* 12.
2. Mayor, "Black Ontario teen cleared in encounter," accessed December 20, 2021.
3. Svetaz et al, "Chapter 42: The Traumatic Impact of Racism and Discrimination on Young People," 325.

4. Kissoondath, "Gene Dziadura," accessed January 22, 2022.
5. Fischer et al, "The bystander-effect," 531.
6. Nelson et al, J.K., "Bystander Anti-Racism," 270.
7. Chavez, "Why Seth DeValve decided to protest national anthem," accessed December 26, 2021.

## Chapter 15: The International Line

1. Cosentino, *Afros, Aboriginals,* 4.
2. Berry, "Leveling the Playing Field," 117.
3. Douglas, "Color of Hockey," accessed January 20, 2022.
4. John Vogl, "Former UB hockey coach recalls road strewn with adversity," *The Buffalo News,* February 6, 2016.
5. John Hanlon, "Japanese Hockey Star Can't Read OR Write," *The Hartford Courant,* February 3, 1972, 50.

## Chapter 16: A Parade for Fergie

1. "Charge Hotel Shows Discrimination," *The Windsor Star,* December 11, 1953, 7.
2. Ira Berkow and N.Y Times News Service, "Again, Jenkins Must Learn To Cope With Tragedy," *Chicago Tribune.* January 10, 1993.
3. Forsyth, "The Lou Marsh Trophy builds on a racist legacy,"accessed January 10, 2022.
4. Ibid.

## Chapter 17: Not Your Mascot

1. McLean et al, "The Whiteness of Redmen," 21.
2. Jeff Gammage and Maddie Hanna, "Many schools holding on to Native American nicknames," *The Philadelphia Inquirer,* September 9, 2020.
3. Office of Governor Janet T. Mills, "Governor Mills Signs Bill to Prohibit Native American Mascots," accessed February 10, 2022.
4. Ibid
5. Ibid

## Chapter 18: Making It Work

1. MacGregor, "Fish are jumpin'," 39.
2. Ron MacLean, "In Their Words," *The Globe and Mail.,* December 21, 2015.

## Chapter 19: Sticks and Stones

1. Parry, "A Brief History of the "Black Friend," accessed December 12, 2021.
2. Ibid
3. Neil Becker, "Six Nations to host sessions targeting anti-Indigenous racism," *Two Row Times,* December 9, 2020.
4. Downey, *The Creator's Game,* 185.
5. Ontario Human Rights Commission, "OHRC working to address anti-Indigenous racism in lacrosse," accessed December 12, 2021.
6. Ibid.
7. Anishinabe Lacrosse, *Anishinabe Baagaadowewin,* accessed November 10, 2021.
8. "Indians May Bar Whites from Tourney," *The Windsor Star,* February 20, 1971, 3.
9. "School discrimination charges said mystery." *The Windsor Star,* January 23, 1973, 6.
10. Don MacTavish, "Report claims discrimination," *The Windsor Star,* September 21, 1972, 1–2.
11. Jacobs, "Assimilation Through Incarceration," 224.
12. Tull, "Cultural Experience, Possible Selves and Subjective Well-Being," 97.

## Chapter 20: Back in the Game

1. Strachey, *The History of Travelle*, 77.
2. Abbott, *The History of the State of Ohio*, 88.
3. Sampson, "Transcript of Interview with Ida Sampson," 4.
4. Native Women's Association of Canada, "Culturally Relevant Gender Based Models of Reconciliation," 11.
5. Miller, *Shingwauk's Vision*, 46.
6. McKinley, *Hockey: A People's History*, 187.
7. Paraschak and Forsyth, "Aboriginal Women 'Working' at Play," 157–173.
8. Stephanie Small, "Outfitting girls a struggle of a different kind," *The Ottawa Citizen*, September 5, 1993, C6
9. Native Women's Association of Canada, ibid, 30.

## Chapter 21: Homecomings

1. McRae, "Japanese Canadian internment and the struggle for redress," acccessed November 4, 2021.

# SOURCES

Abbott, John S.C. *The History of the State of Ohio: From the Discovery of the Great Valley, to the Present Time*. Detroit: Northwestern Publishing Company, 1875.

Adachi, Ken. *The Enemy That Never Was: A History of the Japanese Canadians*. Toronto: McClelland & Stewart, 1976.

Adams, David Wallace. "More than a Game: The Carlisle Indians Take to the Gridiron, 1893-1917." *The Western Historical Quarterly*. 32, no. 1, 2001.

Alliet, Rosetta. "Transcript of Interview with Rosetta (Rosie) Alliet." *Telling the Stories of Race and Sport in Canada: A Symposium*. Last modified August 10, 2018. University of Windsor. http://cdigs.uwindsor.ca/omeka-s/s/rsc/media/9448

Anderson, Chloe. (2020). "The Appropriation of Lacrosse: Competitive Lacrosse and The Creator's Game" Thesis. Augustana College. 2020.

Anishinaabe Baagaadowewin. *Anishinabe Lacrosse*. https://anishinabebaagaadowewin.org/

Assembly of First Nations. "Heroes of Our Time Scholarships 2015." *Assembly of First Nations*. Last modified March 24, 2015. https://www.afn.ca/heroes-of-our-time-scholar-ships-2015/

Bailey, Jordyn. "Arrival of the Fittest: German POWs in Ontario during the Second World War." MA thesis. University of Western Ontario. 2019.

Bangarth, Stephanie. "The Long, Wet Summer of 1942: The Ontario Farm Service Force, Small-Town Ontario and the Nisei." *Canadian Ethnic Studies*, 37, no. 1, 2005.

Beal, Jeremy. "As 2011 dawns, Ontario's extreme fighters prepare to fight—legally." *This*. Last modified January 3, 2011. https://this.org/2011/01/03/mma-ontario/

Berry, Matthew S. "Leveling the Playing Field: African-Americans and Collegiate Athletics." *Historia*, 4, 2004.

Beers, William George. *Lacrosse: The National Game of Canada*. Montreal: Dawson Brothers, 1869.

Berry, Matthew S. "Leveling the Playing Field: African-Americans and Collegiate Athletics." *Historia*, 4, 2004.

Biggar, E.B. *Anecdotal Life of Sir John Macdonald*. Montreal: J. Lovell and Son, 1891.

Bonner, Claudine Y. "This Tract of Land: North Buxton, Ontario, 1873-1914." PhD diss. University of Western Ontario. 2010.

Brand, Dionne. *No Burden to Carry: Narratives of Black Working Women in Ontario, 1920s–1950s*. Toronto: Women's Press of Canada, 1991.

Brown, Matthew. "Boxing Darwin's Shadow: Jack Johnson and Joe Louis's Historical Challenges to American Racism." BA thesis. Wesleyan University. 2007.

Canadian Parliament. *Official Report of Debates, House of Commons*. Ottawa: Queen's Printer. 1883.

———*Annual Report of the Department of Indian Affairs for the Year Ended March 31,1919*. Ottawa: J. De Labroquerie Taché, 1920Cartier, Art. *Politics & Other Games and Notes Volume Two*. London, ON: self-published, 1966.

Cartier, Art. *Politics & Other Games and Notes Volume Two*. London, ON: self-published, 1966.

Chandler, Graham. "The Happiest Prisoners." *Legion Magazine*. Last modified March 15, 2012. https://legionmagazine.com/en/2012/03/the-happiest-prisoners/

Chatham-Kent Black Historical Society. "Chatham-Kent." *On This Spot*. https://onthisspot.ca/cities/chathamkent

Chatham This Week. "Japanese-Canadian internment a less-than-glorious part of our history." Chatham-Kent This Week. Last modified November 15, 2013. https://www.chathamthisweek.com/2013/11/15/japanese-canadian-internment-a-less-than-glorious-part-of-our-history

Chavez, Chris. "Why Seth DeValve decided to protest national anthem." *Sports Illustrated*. Last modified August 22, 2015. https://www.si.com/nfl/2017/08/22/seth-devalve-national-anthem-protest-cleveland-browns.berry

Cosentino, Frank (1998). *Afros, Aboriginals, and Amateur Sport in Pre World War One Canada*. Ottawa: Canadian Historical Society, 1998.

Davis, Timothy. "Race and Sports in America: An Historical Overview." Legal Studies Paper No. 1141868. *Virginia Sports & Entertainment Law Journal*, 2008.

Day, Robert Douglas. "Impulse to Addiction: A Narrative History of Sport in Chatham, Ontario, 1790-1895." MA thesis. University of Western Ontario. 1977.

Detroit Historical Society. "Encyclopedia of Detroit: Race Riot of 1943." *Detroit Historical Society*. https://detroithistorical.org/learn/encyclopedia-of-detroit/race-riot-1943. Accessed January 20, 2022.

DeValve, Erica Harris. "I'm Proud of My Husband for Kneeling During the Anthem, but Don't Make Him a White Savior." *The Root*. Last modified August 24, 2017. https://www.theroot.com/i-m-proud-of-my-husband-for-kneeling-during-the-anthem-1798374605. Accessed December 27, 2021.

Douglas, W. "Color of Hockey: Wright was NCAA pioneer at Buffalo." *NHL.com*. Last modified July 27, 2020. https://www.nhl.com/news/color-of-hockey-wright-was-ncaa-pioneer-at-buffalo/c-317614338

Downey, Allan. *The Creator's Game: Lacrosse, Identity, and Indigenous Nationhood*. Vancouver: UBC Press, 2018.

Drake, Benjamin. *Life of Tecumseh and of His Brother the Prophet: With a Historical Sketch of the Shawanoe Indians*. Cincinnati: E. Morgan & Co., 1841.

Eamon, Michael, and Tabitha Marshall. "First Nations and Métis Peoples in the War of 1812." *The Canadian Encyclopedia*. Last modified January 26, 2017. https://www.thecanadianencyclopedia.ca/en/article/first-nations-in-the-war-of-1812.

Effron, Daniel A. (2014). "Making Mountains of Morality from Molehills of Virtue." *Personality and Social Psychology Bulletin*, 40, no.8, 2014.

Fetter, Henry D. "The Fight of the Century—Really." *The Atlantic*. Last modified July 3, 2010. https://www.theatlantic.com/entertainment/archive/2010/07/the-fight-of-the-century-really/59134/

Fischer, Peter, Joachim I. Krueger, Tobias Greitemeyer, Claudia Vogrincic, Andreas Kastenmüller, Dieter Frey, Moritz Heene, Magdalena Wicher, and Martina Kainbacher. M. (2011). "The bystander-effect: A meta-analytic review on bystander intervention in dangerous and non-dangerous emergencies." *Psychological Bulletin*, 137, no. 4, 2011.

Forsyth, J. "The Lou Marsh Trophy builds on a racist legacy, tainting the award's meaning." *The Conversation*. https://theconversation.com/the-lou-marsh-trophy-builds-on-a-racist-legacy-tainting-the-awards-meaning-154322

————*Reclaiming Tom Longboat: Indigenous Self-Determination in Canadian Sport.* Regina: University of Regina Press, 2020.

Flynn, Karen. "Beyond the Glass Wall: Black Canadian Nurses, 1940-1970." *Nursing History Review.* 17, no. 1, 2009.

————"'Who would play with me?' Childhood Narratives of Racial Identity." *Southern Journal of Canadian Studies.* 5, no.1-2 (2012).

Gemmell, Jon. *Cricket, Race and the 2007 World Cup.* London: Routledge, 2008.

Gilligan, Patrick Lawrence. "The enslaved jockey who got the better of this U.S. President—time and again." *Thoroughbred Racing Commentary.* Last modified February 24, 2021. https://www.thoroughbredracing.com/articles/enslaved-jockey-who-got-better-us-president-time-and-again/

Gilmore, Al-Tony. "Black Athletes in an Historical Context: The Issue of Race." *Negro History Bulletin.* 58, no. 3/4, 1995.

Graham, Elizabeth. *Medicine Man to Missionary: Missionaries as Agents of Change Among the Indians of Southern Ontario, 1784-1867.* Toronto: P. Martin Associates, 1975.

Griffith, Jon. "Sports in Shackles: The Athletic and Recreational Habits of Slaves on Southern Plantations." *Voces Novae.* 2, no. 11, 2018.

Hanley, Eleanor. "Chatham's Early Musical Life 1840-1850." *Kent Historical Society Papers and Addresses.* 8, 1985.

Harding, Wilfred. "Transcript of Interview with Wilfred 'Boomer' Harding." *Breaking the Colour Barrier: An Oral History of the Chatham Coloured All-Stars.* University of Windsor and Chatham Sports Hall of Fame. Last modified February 18, 2017. http://cdigs.uwindsor.ca/BreakingColourBarrier/items/show/719

Harmon, Maya. "Blood Quantum and the White Gatekeeping of Native American Identity." *California Law Review.* Last modified April, 2021. https://www.californialawreview.org/blood-quantum-and-the-white-gatekeeping-of-native-american-identity/

Harness Racing Museum. "Lewis D. Williams." *Harness Museum & Hall of Fame.* Last modified 2008. https://harnessmuseum.com/content/lewis-d-williams

Harris, Cecil. *Breaking the Ice: The Black Experience in Professional Hockey.* Toronto: Insomniac Press, 2007.

Harris, Will. "Looking Back at the Legacy of 'The Great White Hope' and Boxer Jack Johnson." [online] *Smithsonian Magazine.* Last modified February 15, 2021. https://www.smithsonianmag.com/history/looking-back-legacy-great-white-hope-180977089/.

Hebscher, Mark. "Mark Hebscher on why Lou Marsh's name must be removed from Canada's top athletic award right now." *The Canadian Jewish News.* Last modified November 26, 2021. https://thecjn.ca/arts/sports/mark-hebscher-vs-lou-marsh-trophy/

Henning, Fred W. J. *Fights for the Championship: The Men and Their Times.* London: Licensed Victuallers' Gazette, 1902.

Henry, Natasha L. *Emancipation Day: Celebrating Freedom in Canada.* Toronto: Dundurn Press, 2010.

Horn, Robert. "Two Champions and Enemies." *Sports Illustrated.* 72, no. 20, 1990.

Howe, S.G. *The Refugees From Slavery in Canada West.* Boston: Wright & Potter, 1864.

Jacobs, Madelaine Christine. "Assimilation Through Incarceration: The Geographic Imposition of Canadian Law Over Indigenous Peoples." PhD diss. Queen's University. 2012.

Jang, Trevor. "Josiah Wilson, the Indian Act, hereditary governance and blood quantum." *CBC News.* Last modified July 9, 2016. https://www.cbc.ca/news/indigenous/josiah-wilson-indian-act-hereditary-governance-1.3668636. Accessed 12 Nov. 2021.

Janzen, Mark. "Canada Sevens Breanne Nicholas – Head Down, Fire Lit, Aim True." *The Scrum*. Last modified July 30, 2020. https://thescrum.aedelhard.com/2020/07/30/canada-sevens-breanne-nicholas-head-down-fire-lit-aim-true/. Accessed November 17, 2021.

Jenkins, Fergie, with Lew Freedman. *Fergie: My Life from the Cubs to Cooperstown*. Chicago: Triumph Books, 2009.

Jenkins, Sally. *The Real All Americans: The Team That Changed a Game, a People, a Nation*. New York: Broadway Books, 2008.

Jenkins, Terry. "Spirit Horses Their Story." *Spirit Horses*. http://www.spirithorses.ca/spirithorsestheirstory.html

Jennessaux, Joseph. "Letter from Walpole Island." History File 8-9. Walpole Island Heritage Centre. 1844.

Johnston, Basil H. *Indian School Days*. Norman: University of Oklahoma Press, 1995.

Jones, Paul W. L. "The Greatest Negro Harness Horse Owner." *The Crisis*. 44, no. 7, 1937.

Jones, Peter. *History of the Ojebway Indians, with especial reference to their conversion to Christianity*. Whitefish: Kessinger Publishing, 2009.

Katz, Bridget. "Larry Kwong, Gifted Athlete Who Broke NHL's Color Barrier, Dies at 94." *Smithsonian Magazine*. Last modified March 21, 2018. https://www.smithsonianmag.com/smart-news/larry-kwong-first-player-asian-heritage-skate-nhl-has-died-94-180968557/

Katz, Sidney. "Jim Crow Lives in Dresden." *Maclean's*. November 1, 1949.

Kissoondath, Deryk. (2010). "Gene Dziadura: Chatham's Own Moonlight Graham." *Canadian Baseball Hall of Fame and Museum*. Last modified August 20, 2010. https://baseballhalloffame.ca/gene-dziadura-chathams-own-moonlight-graham/

Kiyoshk, Robert. "Transcript of Interview with Robert Kiyoshk." *Indian History Film Project*. University of Regina. Last modified January 4, 1979. https://ourspace.uregina.ca/handle/10294/2228

Krasowski, Sheldon. "*A Numiany* (The Prayer People) and the Pagans of Walpole Island First Nation: Resistance to the Anglican Church, 1845-1885." MA thesis. Trent University. 1999.

Lambertson, Ross. "'The Dresden Story': Racism, Human Rights, and the Jewish Labour Committee of Canada." *Labour / Le Travail*. 47, Spring, 2001.

Landon, Fred. "Canadian Negroes and the John Brown Raid." *The Journal of Negro History*. 13, no. 2, 1921.

Laskaris, Adam. "Advances, struggles in anti-racism work in hockey to be focus of virtual event." *Windspeaker*. Last modified March 15, 2021. https://windspeaker.com/news/sports/advances-struggles-anti-racism-work-hockey-be-focus-virtual-event. Accessed November 17, 2021.

Lavoie, E. J. "Angler & Prisoners of War (Chapter 3 of 7)." *E.J. Lavoie's Blog*. Last modified September 4, 2017. https://ejlavoie.wordpress.com/2017/09/04/angler-prisoners-of-war-chapter-3-of-7/.

Legislative Assembly. *Journals of the Legislative Assembly of the Province of Canada*. Cambridge, MA: Harvard University, 1856.

Loewen, James W. *Sundown Towns: A Hidden Dimension of American Racism*. New York: The New Press, 2018.

Louis, Joe, with Edna Rust and Art Rust Jr. *Joe Louis: My Life*. Hopewell: Ecco Press. 1997.

MacDowell, Laurel Sefton, and Ian Radforth (eds). *Canadian Working-Class History: Selected Readings*. Toronto: Canadian Scholars' Press, 2006.

McCafferty, Dan. *Tommy Burns: Canada's Unknown World Heavyweight Champion.* Toronto: James Lorimer & Company Ltd, 2001.

McDougall, Allan K., Lisa Philips Valentine and H.C. Wolfart (ed). "Treaty 29: Why Moore Became Less." *Papers of The Thirty-Fourth Algonquian Conference.* Winnipeg: University of Manitoba Press, 2003.

MacGregor, Roy. "Fish are jumpin'." *Maclean's,* August 17, 1981.

McKinley, Michael. *Hockey: A People's History.* Toronto: McClelland & Stewart, 2009.

McLean, Sheelagh, Alex Wilson, and Erica Lee. "The Whiteness of Redmen: Indigenous Mascots, Social media and an Antiracist Intervention." *Australasian Journal of Information Systems,* 21, 2017.

Macnab, Maddie. "Hugh Burnett." *The Canadian Encyclopedia.* Last modified April 18, 2018. https://www.thecanadianencyclopedia.ca/en/article/hugh-burnett

McRae, Matthew. "Japanese Canadian internment and the struggle for redress." *Canadian Museum for Human Rights.* https://humanrights.ca/story/japanese-canadian-internment-and-the-struggle-for-redress.

Malcomson, Scott L. "Jack London's Endless Journey." *The Village Voice.* Last modified February 1, 1994. https://www.villagevoice.com/2020/10/17/jack-londons-endless-journey/. Accessed December 12, 2021.

Markovic, John-Michael. "A Place to Call Home: African American Immigration and the Aftermath of the Underground Railroad 1850-1870." MA major research paper. University of Windsor. 2018.

Mayor, Lisa. "Black Ontario teen cleared in encounter with police says officers should have body cameras." *CBC News.* Last modified November 17, 2016. https://www.cbc.ca/news/canada/jake-anderson-police-video-body-cameras-1.3836882

Miles, Rollie. (1960). "About Racial Prejudice." *Maclean's.* May 7, 1960.

Miller, J.R. *Shingwauk's Vision: A History of Native Residential Schools.* Toronto: University of Toronto Press, 1996.

Missionary Diocese of Algoma. *Twenty-Second Annual Report of the Shingwauk Wawanosh Homes.* Toronto: The Bryant Press. 1897.

Molski, Max. "Get to Know the History of Native Americans in Baseball." *NBC Chicago.* Last modified November 10, 2021. https://www.nbcchicago.com/news/sports/nbcsports/get-to-know-the-history-of-native-americans-in-baseball/2680274/

Montgomery, Marc. "History - May 14, 1874 How Canada created American football." *Radio Canada International.* Last updated January 4, 2021. https://www.rcinet.ca/en/2015/05/14/history-may-14-1874-how-canada-created-american-football/. Accessed December 2, 2021.

Morrison, James. "Upper Great Lakes Settlement: The Anishnabe-Jesuit Record." *Ontario History,* LXXXVI, no, 1, 1994.

Mulvaney, Kieran. "When Joe Louis Boxed Nazi Favorite Max Schmeling." *History.* Last modified June 2, 2021. https://www.history.com/news/joe-louis-max-schmeling-match. Accessed January 20, 2022.

Narraway, Andrew. "Settler Colonial Power and Indigenous Survival: Hockey Programs at Three Indian Residential Schools in Northwestern Ontario and Manitoba, 1929-1969." MA thesis. Carleton University. 2018.

National Baseball Hall of Fame. *About Wendell Smith. National Baseball Hall of Fame.* https://baseballhall.org/discover-more/stories/wendell-smith/345.

National Farmers Union (2009). *NFU - In Union Is Strength - Voices of the National Farmers Union of Canada*. Last modified March 24, 2011. https://youtu.be/Wd0CQn0rg7s.

Native Womsen's Association of Canada (2010). "Culturally Relevant Gender Based Models of Reconciliation." Ottawa: Native Women's Association of Canada, 2010. https://www.nwac.ca/wp-content/uploads/2015/05/2010-NWAC-Culturally-Relevant-Gender-Based-Models-of-Reconciliation.pdf

Nelson, J.K., K.M. Dunn, and Y. Paradies, "Bystander Anti-Racism: A Review of the Literature." *Analyses of Social Issues and Public Policy*. 11, no. 1, 2011.

Nestor, Rob. (2018). "Pass System in Canada." *The Canadian Encyclopedia*. Last modified July 13, 2018. https://w0bww.thecanadianencyclopedia.ca/en/article/pass-system-in-canada

Nin.Da.Waab.Jig. (Group). *Walpole Island: The Soul of Indian Territory*. Wallaceburg: Walpole Island, 1987.

Nock, David. A. *A Victorian Missionary and Canadian Indian Policy: Cultural Synthesis vs. Cultural Replacement*. Waterloo: Wilfrid Laurier University Press. 1988.

Nzindukiyimana, Ornella. "'And, Needless to Say, I Was Athletic, Athletic, Too': Southern Ontario Black Women and Sport (1920s-1940s)." PhD diss. University of Western Ontario. 2018.

Office of Governor Janet T. Mills (2019). "Governor Mills Signs Bill to Prohibit Native American Mascots in Maine." *State of Maine*. Last modified May 16, 2019. https://www.maine.gov/governor/mills/news/governor-mills-signs-bill-prohibit-native-american-mascots-maine-2019-05-16

O'Hagan, Michael. "Beyond the Barbed Wire: POW Labour Projects in Canada during the Second World War." PhD diss. University of Western Ontario. 2020.

————"POWs and 'the good ol' hockey game.'" *POWs in Canada*. Last modified February 8, 2019. https://powsincanada.ca/2019/02/08/pows-and-the-good-ol-hockey-game/

Ohayon, Albert. "Dresden Story: Racism in 1950s Canada | Curator's Perspective." *NFB Blog*. Last modified February 4, 2021. https://blog.nfb.ca/blog/2021/02/04/dresden-story-racism-in-1950s-canada-curators-perspective/. Accessed October 2, 2021.

Olbey, John. "Transcript of Interview With John Olbey, joined by Olive Olbey and Dorothy Wallace." *Breaking the Colour Barrier: An Oral History of the Chatham Coloured All-Stars*. University of Windsor and the Chatham Sports Hall of Fame. Last modified July 6, 2016. https://cdigs.uwindsor.ca/BreakingColourBarrier/files/original/42ab0475d18bae3c-0868315ce7573506.pdf

Ontario Human Rights Commission. (2020). "OHRC working to address anti-Indigenous racism in lacrosse." *Ontario Human Rights Commission*. Last modified December 1, 2020. http://www.ohrc.on.ca/en/news_centre/ohrc-working-address-anti-indigenous-racism-lacrosse.

Paikin, Steve. "Facing Racism: Finding Comfort - Breaking Barriers: Dealing with Racism." *The Agenda with Steve Paikin*. Last modified February 29, 2016. https://www.tvo.org/video/breaking-barriers.

Paraschak, Vicky, and Janice Forsyth. "Aboriginal Women 'Working' at Play." *Ethnologies*, 32, no. 1, 2011.

Parry, Tyler. (2018). A Brief History of the 'Black Friend.'" Black Perspectives. Last modified July 30, 2018. https://www.aaihs.org/a-brief-history-of-the-black-friend/

Poole, Carmen. (2015). "Conspicuous Peripheries: Black Identity, Memory, and Community in Chatham, ON, 1860-1980." PhD diss. University of Toronto. 2015.

Powers-Beck, Jeffrey. "'Chief': The American Indian Integration of Baseball, 1897-1945." *The American Indian Quarterly*. 25, no. 4, 2001.

Queen's University. "Uncovering the Stories of Black Heroes." *Queen's University Alumni*

*Association*. Last modified February 6, 2017. https://www.queensu.ca/alumni/news/uncovering-the-stories-of-black-heroes

Rementer, Jim. (1993). "Pahsahëman - The Lenape Indian Football Game." *Archaeological Society of New Jersey*, Bulletin #48, 1993.

Rhyno, Art. "Internment, Racism and Baseball in Southwestern Ontario: Japanese-Canadian Farm Labourers During World War II." *Telling the Stories of Race and Sports in Canada*. Windsor: Univertiy of Windsor, 2018.

Rice, Ed. *Baseball's First Indian: The Story of Penobscot Legend Louis Sockalexis*. Camden: Down East Books. 2019.

Robbins, Arlie C. *Legacy to Buxton*. Chatham: self-published, 1983.

Robertson, Karli. "Indigenous Women's Experiences of the Canadian Residential School System." *Journal of Multidisciplinary Research at Trent*, 1, no. 1, 2018.

Robidoux, Michael A. "Imagining a Canadian Identity through Sport: A Historical Interpretation of Lacrosse and Hockey." *Journal of American Folklore*, 115, no. 456, 2002.

Robinson, Gwendolyn, and John W. Robinson. *Seek The Truth: A Story of Chatham's Black Community*. Chatham: self-published, 1989.

Robinson, Jackie, with Alfred Duckett. *I Never Had It Made: An Autobiography of Jackie Robinson*. Hopewell, NJ: Ecco Press, 1995.

Royal Commission on Aboriginal Peoples. *Report of the Royal Commission on Aboriginal Peoples*. Ottawa: Government of Canada, 1996.

Sampson, Ida. "Transcript of Interview with Ida Sampson: December 21, 1978" *Indian History Film Project*. https://ourspace.uregina.ca/handle/10294/2226

Scanlan, Wayne. "Mike Marson on challenges he faced as NHL's second black player." *Sportsnet*. Last modified February 14, 2020. https://www.sportsnet.ca/hockey/nhl/mike-marson-challenges-nhls-second-black-player/

Shanahan, David. "Chenail Ecarte Purchase: September 7, 1796." *Anishinabek News*. Last modified September 24, 2021. http://anishinabeknews.ca/2021/09/24/chenail-ecarte-purchase-september-7-1796/

Sheffield, R. Scott. "'Of Pure European Descent and of the White Race': Recruitment Policy and Aboriginal Canadians, 1939–1945." *Canadian Military History*. 5, no. 1, 1996.

Simpson, Donald George. "Negroes in Ontario from Early Times to 1870." PhD diss. University of Western Ontario. 1971.

Strachey, William. *The History of Travelle into Virginia Britannia*. London: The Hakluyt Society. 1849.

Staurowsky, Ellen J. "An Act of Honor or Exploitation? The Cleveland Indians' Use of the Louis Francis Sockalexis Story." *Sociology of Sport Journal*. 15, no. 4, 1998.

Stephens, Christianne V. "'Speaking the Pictures in my Head': Residential School Discourse for Theorizing the Past as a Vehicle." *Actes du Trente-Septième Congres des Algonquiniste*, 2006.

Svetaz, M.V., T. Coyne-Beasley., M. Trent, R. Ward Jr, M.H. Ryan, M. Kelley, and V. Chulani. "Chapter 42: The Traumatic Impact of Racism and Discrimination on Young People and How to Talk About It." In *Reaching Teens, 2nd Edition*, edited by Kenneth R. Ginsburg. American Academy of Pediatrics, 2020.

Tanser, H.A. "Intelligence of Negroes of Mixed Blood in Canada." *The Journal of Negro Education*. 10, no. 4, 1941.

———*The Settlement of Negroes in Kent County, Ontario, and a Study of the Mental Capacity of their Descendants*. Chatham: The Shepherd Publishing Co, 1939.

Te Hiwi, Braden, and Janice Forsyth. "'A Rink at this School is Almost as Essential as a Classroom': Hockey and Discipline at Pelican Lake Indian Residential School, 1945–1951." *Canadian Journal of History*, 52, no. 1, 2017.

Titley, E. Brian. *Narrow Vision: Duncan Campbell Scott and the Administration of Indian Affairs in Canada*. Vancouver: UBC Press, 1992.

Truth and Reconciliation Commission of Canada. *Honouring the Truth, Reconciling for the Future: Summary of the Final Report of the Truth and Reconciliation Commission of Canada*. Winnepeg: National Centre for Truth and Reconciliation, 2015.

Tull, Graham G. "Cultural Experience, Possible Selves and Subjective Well-Being Among Anishnabe Youth." PhD diss. University of Windsor. 2013.

Turmel, Theresa. *Mnidoo Bemaasing Bemaadiziwin: Reclaiming, Reconnecting, and Demystifying Resiliency as Life Force Energy for Residential School Survivors*. Winnipeg: Arbeiter Ring Publishing, 2020.

———"Reflections and Memories: 'Resiliency' Concerning the Walpole Island Residential School Survivors Group." PhD diss. Trent University. 2013.

van Waas, Courtney Hope. "The Grand Experiment: Jerome Dwight Davis and the Young Men's Christian Association's War Prisoner Aid Sports Programming for German POWs in Canadian Camps During World War Two." PhD diss. University of Western Ontario. 2019.

Vinci, Alexandra. "A Study of Race-Relations Between Blacks and Whites Over Issues of Schooling in Upper Canada, 1840-1860: White Prejudice, Black Anti-slavery and School Reform." MA thesis. University of Toronto. 2010.

Ullman, Victor. *Look to the North Star: A Life of William King*. Toronto: Umbrella Press, 1994.

Wilson, E.F., ed. *Our Forest Children: Published in The Interest of Indian Education and Civilization*. Owen Sound: Jno. Rutherford, 1890.

Walker, James W. St.G. *A History of Blacks in Canada: A Study Guide for Teachers and Students*. Ottawa: Minister of State Multiculturalism, 1980.

Walker, Rhiannon. "The day Jack Johnson became the first black world heavyweight champion." *Andscape*. Last modified December 27, 2017. https://andscape.com/features/the-day-jack-johnson-became-the-first-black-world-heavyweight-champion/.

Walters, Jared V. "Narratives of Canadian Identity at the Ultimate Fighting Championship." PhD diss. University of Western Ontario. 2019.

Washington, Jesse. (2018). "Joe Louis and Jackie Robinson's Pittsburgh story." *Andscape*. Last modified February 28, 2018. https://andscape.com/features/book-smoketown-joe-louis-and-jackie-robinson-pittsburgh-story/

Waterstone, Gordon. "Being Black in Harness Racing." *HarnessRacing Weekend Preview*. June 19, 2020.

Waxman, Olivia B. (2019). "'Lucy Stone, If You Please': The Unsung Suffragist Who Fought for Women to Keep Their Maiden Names." *Time*. Last modified March 17, 2019. https://time.com/5537834/lucy-stone-maiden-names-womens-history/. Accessed November 27, 2021.

White, Paul. "The Chin Brothers: Dominant in Hockey Drawing Attention From the NHL." *History-Articles.com*. https://www.history-articles.com/Chin-Brothers.html

Wiggins, David K. (1983). "Wendell Smith, the Pittsburgh Courier-Journal and the Campaign to Include Blacks in Organized Baseball, 1933-1945." *Journal of Sport History*. 10, no. 2, 1983.

Zukerman, Earl. "This Date in History: First football game was May 14, 1874." *McGill University: Channels*. Last modified May 14, 2012. https://www.mcgill.ca/channels/news/date-history-first-football-game-was-may-14-1874-106694. Accessed October 12, 2021.

# INDEX